Nancy Eshelman: A Piece of My Mind

Columns from The Patriot-News

by

Nancy J. Eshelman

Bloomington, IN 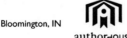 Milton Keynes, UK

authorHOUSE®

AuthorHouse™
1663 Liberty Drive, Suite 200
Bloomington, IN 47403
www.authorhouse.com
Phone: 1-800-839-8640

AuthorHouse™ UK Ltd.
500 Avebury Boulevard
Central Milton Keynes, MK9 2BE
www.authorhouse.co.uk
Phone: 08001974150

First published by AuthorHouse 10/1/2007

ISBN: 978-1-4343-0985-3 (sc)

Library of Congress Control Number: 2007904829

Printed in the United States of America
Bloomington, Indiana

This book is printed on acid-free paper.

CONTENTS

INTRODUCTION

Plenty of people have come up to me over the years and said, "You ought to write a book."

My response has always been to ask them to imagine they are a hairdresser. All day they work in a salon, cutting hair, coloring hair, styling hair. Now, I ask, "When you go home at night do you want to cut hair, color hair and style hair?"

The last thing I wanted to do after a long day in the newsroom was construct sentences, edit paragraphs and compile a manuscript.

Then one day I had an awakening. All those words I had been stringing together in columns in The Patriot-News since 1989 were just hanging around in a computer library. A few were clipped from newspapers and shoved in people's drawers. Some dangled from magnets on refrigerators. Why not gather a bunch of them together and create a book?

And so this work began taking shape.

A lot of what I write as a columnist is timely. Some politician does something really stupid and a column is born. Living in Pennsylvania, a columnist could give birth to quadruplets most weeks. But who's going to remember those foibles a year from now when so many others have been born since?

And so I began thinking about the timeless quality of relationships.

People often tell me they remember a column I wrote about something one of my grandchildren did or what I said when one of my parents passed away. They call or write to tell me their child did the same thing or they felt the same way. These columns seem to touch people where they live, in their homes and in their hearts.

So I decided to compile columns written over the years about the joys and sorrows that come from caring about someone and about the changes I've experienced in passing from child to adult, from daughter to mother to grandmother.

Maybe my columns leave readers grateful that my family isn't theirs. Maybe they see my family in their own or their life in mine. But what I've always hoped is that the words touch readers in some way.

People are packaged in all shapes, sizes and colors. Some are very bright, some less so. We do all manner of work. Some are born with a silver spoon in their mouths. Others wonder where they'll find their next meal. But the thing we all share is a relationship with others, either by blood or by choice. And that, I believe, is what makes the words that follow relevant and timeless.

ACKNOWLEDGEMENTS

Although she is no longer with me, my Mother more than anyone else, encouraged me to read, which led me to write. I miss her and my Dad every day. My elder son Michael Plank pushed me to collect these columns in a book, and Cate Barron and David Newhouse at The Patriot-News smoothed the way for me to do that.

I also have to thank Patriot-News photographer Christopher Millette for his patience in shooting the photograph that appears on the cover and my family and friends for letting me hold them up to public scrutiny. I also would be remiss if I didn't thank Doug Dohne, who for many years copy-edited my columns and wrote brilliant headlines for them. Watching him work made me a better writer.

But most of all I have to thank the readers of The Patriot-News, especially those who stopped me in supermarkets or sent emails or called to let me know that someone was enjoying what I have to say.

THOSE WHO CAME BEFORE

September 19, 1990

WHOJIGGIES BROKE?
WHO DO YOU CALL?

For most of my adult life I was carefree. That's because for most of my adult life I rented whatever home I happened to be living in.

Ah, those were the days.

It was always so easy when something broke.

In those days I simply picked up the phone, dialed the landlord and said, "It broke. Fix it."

Then a year or so ago I was looking to move again. That's when a real estate agent convinced me that buying was oh so much more logical for someone in my situation.

He was right, I know.

I'm building equity, looking out for my future, putting down roots. I have something to call my own.

But that something is a lot of work.

Take my wallpaper. All of it. It's dirty, grimy and doesn't suit my tastes. So instead of picking up the phone and saying, "Change it," I'm doing it myself.

Room after room of scraping, sanding, measuring, cutting and applying.

My back aches, my fingernails are non-existent and I swear my arms are 3 inches longer than they used to be. But the walls look nice. They really do.

But there's so much more to home ownership than nice walls.

When something is really yours (well, mine and the bank's) it's easy to convince yourself that this improvement or that would make

2

life so much nicer, and, of course, increase the value of the initial investment.

And being the optimist I am, it's easy for me to convince myself that I can do anything I set out to do. It's only in the midst of a project that I find I can't.

A couple of weeks ago, for example, I was sitting on the bathroom floor installing carpeting when I heard a hissing sound. Investigation revealed it was the toilet tank, slowly leaking.

Since homeowners pay their own water bills, I set off for the hardware store, where a friend and I spent a half-hour comparing the merits of various toilet tank systems.

And people think I don't have an exciting life.

After bringing a clerk into our discussion, I settled on a system and headed home to save lots of money.

I got all the stuff apart, but then I couldn't get it back together.

With company coming and my toilet disassembled all over the bathroom floor, I did what any self-respecting, grown-up person would do.

I called my Dad.

He was there in a flash, toolbox in hand and had things working before you could say "Ty-D-Bol Man."

Dad came through again last weekend when I got it in my head that I could build a linen closet. He sawed and nailed and pounded most of Sunday afternoon.

Then he answered a distress call Monday when I couldn't get the darn whojiggies that hold the shelves in the walls to stay where they were supposed to go.

This time he came right from work, so he didn't have his tools. I let him use mine, the ones with the pink handles.

He cursed at my hammer and shook his head at my screwdriver, but he got the whojiggies to stay where they were supposed to be.

I watched him, just as I always do, so that next time I'll know how to do the job myself.

Observing as my Dad completes my home improvement projects gives me the knowledge and the confidence I need.

But not as much confidence as I get from the knowledge that good old Dad is always just a phone call away.

KIDS NEED GUIDANCE OF A FATHER

The first thing people usually notice about my father is his hands.

Having been on the receiving end of a swat on the backside more than once as a kid, I know they are not just large hands, they're strong hands too.

Those hands also are helping hands, particularly now that I'm in the throes of making an old house livable.

A lot of power behind those hands went into a weekend project to build a deck recently. And that strength came in handy after the painters departed, leaving all the windows in what was — until Dad came along — a permanently closed position.

I think about my father's hands as the special day for dads approaches Sunday.

They're hands that can caress a child, tickle a tiny tummy or sail a swing skyward. They're hands that can sprinkle powder on a baby's bottom or dump bags of mulch around the yard.

I know how fortunate I am to have my Dad, and if I ever should forget, I need just to look around me.

So many children grow up without the guiding hands of a father.

Some of these children have a father in the home, but he's not really there. A lot of men, it seems, would rather wrap their hands around a golf club than pitch a softball to a waiting child, read the stock pages instead of a child's book or stare aimlessly at the tube when they could be watching their children grow and change.

Other fathers leave their children's lives when they leave their children's mother, creating a wall of resentment and disgust that the children carry with them to adulthood.

It must be — I think from sharing their pain — more difficult to have a living father who apparently doesn't care than to have lost a dad to war or illness or accident.

Fathers who deserve extra credit on the annual day set aside for dads are those who work at relationships with children who don't live under their roof. That's a tough situation for all concerned, particularly when mom and dad find it difficult to be civil to one another.

Many of these dads do a great job of fathering, despite the obstacles. Some find a way to make their kids at home in their home. Others are in regular attendance at school functions. And many work the kids into their summer vacation plans.

Their accomplishments are all the more impressive when one considers that fathering is a job for which an awful lot of dads seem to have no training and no respect.

Too many fathers, it seems, find it easy to throw up their hands and walk away. What they leave behind is hurting, hurtful kids who keep wondering what they did wrong.

I am lucky, I know, not to be one of them.

If my Dad and I are bonded, it's because Mom is the glue that holds us together. They've been working at their relationship for 45 years, and at their relationship with me for only slightly less time.

If I don't always seem to appreciate how special that is, it's because they always have been there — no matter what.

I discover that is not the norm when I hear friends talk about family ties that have come undone or hear kids say father not only doesn't know best, he doesn't know them — and apparently doesn't want to.

For my dad and all the dads who keep a hands-on relationship with their kids, who stayed through the terrible twos and the tumultuous teens, thanks.

We don't always say it, but we're glad you're here.

THANKS GIM, FROM ALL OF US

What makes my mother unique?

Everything and nothing.

Like thousands of other moms, she is about home.

But to our little family, her home is a spotless place where we are always welcome, where we can always get a meal and a sympathetic ear.

Mom grew up in the Depression, kept the home fires burning during World War II. Married to the same man for almost 48 years, she's about devotion and trust.

And while her standards were firmly planted in the past, she's adjusted to divorce and single-parent families and couples who live together. She may not understand, but she accepts.

Her name is Agnes, but to her family she's Gim, a name bestowed many years ago by a fat-cheeked tot who just couldn't manage the word "Grandma."

So while there are thousands of moms and grandmas, there is only one Gim.

Gim is the person we all count on, regardless of the season.

When her grown grandson requests a particular type of chocolate chip cookies for Christmas, she bakes him up a mega-batch, packages them in a decorative can and puts them under the tree.

And when he blows into town for an overnight visit, she stands over the oven in the heat of summer and makes the same cookie again, without being asked.

Like thousands of other families, we take her talents for granted, I think. We pull into the driveway and bolt into the house, forgetting to stop and smell the roses and the dozens of other flowers blooming in her yard.

She nurtures them, the way she nurtures all of us.

Too often we take that for granted.

She announces at dinner that the salad we're eating went straight from her garden to the table. We mutter a few words, too few for the work and the care involved.

In fact, we say too little to her most of the time.

How can "Thanks" repay her for hours spent on a needlepoint picture she casually offers?

How can "Great dinner" compensate for the shopping and the planning and the cooking and the clean-up?

How can muttered words of gratitude let her know how much we appreciate the small loans and outright gifts that get us through tough financial times?

What knickknack or item of clothing wrapped in flowery paper and handed to her today can express enough gratitude to a woman whose life revolves around the rest of us?

Sometimes on Sunday afternoons she sits on the floor and plays card games with the youngest generation. Her undivided attention makes them feel special, the way it did my sons, and, before that, me.

And sometimes, sitting in the house where she's lived for 41 years, she jokes about how often the rest of us move.

"Everything you own is on wheels," she says, shaking her head.

Mom has played card games on the same floor with three generations of kids.

All those generations look on her home as a refuge not because it's the same house, but because it's where Gim is.

You see, my mom is unique.

A GOLDEN EXAMPLE OF STABILITY

This is a story about stability.

The couple in the story haven't won any awards for heroism. They aren't famous. No one asks for their autographs. They are simply the kind of people who do what's right because they can't imagine doing anything else.

They grew up in the Depression, graduated from high school and went to work.

Sometime after the bombs fell on Pearl Harbor, the man left his home, his job, his family, his sweetheart and everything familiar and went off to do his duty.

His sweetheart stayed behind, going to work every day, keeping close to his family, writing encouraging letters.

Eventually, there was peace on earth.

On May 13, 1946, the man took off his Navy uniform for the last time. He returned to his job and his family. Six weeks later, he married his sweetheart.

They exchanged simple gold bands, had a reception at her apartment, and honeymooned briefly in New York City.

A year later, they became the parents of a daughter.

The years after World War II brought great change. A generation of men returned home; the economy boomed; suddenly people could buy things.

And there were so many new things to buy: cars, your first television, household appliances designed to make life easier.

Our couple bought things. Slowly, as they could. A used car. Furniture. A TV.

There was no MasterCard then. No Visa. No rent-to-buy. Her parents were dead, his poor. No one gave them anything. They didn't ask.

One day his employer announced that his department and all the workers who wanted to keep their jobs would be moving to another state.

They left behind brothers, sisters, friends and everything familiar to move to Pennsylvania. When you had a child, you did what you had to do.

A year later, when they bought a house, they lay awake at night, terrified at the prospect of missing a mortgage payment.

Of course, they never did.

They never missed a payment on anything in their lives. Never forgot a loved one's birthday or let the grass grow too long. Never called in sick when they weren't or said no to anyone who needed help.

There's a plaque you see in gift shops that says: "The most difficult year of marriage is the one you are in."

It's true of any marriage.

Every year brings its own pressures: family members die, children are born, bills mount, someone is seriously ill, the car stops running. You worry about your kids and your grandkids and, eventually, your great-grandkids.

The couple in this story, like thousands of others who grew up in the Great Depression and wed when the men came home from World War II, weathered all those crises and aced the true test of marriage — day-to-day living. They've shared more than 18,000 breakfasts and 18,000 dinners and still find something to talk about over meals.

They've been through sickness and health, been richer and poorer. Still, they like each other.

Saturday, the couple in this story will mark 50 years of being together and being the glue that holds a family together.

They may not be famous, no one will stop them on the street and ask for their autographs, but they're my heroes.

Happy 50th anniversary, Mom and Dad.

And thanks.

MEMOIR PUTS ANCESTOR'S
LIFE IN FOCUS

Imagine being 21 years old and alone in New York City, with no money, no job, no friends or family. Imagine you can't speak the language.

That is the situation in which my great-grandfather found himself in 1886.

I know this now because of a wonderful journal he left behind.

My mother came into possession of his journal recently and gave me a copy. When I read it, I found myself enamored of a man I never met.

I discovered a very precise, very intelligent, very proud man who grew up on a farm in 19th century Germany.

With words, he shared his world.

"It is the custom in Germany that every boy after leaving public school at the age of 14 learn a trade or go to higher schools for study," he wrote.

Being from a poor family, he was apprenticed to a shoemaker. For the next several years, the youth who would become my great-grandfather worked from 6 a.m. to 9 p.m., "very often until 12 and 1 o'clock nights, always Saturday nights," so customers' shoes would be ready for church on Sunday.

At 17, he mastered his craft by making a pair of ladies shoes that a panel of examiners declared "cleanest and best of all."

But soon he would begin a journey from shoemaker to student in what we know today as college.

A man not shy about his talents, my great-grandfather wrote that a former teacher arranged a scholarship for him: "He spoke very highly of me and my graduation test made a very good impression on him."

But college didn't ease his life. Classes began at 6 a.m. and lasted until noon. Afternoons were spent working in the fields or the gardens, with the animals, or in the buildings, where students cleaned and shined and polished until it was time for the evening meal, which he called lunch.

After three years of studying to be a school teacher, he was asked if he would like to go to an American seminary and study for the ministry. He joined a group of students and left his homeland. After sailing for 17 days, they landed in New York, where he spent the last dollar he had on a room and a meal.

Only then did the students learn that, despite what they had been told, their passage had been paid only to New York. Since he alone had no money for a train, the others went on without him.

Suddenly, I realized the twist of fate.

Because he lacked train fare, I am here. Had he continued on to St. Louis, he wouldn't have met the woman who would become my great-grandmother.

But the journal made me realize something even greater — the importance of sharing the story of your life.

His descriptions of his German village and the America he found, of lugging water from the town well and polishing the oil lamps, enthrall a child who grew up with indoor plumbing and electric lights.

I share this discovery in the hope of convincing others of the importance of leaving a similar gift to generations they will never meet.

No life is too boring. No details too mundane. Decades from now, in a different world, your words and your life will fascinate.

FINDING SHE'S A BEST
FRIEND ISN'T CLOSE CALL

Most days, I call my mother. It's something I've been doing ever since I moved out of my parents' home.

At first, it was self-preservation.

"Hi, Mom, how do you cook pork chops?"

"Hey, Mom, I bought this roast and now I don't know what to do with it."

While the topics changed over the years, for a long time they remained peppered with advice — some of it unsolicited.

We spent a lot of years talking about my kids. Usually she gave child-rearing advice. Sometimes I listened.

Other times we discussed my life. Sometimes she gave advice. Seldom I listened.

Now that my kids are grown and I have, too, we talk more about the stuff girlfriends discuss: What's for dinner. What's on TV tonight. What store's offering good bargains. Kids. Grandkids. The weather. Our moods.

My mom's as quick as my two best friends. Like them, she can tell from a simple hello if I'm tired, sick, mad, disgusted or preoccupied. And, like them, she always offers to help.

I suppose the transformation from mom to friend happens when kids grow up.

I remember going to a party at my son's house in Philadelphia and chatting with another guest in the backyard. I was shocked when she asked how long I had known our host. She figured I was a friend or acquaintance.

I assumed I had "Mom" tattooed across my forehead.

My mom blends in with my friends just as easily. I'm always comfortable inviting her to a cookout or asking her to come along if I'm going shopping with a girlfriend. She's pretty hip for a gal her age.

She provides an added bonus when she refers to my friends and me as "you young people."

No one else calls us that.

She may have us by a generation, but she's got a memory that shames my long-time buddy and me. She dredges up stories from our teens that we've long forgotten.

We get back at her by confessing that we left out certain parts when we first shared those stories 30-odd years ago.

Then we all share a laugh.

Mom makes little gifts for my friends, drops them notes and treats them like royalty when they visit. She's always let it be known that any friend of mine is welcome in her house.

Despite our mutual affection for my friends, Mom and I are nothing alike. Not at all.

I always thought if we were flowers, she would be a violet: pretty, delicate, subdued.

I would be a dandelion: stubborn, hearty and generally annoying.

Maybe, because I'm a bit more wild, I lead her to places and things she would avoid on her own.

Perhaps, because she's more manicured, she keeps me in check occasionally.

All I know is that somehow our relationship works.

Lately I've been seeing a commercial in which a woman brags about a phone plan that lets her talk to her mother every Sunday for only 5 cents a minute.

It always makes me feel sorry for her because she talks to her mom just once a week.

This Sunday, moms' special day, sons and daughters will jam the phone lines, making obligatory calls to their mothers. People will hustle to mail cards or order flowers or dash madly through the mall looking for gifts for their mothers because the holiday demands it.

I'll be seeing Mom Sunday, probably calling her, too. But there's nothing unusual about that. I call her just about every day.

I call because I want to. I call because she's my friend.

CARRYING ON TRADITIONS DESPITE VOID

This kickoff day to the holiday season is a time when we're supposed to give thanks.

And I do, for the food on the table and the folks gathered 'round it.

But my family starts this holiday season with a void we can never fill.

My mother left us a month ago today. She fought cancer for more than three years. She won a couple of battles. She saw a grandson get married, took a long-anticipated trip to Hawaii, went to Florida for a family wedding.

But cancer won the war. She won't be with us this holiday season, and she won't share the joy next year when another great-grandchild is born.

My mother lost her mother when she was just 15. She spoke about it often. The loss stayed with her through her adult years.

I give thanks that I had my mother for so much longer and that we had time to grow to be friends. But I know her loss will stay with me for the rest of my days.

I am an only child. It's a role that can be both a burden and a blessing. As a child, some days I longed for a sibling to divert the attention away from me. As an adult, I realize I blossomed because of that attention.

As my mother was slipping away, I longed for a sibling to share my pain. But the selfish part of me was glad I didn't have to share her last days with a sister or brother.

During those days, our family dynamics changed. Suddenly, I became the grownup, the family matriarch. I had to make decisions, make phone calls, make arrangements, support the father who had always supported me.

While I was growing into my new role, my older son assumed a new role, too. He's been an adult for a long time now. He's seen his 30th birthday. But he's always been my kid, someone I should nurture.

Suddenly, he was taking care of me, reminding me to sleep, to eat, to leave my mother's room and walk in the sunshine. We sat at her bedside together and cried together as friends.

When she left us, her great-grandson predicted the sadness that will hang over this holiday season.

Christmas will never be the same, he said, because he had spent every Christmas of his life at his great-grandma's house. All 10 of them.

Those words of pain from a child made me realize that I, too, had spent every Christmas of my life at my mother's house. Fifty of them.

Sustaining a half century of tradition will be tough. As matriarch, it falls to me to try. I know what my mother always did, but I doubt my ability to live up to her standards. Where I can't duplicate, I'll substitute or delegate.

I'll cook a turkey today and serve pies purchased at the farmer's market. I didn't inherit my mother's love for the kitchen.

When Christmas arrives, we'll have a tree and gifts and a traditional dinner. My daughter-in-law offered to try Mom's cookie recipe. She asks only that we not make comparisons.

My mother's last wish was to buy a Christmas gift for each person that she loved. I took her to the mall, and when she grew too weak for that, I helped her order items from catalogs. I wrapped them as they arrived, and she summoned the strength to write the recipients' names on the gift tags.

Some of the items arrived after she was gone. I wrapped those, too, and signed the tags with her name.

We'll open them on Christmas, greedy to have some part of her with us one more time.

As a family, we'll pull together and get through the holidays. It won't be easy.

But we'll do it for her and for each other, because her last wish was for us to have a happy holiday.

A WAR STORY, WITH RESPECT
AND GRATITUDE

Those of us born in the shadow of World War II grew up on war stories. Whenever our fathers got near another veteran, the tales would begin.

Sailing the Pacific. Japan after the surrender. R&R in Hawaii. Tanks in Africa. Battles in Europe. The stories were the background noise of our growing up years.

I remember sulking in my room as a child because my father had the only TV in our house tuned to "Victory at Sea." While he sat mesmerized by the black and white films of ships cresting waves, their big guns booming, I grumbled because he was depriving me of "Lassie."

As I grew, the telling of war stories tapered, although they never disappeared. My parents would visit with friends, and while the women talked kids and recipes and shopping, the men relived the war years.

Then, an interesting thing happened. As an adult, I started listening. Slowly I began to realize that the entire generation that preceded me spent a portion of their young adult years living with terror. Young men knew that anytime, anyplace, they could die. Women knew any knock on the front door could be someone delivering devastating news.

I developed a respect for my parents' generation.

I began asking questions about the places my father had been and the things that he had seen. It was the adult equivalent of "What did you do in the war, Daddy?"

I went so far as to suggest he write about his experiences, pointing out that some great-grandchild might someday find them fascinating history.

Recently, he told a story I had never heard before. Today, the day after Veterans Day, is an appropriate time to retell it.

Dad had completed a training school in Gulfport, Miss., and had a few days leave before he had to report to Richmond, Va. So he and another sailor hopped a train in their white uniforms and headed for New York City and home.

It was summer and it was hot, and they spent a couple of days sitting on the train, sleeping in their seats when they could, eating what they could. Grime from the coal-powered engine and dirt from the tracks blew through the open windows.

When they finally arrived in Grand Central Station in New York City, my father looked for a way to clean up before he took a bus across the river to his family's home. He walked into a barber shop wearing a white uniform turned almost black and asked for a shave and a trim.

The barber tended to him with hot towels and a sharp razor, and when my father was as tidy as he could be under the circumstances, he reached into his pocket and asked what he owed.

In broken English, the Italian barber told my father, the son of Italian immigrants, that he would accept no money. He appreciated what the servicemen were doing, he said, and adamantly refused either pay or tips.

"So even though I had a dirty uniform, I had a clean shave and a haircut," my father recalled.

Because the barber's appreciation for my father's sacrifices has stayed with him for 50-plus years, I realize that it's never too late to say thank you. That's what Veterans Day is all about.

Those of us who skipped the observances yesterday in favor of a chance to lounge at home or walk through the mall can still express our gratitude today — or tomorrow. It's simple. Just turn to someone who once wore a uniform and say, "Thanks, for a job well done."

1-CENT UTILITY BILL SEEMS,
WELL, SENSELESS

The cable company might offer us a zillion channels, and the electric company deserves credit for holding up its end during the summer sizzle, but most of us still dislike the companies that provide us with basic services.

In fact, somewhere a scientist probably is spending a $6 million government grant to study whether we're born with an anti-utility company bias or it's learned behavior.

I favor the learned theory. No matter how nice or polite the cable company employees seem now that they're competing with video stores and cheap little satellite dishes, a lot of us remember the days when you had to stay home from work for a month and a half and wait until the company was darned good and ready to send an installer to your house.

And you had to drive out to the cable company's office and wait in a line of Disney World proportions to return a black box if you wanted to move or change your service.

We also recall the days before the phone company had competition. Back then it was mandatory for employees to attend classes on how to be rude to customers, so they could explain that their people would install your phone when they got around to it — and if you gave them any lip, you'd wait another week.

Now, butter melts on their tongues.

They ask: "Are you satisfied with the results of your call to our phone company today?" And then they thank you for selecting them.

Yeah, right. Somehow you just know the person on the other end isn't sincere.

In fact, when I called the cable company recently, I could just imagine the cable employee making "Boy-are-you-dumb faces" at the phone receiver.

My father moved out of his house recently after 45 years in the same place. Every month for 45 years, his bills were paid on time and in full. Trust me on that.

So when he moved, the utility companies could have showed a little class. Maybe a "thank you for being an all right guy" would have been in order.

What did he get from the cable company?

A bill for one cent.

Honestly.

The company spent 24.3 cents to mail him a bill for a penny.

The bill says payment is due on receipt and DO NOT SEND CASH. Only a check in a stamped envelope will do. And Dad doesn't get a discount like those companies do. He has to pay 33 cents for his stamps.

I called the cable company and, after working my way through a series of instructions from a disembodied voice, a disinterested woman told me it's not necessary for Dad to pay the penny. But she promised that the bills would keep coming for a few months until the company gives up on him.

Eventually they give up whenever anyone owes them less than 5 bucks, she said.

So, I said — and this made sense to me — "Why don't you just go into your computer and wipe out his one-cent debt? Save yourself some postage." I didn't even mention the envelope, return envelope, sheet of paper for the bill or the cost of the glossy paper that tells you what movies you can buy in the month ahead.

She gasped and said she can't adjust what's in the computer, and even if she could, it's company policy to keep going after that cent.

And they have kept coming. In fact, my deadbeat Dad got another envelope and bill and glossy list of upcoming movies delivered courtesy of 24.3 cents postage just the other day.

He wadded it up and threw it in the trash.

He may have a solid-gold credit rating, but a guy who grew up during the Great Depression isn't about to write a check and lick a stamp to pay somebody a penny.

It just doesn't make cents — or sense.

SHORT-STAFFED HOSPITALS
NURSE SELVES THROUGH

To be honest, I've gotten phone calls.

People — strangers, readers — have complained about excruciatingly long waits in local emergency rooms. I've listened politely, thanked them and promptly forgotten about it.

Then it became personal.

When it's your father who's waiting, suddenly you wonder what the heck is the holdup.

The doctor said my father needed to be in the hospital. He told me to take Dad into the emergency room at Harrisburg Hospital one day last week.

Dad was evaluated promptly. He showed them his insurance cards.

Then he waited. Lots of other people were waiting, too.

Eventually, they called Dad into the inner sanctum. He was assigned to a gurney in the hallway. It was a step up from a bench in the waiting room. Not quiet, not private, but a small step up.

They told me he would be admitted to the hospital proper just as soon as a bed became available.

I'm a journalist, trained to ask questions. So I asked: How long until he gets a room?

Hopefully, it would be hours, they said.

Hours is good. Apparently, it's not unusual for patients to spend days waiting for a bed.

Now I'm looking around a large metropolitan hospital with a fancy new entrance and lots of new signs and a tunnel over to the parking garage, and I'm hearing it could take days to get a room.

Houston, we have a problem.

About six hours after we arrived at the emergency room, Pop was upgraded again. They took him from his gurney in the hallway to a real bed in a cubicle. He even had a curtain for privacy.

No TV though. He faced a long evening. I went home.

He called at about 11 p.m. He had just gotten a room. Hallelujah! He was fast-tracked to a room in just 10 hours.

Don't get me wrong. I have no complaints about the staff. Everyone was pleasant and efficient, considering the circumstances. My question was for the powers-that-be. I'm a journalist, trained to ask questions. So I called and asked: What the heck kind of place are they running?

I suspected, like a lot of people, that this problem stems from merging Polyclinic and Harrisburg hospitals under that big Pinnacle umbrella. Let me guess, I told their PR guy, you got rid of too many beds. Bad planning. No long-range vision.

Not so, he said. It's nurses. They don't have enough. Nobody has enough. We're desperate, the PR guy admitted.

Pinnacle is recruiting in Canada. A hospital in a neighboring city just hired a bunch of nurses from the Philippines.

If Harrisburg Hospital could find 100 qualified RNs who wanted to work there, they'd scoop them up in a heartbeat, he said.

The hospital has empty beds, but without nurses, you can't put patients in them.

So everything backs up. People wait in the emergency room for hospital beds. That forces others to languish in the waiting room until an emergency room bed becomes available.

You might call the whole thing a sick joke, except there's no punch line and no antidote in sight.

So I'll offer some advice: Don't get sick. If you must get sick, do it in nice weather. The hospital is less busy then.

And tell your kid to be a nurse. There's plenty of opportunity in the field.

P.S.: Dad's home and vows to stay out of the hospital — if he could ever get in again — for a long time.

WHEN IT'S TIME TO TAKE DAD'S HAND

People have always remarked on the size of my father's hands. He doesn't shake your hand; rather, his envelops yours.

All my life, I've wondered why his huge hands surprise people. At 6 feet 4, he would look odd with tiny hands dangling from his powerful arms.

For seven weeks now I've been holding those hands, day after day, as he lies in a hospital room surrounded by beeping machines.

His hands are bruised from the injections and the IV lines. But even though his body is weak, I can still feel the strength in his hands when he squeezes mine.

Sometimes as I sit there, I close my eyes and drift to another time.

It's a sunny day somewhere in New Jersey. In front of us stretches the Atlantic Ocean, vast and powerful. For a child, the allure is awash in terror.

I might have been 5 then. I wanted to march in, to feel the waves lapping first on my feet, then on my legs. But I was afraid.

When my father took my hand, the fear drained out of me.

Many times we strode into the ocean together, Daddy and me. We'd get our legs wet, then our chests and our shoulders.

Then he would support me and I would float as the briny waves bobbed by.

He told me he wanted me to swim like Esther Williams. He said I could be an Olympic champion.

I disappointed him on that score. But he taught me enough to make me love the ocean and respect it so I could enjoy it as a child and as a teen, and eventually as a mother leading her own little ones into the swells.

I realize now that the ocean is a metaphor for life. You have to plunge in, but you also have to respect it if you want to continue to enjoy it.

He taught me that too, not with words, but by holding my hand every time I needed encouragement to wade into something new.

Now he and I are up to our necks in the uncertainty of his illness.

It's a new challenge.

All around us the machines sound off, one beep of reassurance, then one of dread. At the end of the day, I cheer him if he's been able to dangle his feet over the bedside. That's the extent of the journey he can make right now.

As I sit in his hospital room clutching his mighty hands, I realize how lucky I am.

Most people have fathers. Not everyone has a dad.

A dad holds your hand when you take your first steps or meet the ocean. He supports your endeavors and convinces you that you can be anything you want — even Esther Williams.

Around me today I see a new generation of dads who are very involved in their children's lives, who go to swimming classes with them and dress them and feed them and encourage them and hold their hands.

My dad did all that before it was trendy.

Sadly, though, I see too many children who don't have a dad like mine. Just walk into the corner bar if you need proof.

Several decades ago, I decided to explore the idea of resettling far from my family and my roots.

Dad drove me to the airport, and when he hugged me good-bye, he whispered, "You'll be back, won't you?"

At that moment, I knew that I would.

At that moment, he taught me that my strength comes from being close to family.

Now, each night when I leave the hospital, I promise, "I'll see you tomorrow."

I'll be back, because he's my dad.

THEY'RE WELL;
THAT'S WHAT TRULY MATTERS

My aunt called Saturday morning and snatched me from the weeds in my garden. Her voiced stretched across 180 miles and soothed me with a verbal hug.

This aunt is my late father's older sister. We didn't talk about my dad, but I know she misses him, too.

We didn't discuss why she called that particular day, but I knew she probably was prompted by Father's Day, what would have been my parents' anniversary last week and the approach of what would have been my dad's birthday.

We exchanged how-are-you's and how is this one and that one.

Everyone's fine.

It wasn't the sort of conversation that contained a lot of news, but it's stayed with me since Saturday.

Her voice brought all the comfort of being wrapped in an afghan on a winter night. But digesting her words reminded me that she is an extremely wise woman, although she would never claim that.

In the exchange of how-are-you's, my aunt assured me she and her husband are just fine. They have passed their 80th birthdays and have the resultant aches and pains, but, thank God, nothing more serious.

All in all, they're good — very good.

I mentioned another aunt, my late mother's sister, who's about the same age. She and I talk almost every week, even though she, too, is 180 miles away.

I told my father's sister that my mother's sister is much the same. She ignores a few aches and pains and remains sharp as a tack. She leaves the house every day to eat lunch with her girlfriends or play bridge or attend to errands.

All of them have more active social lives than I, leading me to the conclusion that should I celebrate an 80th birthday I would love to be as vibrant as any of them.

They go to casinos. They play cards and eat their meals out.

My father's sister and her husband stay active with senior citizens' and veterans' groups. Not a holiday goes by without their participation in a parade or a celebration.

My mother's sister gravitates toward the country club and she still models once a year in her Zonta Club fashion show.

With all that they do, sometimes it's hard to find them at home.

My father's sister was glad to hear that my mother's sister is well and keeping busy.

Then she shared the most important words I had heard all week: What more could someone their age want?

She's watched a lot of years tick by and lost a lot of people she loved. But she reminded me that she has her health, her mind and family close by — children, grandchildren, great-grandchildren, sisters and more.

A woman really couldn't want more, she said.

So simple, so true.

The weeds in my garden really weren't so bad.

I washed my hands and decided to spend the rest of my weekend enjoying the people I love.

KIDS AND GRANDKIDS

SOMETIMES IT'S TOUGH TO CHEER

When a little girl who is very special is excited about something, those who love her want to share her excitement.

But when that little girl, who is a hair short of 7, is excited because she's become a cheerleader, it takes a hard swallow for this person to generate any enthusiasm.

I've always admired athletic women, gals who can hammer a softball, return a tennis volley or swing a golf club for 18 holes. Me, I grew up doing traditional girl things, and sports weren't traditional for girls in that time and place. So, I flinch if a ball whizzes by me, reject tennis because it requires too much running and find golf requires me to remember too many things, like how to hold the club and where to place my feet.

But I truly expected girls today to be different. I guess I thought the women's movement had filtered down into kindergarten and that a tot would be more interested in playing a game than cheering while someone of the male persuasion takes to the field.

I guess I was wrong.

This special little girl burst into my house the other day wearing an orange and black pleated skirt, an orange shirt bearing a team's name and carrying a pair of matching pompons. Then, to make matters worse, she showed off one of her cheers, something to do with shaking her 6-year-old booty.

This is a child I've been brainwashing since birth.

Before she could talk, I was telling her not-so-subtle stories emphasizing that education gives a woman the opportunity to take a leadership role and make big bucks.

When she picked up a miniature stethoscope to play nurse, I reminded her that she could be a doctor.

When she sat her little sister down with crayons and paper and began playing teacher, I explained that being principal or superintendent is an option.

When she packed a couple of baby dolls into a stroller and played mom, I assured her that she could find fulfillment in life without children, or should at least wait until she is 35.

But I knew my words were falling on deaf ears when she began focusing her attention on that floozy Barbie and acquiring various clothes and paraphernalia. For the past year now, she's been combing and styling Barbie's unnaturally blond hair and pulling this and that outfit over Barbie's unnaturally shaped body.

When she showed me the Barbie lunchbox she had bought to start school, I should have known it was just a matter of time until she started styling her own hair and imitating the lifestyle of that doll.

Well, it sure didn't take long. Here she is now, a cheerleader, a girl who spends her time on the sidelines cheering for the boys, waving her ponytail and pompons, shaking her booty and cartwheeling across the grass.

From my back yard comes the sound of "Hello, hello, just came to say hello," and the swish, swish, swish of the pompons. She leaps in the back door and cheers her way through the kitchen, stopping to remind me that I promised to buy a $1 ticket to support the cheerleaders and, gee, wouldn't I like to come to a game.

I want to cry.

But instead I smile and say, "Sure, honey," and tell her how cute she looks.

Then I try to think of ways to make sure she's busy Saturday, or at least in bed before the Miss America pageant comes on TV.

I'm dealing with cheerleader. It's tough, but I'm trying.

But I draw the line at beauty queen. I really do.

KIDS FIND OWN TURF AT CHUCK E'S

It was the day of reckoning.

For months, three munchkins had been after me, begging in high-pitched little voices, "Will you take us to Chuck E Cheese's?"

Always, it had been on my turf, in my town, and the excuses came like machine-gun fire:

"There's not enough gas in the car."

"I've got dinner cooking."

"I'm expecting an important call."

"Chuck E's on vacation."

This time they had me. Chuck E had just started peddling his cheese in their town. They knew where he was and they knew he was open.

I was trapped by a rat.

I climbed in the car with my grown son and three munchkins to keep an overdue date with an oversized rat. The squeals started as we pulled into the parking lot.

"Chuck E's here." "Chuck E's here." "Chuck E's here."

Three munchkins spilled out of the car and leaped toward the door, hopping, jumping, dragging two adults into a colorful room filled with dozens of squealing munchkins and a bunch of dazed-looking adults.

We stood behind a velvet rope — the kind you see in theaters — while they found us a table.

Correction. My son and I stood there. The munchkins slipped under the rope, tore off their shoes and disappeared in a cage full of brightly colored plastic balls.

The menu offered a choice of pizza, pizza or pizza. We ordered pizza and went looking for the munchkins.

Blond heads popped in and out of the colored balls or appeared briefly in the plastic tunnels that surround the cage.

Sometimes the blond heads were our munchkins. Sometimes they were someone else's. Most times they moved too quickly to tell.

Kids ran through the restaurant like commandos on a mission. Adults froze, mesmerized by sensory overload. Music blared. A fuzzy gray creature kept shaking people's hands.

I quickly figured out that, except for the cage full of balls, if munchkins want to play they have to pay with tokens.

I formulated a plan.

"No tokens until you eat your pizza," I told the bobbing blond heads.

Three munchkins chomped down a slice apiece and suddenly were ever-so-full.

The best laid scheme of woman destroyed by a mouse.

I sighed and divvied up the tokens. A trio of munchkins scattered as if someone had dropped a bomb.

To my left, curtains opened and some furry creatures on a stage professed in song how happy they were to see us.

They weren't real.

To my right, a bunch of teens in uniform gathered around a table of 12 and sang birthday greetings to a munchkin.

They weren't sincere.

I tallied up the cost of our pizza, five drinks and the tokens and decided the birthday kid's parents must have robbed a bank.

I found our munchkins dropping tokens into Skee-Ball and basketball machines. At the end of each game, the machine popped out a couple of tickets.

Realizing that the tickets brought shrieks of joy, I helped the littlest munchkin acquire a few by throwing plastic balls into two garbage cans as the lids popped on and off.

When the leftover pizza was cold and the machines had eaten all their tokens, the munchkins traded their tickets for treasures.

They got a couple of plastic cups, some combs, a ponytail holder.

I got three hugs, three thank-yous and one very large headache.

REAL ISSUES
ILL-ADDRESSED BY COSTUMES

Saturday, I have a date to take three munchkins shopping for Halloween costumes.

Having done this several times before, and with more than one generation of kids, I'm pretty sure how it will go. If they're totally happy, I won't be. If I'm totally happy, they won't be.

Before it's over, they'll whine, they'll pout. I'll whine, I'll pout.

In the end, we'll compromise.

To me, Halloween is about fantasy. For a day, or an evening, a kid gets to be what he or she wants. Problem is, I'm not always thrilled with what they want to be.

Take Ninja Turtles.

A couple of years ago, they were really big. I didn't know exactly what they were. Then I saw the movie.

They lived in a sewer, ate lots of pizza, kicked and punched people. Kind of like college boys with shells on their backs.

Granted, they seemed to limit their kicking and punching to bad people, but I wasn't really pleased about the message that sent. Seems there should be better ways to resolve differences.

When Ninja Turtles became passe, Power Rangers emerged.

I expected the first-grade boy with his front teeth missing would want to be one since they kick people too.

What I didn't realize was there was something called a Pink Ranger. A girl Power Ranger.

So last year three kids were pleading for Power Ranger costumes.

Again, a dilemma.

We rented some Power Ranger videos. Yes, they were the good guys and gals, and they all seemed to have a sense of humor, but they solved their problems like Ninja Turtles with kicks and swirls and bad guys knocked senseless on the ground.

Still not exactly the way I envision problem-solving.

But when shopping for Halloween costumes, one has to consider the alternatives.

If the girls don't want to be Pink Rangers, they want to be Barbie.

Ugh.

Nothing more I would want for them than to grow up to be disproportionately endowed airheads who spend their lives changing clothes and hanging around a swimming pool with Ken.

It's about as appealing as having them enter the Miss America contest.

And if the boy whose front teeth are finally coming in this year can't be a Power Ranger, he'll want to be Batman.

Yuck.

Batman is just a bit too much like Michael Jackson for my taste. He's incredibly rich, runs around in black tights and spends an awful lot of time with a young boy named Robin.

Not exactly the role model I'd pick for an impressionable kid.

So considering the alternatives, I suppose I'll give in and let the boy be a Power Ranger or Spider-Man. In my mind, those mythical beings are slightly preferable to the real people who populate WWF Wrestling, which the kid and his dad have been known to watch.

But those girls, oh those girls, really present a problem.

How do you explain to a 6-year-old that Cinderella should have gone to college or had some specialized training before she tried on the glass slipper? That way, if Prince Charming turned out to be Ken with a foot fetish she would have something to fall back on.

And should you take the magic out of Pocahontas by telling them she never married John Smith, although she did get to England, where civilization in the form of smallpox killed her at the tender age of 22?

Decisions, decisions.

Maybe I'll just meet them at the cash register, close my eyes and pay.

FIELD (TRIP) OF DREAMS
FOR THE CHAPERON

Before me were 80-plus reasons why schoolteacher was not my career of choice: four classrooms of second-graders, squealing, squirming and shoving.

One-on-one, a second-grader can be sweet and surprisingly bright, which is how I managed to find myself on a second-grade field trip yesterday. In groups, second-graders are silly and somewhat wild creatures who like to push, shove and disappear, a recipe for disaster for an adult who's been sweet-talked into serving as a chaperon on a field trip.

I'd been down this (rail) road before, about 20 years ago when the sweet-talker's father was one of the squirming, shoving mass. Yesterday, it loomed again, as I stood at 8:30 a.m. sharp in a school yard in Lancaster, waiting for a bus and watching this amazing group of little people swing, jump, climb and run, while I focused most of my energy simply on staying awake at what is, to me, an absurd time of day.

A blinking red light kept catching my eye. Blink. Blink. Blink-blink.

A sneaker. Every time the kid's toe hit the ground, his sneaker blinked.

That's something they didn't have on field trips 20 years ago.

Back then, you also didn't see a sawed-off kid wearing a shirt large enough to fit his father. Or shorts hung so low they almost hit the kid's ankles.

Boys didn't wear baseball hats backward, and girls didn't come to school with their midriffs exposed. And I'm sure the language I heard yesterday didn't permeate the playground back then.

But those who needed a bar of soap inserted between their lips cleaned up their mouths once their teachers appeared, and kept them 99 and 44/100 percent pure for the rest of the day.

Since these city kids walk to school, riding a school bus is a big deal. That may explain why they shoved so hard to get on, and off. And on again, and off again. And on one more time, and off when their field trip ended.

It also explains why I spent so much time opening bus windows for kids who had no idea how to operate them.

Destination one was the Strasburg Railroad, where each chaperon's task was to herd three kids, keep them from being mashed by moving trains, guarantee they would be in the prearranged place at the prearranged time, let them finger every item in the gift shop before deciding which to purchase, and eat sugary treats so they could replenish all the energy they expended running, jumping, shooting imaginary basketballs and tapping other second-graders on the head.

Riding the train, the city kids had more than a few words to say about the country smell of manure. But then, smells and bathroom jokes are pretty popular topics in second grade.

We saw farms, a couple of Amish people, lots of cows. More importantly, we got all the second-graders on the train, off at the picnic grove, back on the train, off at the station, and back on their buses, without anyone being mashed.

In fact, the only injury I witnessed occurred at the picnic grove where someone was hit hard in the stomach, either by a piece of playground equipment or a fellow student.

Depends on whom you talked to.

The next stop brought more injuries.

The group wasn't in Long's Park more than 10 minutes before blood poured from a split lip and a kid got the wind knocked out of him when he ran hard into the side of a park bench.

The teachers came prepared, with ice packs and bandages and wet wash cloths in plastic bags. They also packed a sense of calm the chaperons lacked.

Along with their first aid kits, and the balls and bats they lugged along for the kids' entertainment in the park, the teachers were carrying a real joy, based on the fact that the number of remaining school days is fewer than the number of fingers on a second-grader's two hands.

TODAY'S 'CAF': REAL
FOOD FOR THOUGHT

Saying no to that little voice on the phone is all but impossible.

So when the munchkin called and invited me to lunch at her school, I agreed.

There I was recently, eating pizza and sitting on a bench about a foot off the floor.

It gave me a great perspective on how much things have changed since the prehistoric days when I attended school.

For one thing, kids eat only what they want these days.

Don't want to finish that pizza? Just dump it. Tired of those green beans? Toss them.

Geez. Back in the old days, we had to clean our plates. And the cafeteria ladies didn't ask if we wanted green beans like they do now. They just plopped them on our plates. We had to sit there until we ate them — and everything else. Which is why to this day I don't eat pickles.

That stems from being forced once to eat pickles and drink milk. Don't ask for details.

Today, if you don't like pickles, or even the main course, you can get something different.

Not a pizza fan? Hoagies or barbecue or a salad bar are available. And a kid can pick up snack foods, such as cookies and ice cream, right there in the cafeteria for an extra 35 cents.

In my day, we had to sneak to the corner store — and risk detention — if we wanted sweets.

The munchkin's school sells supplies, too.

My visit happened to coincide with a school store day. A couple of times a week, the kids can visit the store and buy pencils and pencil sharpeners and folders and other supplies.

Of course, if you invite a guest who has her wallet handy, it's an opportune time to shop.

Ten minutes and $3.95 later, I had the chance to visit a couple of classrooms. That's where I saw the really big changes from my days in school. The computers are the most obvious addition, a bank of them in every classroom.

Then as I looked around, I noticed each classroom has a telephone, a television and a VCR.

Classrooms didn't have phones and TV's when I was a student. And VCR's weren't invented. If a teacher wanted to get a message to the office, one of us got to saunter up there carrying a note and wait for a reply. Generally, that mission was reserved for teacher's pets.

Fetching the movie projector, however, was a task delegated to the two or three huskiest boys in the room. They were sent with a key to a locked closet, where they wheeled out the projector, propelled it through the halls and shoved it into the back of our classroom.

Any of you who remember those days also will recall that the sound and the picture generally were out of sync and the reel of film broke at least four times during every movie.

We watched our movies in drab classrooms darkened by shades that had discolored to a nasty shade of tan.

The munchkin's teacher has decorated her third-grade classroom like home sweet home. She's hung colorful valances on the windows, pictures of cats on the walls and put her own piano in the corner. She also keeps a small refrigerator near her desk.

In fact, the whole building is delightful, with an aquarium of colorful fish in the lobby and a traffic light outside the cafeteria that flashes red or green to let kids know whether they can go to the playground after lunch.

And the playground. Wow. Following the munchkin's older sister outside, I saw kids climbing, kids swinging and kids sliding. Underneath them all, that shredded stuff waited to pad the impact if one of them happened to fall.

A group of boys played football on a field, while another bunch of boys shot basketballs at hoops nearby.

Racing in and around the equipment, the fifth-grade girls spent their lunch break chasing the fifth-grade boys, poking them, teasing them. The girls giggled. Then they giggled some more.

Ah, yes, the more things change, the more they remain the same.

MUNCHKINS ON A MISSION FOR FUN

Diary of a weekend:

Friday, 5:30 p.m. Pick up the munchkins who are to be my weekend houseguests.

Friday, 6:30 p.m. Explain to them that, yes, I promised to take them to a high school football game, but they agreed we would cancel if it was raining.

Friday, 7 p.m. Put on my father's size XXL raincoat, pull up the hood and walk into the soggy stadium, hoping not to see anyone I know.

Friday, 8 p.m. Skirt the puddles on outing to satisfy munchkins' cravings for french fries, pretzels and sodas.

Friday, 9 p.m. Wrap the littlest munchkin in a large sheet of plastic. Watch her teeth chatter.

Friday, 9:30 p.m. Console munchkins on their team's loss. Explain philosophically that someone always wins and someone else always loses.

Friday, 9:31 p.m. Admit that the littlest munchkin is right. Sometimes teams tie.

Friday, 10:30 p.m. Pull into my driveway. Bask in the thought that they will be asleep soon and I can curl up in an afghan and watch part two of the three-part, season opening episode of "Homicide" I am taping.

Friday, 10:32 p.m. Discover the power has been off, the cable is out and "Homicide" is no longer an option.

Friday, 11 p.m. Learn from a representative of Suburban Cable that a car crash caused the outage and they are working on it.

Saturday, 10:30 a.m. Try to tune in kiddie shows on TV.

Saturday, 11 a.m. Learn from a representative of Suburban Cable that they are still working on it.

Saturday, noon. Drive in the rain to Wal-Mart, Hills and Kmart in pursuit of Halloween costumes. Find aisles clogged with pushy parents, whiny kids, and masks and costumes that have slid onto the floor.

Saturday, 2 p.m. Arrive home with costumes that cost a lot more than I wanted to spend.

Saturday, 3:30 p.m. Notice rain has stopped. Go to Balloonfest at Hershey. Pay $5 to park.

Saturday, 4:30 p.m. Watch the balloons lift off. Watch the kids eat pierogies and Lebanon bologna and hot dogs and candy apples and onion rings. Watch the oldest ride the "Ring of Fire" and pray that she doesn't suddenly feel the effects of all that food while dangling upside down.

Saturday, 5:30 p.m. Walk to Chocolate World so the munchkins can go on the chocolate ride for about the 50th time in their lives.

Saturday, 6:30 p.m. Walk back to the $5 parking space and leave for the Hershey outlets, where trick-or-treating, with candy courtesy of the nearby factory, is scheduled from 6 to 8.

Saturday, 7 p.m. Accompany munchkins in a trick-or-treat attempt, only to find that most stores are out of candy.

Saturday, 7:10 p.m. Listen to myself whine, "Is Bethlehem out of steel? Is Philadelphia out of cheesesteaks? How can Hershey be out of candy?"

Saturday, 7:20 p.m. Head to an empty storefront for refreshments and costume judging. Hear organizers declare refreshments off limits until the judging ends. Watch hundreds of kids squeal and twist while waiting to be judged. Feel relief when munchkins beg to leave.

Saturday, 8 p.m. Go to the sweets shop and find plenty of chocolate — for sale. Spend more than I care to on oversized chocolate chip cookies and milk shakes.

Saturday, 8:15 p.m. Walk back to the car, where munchkin No. 2 discovers he has lost his $4 mask.

Saturday, 8:20 p.m. Search for the mask.

Saturday, 8:25 p.m. Give up; drive home.

Sunday, 7:30 a.m. Open one eye and find munchkins staring at me.

Sunday, 8 a.m. In a stupor, cook bacon and eggs.

Sunday, 10:45 a.m. Drive the munchkins home in the pouring rain.

Sunday, 11:30 a.m. Receive big hugs from munchkins who proclaim their love and promise to visit again soon.

Sunday, 6 p.m. Miss them.

'MOM' BACK IN THE SWIM AS KIDS VISIT

I forgot.

Sure, I raised two boys. But they've been grown for a long time now, and I forgot how much work is involved.

Or maybe it just gets harder as you get older.

Friday afternoon I arrived home from work to find four munchkins. It wasn't hot enough, but they had been swimming. Then they had toweled off, dropped the wet towels, dressed and jumped into the car for a trip to McDonald's.

When they came back, it was pool time again, even though it was still too cold.

They fell into a pattern: Take off clothes. Put on bathing suit. Get in pool. Freeze. Get out of pool. Wrap up in towel. Drop wet towel. Drop wet suit. Shower in hot water. Dress in clean clothes. Say, "I'm hungry. What have you got to eat?" Eat. Repeat process.

Evening arrived.

They fought over who would sit in the front seat during the drive to the video store. They rented movies. They fought over whose to watch first. They stayed overnight.

I slept like a log.

My neighborhood had a yard sale Saturday. They got up really early, bought everybody's junk and hauled it to my house.

They wanted grilled cheese sandwiches for lunch. Then, they wanted more. I used an entire loaf of bread.

One kid went home. The others went swimming. See paragraph six for a description of the afternoon.

I made dinner. Two like hamburgers; one hates them. Two like angel hair pasta; one hates it. One likes rice; two hate it. Nobody likes tomatoes.

My washer washed. My drier dried. My dishwasher screamed for mercy.

So did I.

But it got worse. Sunday it rained.

I forgot. What do you do with three kids when it rains?

Two wanted to go to the mall; one wanted to go bowling.

We went to the mall to eat. Two wanted McDonald's; one wanted pizza.

Then we went bowling. They all wanted to go first.

After three games, we went back to the video store.

By then, I had a system: One sat in the front seat going to the mall; another going to the bowling alley; the third en route to the video store. Then we started over.

We stopped at the grocery to pick up snacks. Two like pretzel goldfish crackers; one likes original flavor. Two like chocolate ice cream; one hates it. One likes vanilla ice cream; two hate it. Everybody prefers ice cream served in a cone.

We bought two kinds of everything and a large pack of cones.

That night, they ate all the snacks.

I fell asleep listening to the drier running.

Monday, glorious sunshine.

They went outside. They went swimming. (See paragraph six.)

They packed up to go home. They hugged me and thanked me and said they had a lot of fun. They asked if they could come again — soon.

I ran the dishwasher, the washer and the drier one last time.

I sat down and tried to remember: Had I really said, "Sure, come back any time."

SCHOOL'S OUT, BUT
LEARNING NEVER ENDS

Disguised as an end-of-the-school-year treat, the three-day excursion to Washington, D.C., was designed to remind the munchkins that education doesn't stop when summer starts.

The White House, the Washington Monument, the Vietnam Memorial and the Tomb of the Unknowns were on my to-do list.

My three companions said sure, they wanted to see all that stuff. But was I really, really sure that the hotel had a pool?

I was, I said. On the roof.

When we arrived late on a Friday afternoon, I figured the pool was a nonissue. A bank thermometer registered 68 degrees, and I needed the intermittent windshield wipers to keep the raindrops from piling up.

I underestimated the kids. They're like miniature postal workers. Neither rain nor cold . . .

I found myself nine stories up, wrapped in a jacket, watching them turn blue and hearing them insist they weren't cold.

When chattering teeth finally made conversation impossible, they agreed to hot showers and a visit to the hotel restaurant, a casual place where no one looks twice if a kid orders a banana split for dinner.

Then they rented a horror movie on the TV in the room, while I laid plans for our assault on the White House.

Up early and out. It was pretty neat, I thought. The tour guide, a Secret Service guy with a wire going into his ear, told stories of residents past and gave us a look at rooms in red, green and blue.

It was OK, the munchkins said.

Middle munchkin liked the Metro ride more than the president's house, although he reminded his sisters repeatedly that it wasn't his first ride on a subway, no way. He had ridden on the subway in Philadelphia with his uncle. Went to a Phillies game, they did. Those girls might be riding a subway for the first time, but not him. He'd been around.

Older sister viewed the subway as transportation to the stars. Money burning in her pocket had filled her with visions of a Leonardo DiCaprio T-shirt. Or the Spice Girls.

A friendly White House guard pointed us to street carts packed with dozens of Leonardo and Spice Girls shirts. Decisions, decisions.

Girl power won out over the heartthrob. She bought two Spice Girls shirts, one to wear that evening and the other the next day.

Smaller sister brought a tie-dyed shirt with a happy face. She likes happy faces. This one says Washington, D.C.

Brother, ever cool, selected a Fubu hat, then stopped at every street cart in the capital searching for the perfect Fubu T-shirt.

He found it at 4:30. In between we saw the monuments — Washington, Lincoln, Vietnam — the Reflecting Pool and a bit of the Air and Space Museum. Someone asked which war came first, Civil or Vietnam.

The tab for lunch at Planet Hollywood could have paid for a war.

Sunday's schedule called for us to go to Arlington, but I got lost. We wound up in Rock Creek Park. They said fine, they'd rather see animals anyway.

We wandered through the zoo, stopping repeatedly at ice cream stands where a dollar bill won't buy you anything.

The munchkins took lots of pictures. Five rolls in all. We have about 60 pictures of the Washington Monument and another 12 of baby ducks in the Reflecting Pool. There's a girl wearing a Spice Girls T-shirt in various poses around the pool, a kid in a Fubu hat flexing his muscles by the pool and little sister eating ice cream at various historic sites.

I actually appear in one picture. I'm the one looking frazzled. If you look closely, you can tell by my expression that I'm the one getting an education.

A STEP BACK BUT NO
FURTHER FROM THE HEART

This adorable guy stole my heart again last weekend.

He does it every time he comes to town. My only complaint is that he doesn't come around enough.

But every time he walks in, I fall in love.

Who wouldn't?

He's bright and blond and his blue eyes sparkle. He's witty and his laugh is infectious.

The things I do to make him laugh amaze me.

Friday night found me on my belly on the floor, making vroom-vroom noises as I rolled a truck to him again and again and again. When he tired of that, I fed him pudding. Every spoonful was an airplane, flying through the air before it landed in his mouth.

It's the same game I played with his father almost 30 years ago.

It's been so long I don't recall if his daddy said, "Ummmm" with every mouthful the way my beautiful grandson did Friday night.

We looked at books about farm animals. We mooed at the cows and barked at the dogs and quacked at the ducks.

I know for a fact his daddy did that.

Saturday, we headed for the backyard. He and I played kickball with a beach ball. He said "ball" over and over and over. Once, before I kicked it, I asked, "Ready?"

Immediately, that became his favorite new word.

I determined that he is amazingly smart. Very precocious. Terribly bright.

That's the joy of being a grandparent. You can say those things. You can say that your grandchild is gorgeous and brilliant and loving and somehow it doesn't sound like bragging.

Well, maybe it does, but people are tolerant. It's not as if you're bragging about your own kid.

Being a grandparent puts you a step away. If you don't see your grandchild for a week or a month, you can marvel at what he's learned in the interim.

When people proclaim that he's cute, you can agree without seeming conceited. You can say he got his blond hair from his dad, and the curls from both his parents. Oh, yes, and grandma has curls and blue eyes, too.

But you're a step removed. He's not your child. You're just the grandparent. You didn't have much to do with it.

All you get from the deal are visits and wet kisses and hugs and laughs. You smile as his face reacts with delight when the dog grabs a biscuit he has offered. You watch as he figures out that if he pushes a certain spot on a certain book, a cow will moo. You can actually see the learning process as he realizes that no matter how many times he pushes, he'll get a moo.

And pretty soon he learns that the light switch at the bottom of the stairs flips on the hall light. And flips it off. And on. And off. And on.

When you're a toddler, every step is an adventure in learning.

When you're a grandparent, every step he takes is amazing. You realize that he knows more today than he did yesterday and less than he will tomorrow.

When he visits, that tomorrow always comes too soon. When it's time for him to go home, a grandparent busies herself by helping to pack up the gear that a grandchild requires — the portable crib and the stroller and the toys and diapers and bags and sippy cups.

The busy work provides grandma with time to back away.

Then it's kisses and hugs and a reminder to come again soon. And when he's gone, grandma's left with fingerprints on glass surfaces and remnants of his wet kisses.

He's left with a piece of her heart.

May 6, 1999

GRANDMAS FEEL THE GRAND
PART OF MOTHERHOOD

Being a mom is a wonderful thing.

But being a grandma is phenomenal. I think sometimes that life keeps moms and dads so busy they don't have time to appreciate the wonder. Grandma has time. Grandpa may, too. But Mother's Day approaches, so it's grandmas who have the spotlight today.

Moms are proud of their tots.

I watched one beam recently as her toddler climbed onto a plastic three-wheeler, settled on the seat, looked up and said, "I've got a bike."

Mom beamed. Grandma was astounded. He had spoken a sentence. He had strung together a noun and verb. The words made sense. We understood them. He had communicated verbally.

He wasn't doing that last month. Last visit we were marveling at his coordination, because he could kick a ball pretty hard and fairly straight. This visit he was talking in sentences. Grandma felt the wonder.

She felt the same wonder sitting with the family's newest mother watching a set of pudgy fingers open and a dimpled hand reach out. With concentration, the infant aimed her hand at Cookie Monster's blue feet and grabbed.

Her mother and I were surprised.

Just yesterday, she wasn't reaching, wasn't grabbing. This was a new skill, one that left grandma slack-jawed with wonder.

Yes, being a grandma brings much wonder. It arrives with e-mails containing pictures of a pudgy-cheeked beauty. It flows with tears of joy when you watch her daddy rock her to sleep. It wafts in with that powdery baby smell that fills your nostrils when you hold the little one close.

Being a grandma is about talking to the almost 2-year-old on the phone and pretending you understand what he's chattering about. Or opening an envelope full of pictures and recalling that silly moment when he put on Grandma's glasses and posed for the camera.

Being a grandma is supervising a 10-year-old who wants to mash the potatoes for dinner. Sure, some of them will fly out of the bowl and onto the counter or floor. So what? For grandma, it's about spending the time with her, creating a memory.

Being a grandma is commiserating with the boy who has to put up with two sisters. Grandma listens to his tales of woe and offers understanding when he wishes he were an only child. Then she takes him to the video store and lets him rent a "boy movie" to watch on the VCR.

Sometimes, if his friends aren't around, he'll even let Grandma soothe him with a hug.

Being a grandma is about being conned by a 12-year-old. After grandma agrees to buy her a blouse, she tries on three — to decide, you know — and declares that she loves them all and simply can't make up her mind. She knows grandma has a MAC card and a hard time saying no.

Grandmas are allowed to spoil. In fact, it's expected. They let the kids stay up late. They sneak them ice cream twice a day. They barter kisses for candy and hugs for cookies.

They tickle and play peekaboo and then say, "Oh, I think your child needs her diaper changed." They feed the little one crumbly cookies and let his parent clean him up.

There's a bumper sticker around that says something like, "If I'd have known grandchildren were this much fun, I'd have had them first."

The explanation is simple. Raising kids is such hard work that it's easy to miss the wonder.

When your own kids become adults, you enter a "wonder" full, less hectic stage of life. Being a grandma allows you the luxury of time to realize how lucky you are to have the little ones around.

HIGH-TECH JOB AS
BABY SITTER GETS HER DOWN

The more things change, the older I feel.

That's my observation after providing a couple of days of child care for my 13-month-old granddaughter.

Let me go on record here and say there's a darn good reason why most women in their 50s don't give birth: We're too old, too tired and too technologically inept.

Baby's Mommy was going out of town for a couple of days, and baby's Daddy had to work. Grandma figured a few days in Philly would be a nice break from work.

I raised two kids, but I guess Mommy thought I might be a bit rusty. She left four pages of instructions on what baby eats when and when baby sleeps.

Of course, baby ate what she wanted when she wanted and slept when she wanted.

I guess she didn't read Mommy's note.

What I could have used were instructions for the high-tech stuff that comes with babies today.

Part of child care is changing baby's diaper. Nowadays you're supposed to put the used diaper in some white thing that twists it, stores it and allegedly removes unpleasant odors.

I tried stepping on various buttons, pushing down on the top and shaking the thing, but I never did master how it works.

I just left the diapers in a pile and asked Daddy to take care of them when he got home.

Then there was the dang car seat.

One day, baby and I went toy shopping at Wal-Mart. When we returned, panic set in as I tried to remove her from her car seat. I simply could not operate the contraption.

Back in the day when my kids were little, we didn't have car seats. They bounced around the back seat like two little rubber balls.

So this harnesslike contraption was beyond my experience. Baby remained calm, but I was heating up as I stretched across the back seat and tried to wedge my left hand under the bar and between her legs while yanking on the straps with my arthritic right thumb.

I'm pleased to report that eventually I removed child from seat without major injury to either of us. I just wish I could remember — for future reference — how I did it.

Another day, I pushed baby to the grocery store in her stroller, which comes with its own set of straps. After mastering them, I had to figure out how to get stroller and baby down the front steps of the house without permanently injuring my back.

Then, at the store, I had to tip and dip the stroller to get in the entrance, which is surrounded by a black cage designed to keep people from stealing the carts.

Daddy had asked me to pick up some milk. He said Mommy prefers organic milk.

Organic milk! That was a new one for me. I thought all milk comes from cows. I'm familiar with whole, 1 percent, 2 percent and skim, but organic?

Of course, I couldn't find it. So baby wound up with ordinary milk. I hope that won't cause permanent damage.

I also hope she doesn't tell Mommy that she and I shared a peanut butter milk shake.

Personally, I used the stairs to justify the calories. Mommy, Daddy and baby live in a three-story house, with baby's room on the second floor and the TV room on the third floor.

(Daddy vows if they're ever robbed, the thieves are going to work for what they get.)

As a result, Time for Teletubbies meant lugging a pudgy princess up two flights of stairs. It was enough to work off two milk shakes.

I love that little girl, but after a couple of days I needed to come back to work. It's a lot less strenuous here.

ALAS, LITTLE GIRLS GROW INTO TEENS

All hail The Queen. Tomorrow she turns 15.

The Queen is the oldest munchkin and No. 1 grandchild. She earned her title by acting like royalty and treating the rest of us as her subjects.

Sometimes, for short, we call her Elizabeth — as in England.

Sunday, Elizabeth cleared her schedule so I could take her shopping and shower her with gifts for her birthday. She allowed her younger sister, The Princess, to go with us, provided she rode in the back seat of the royal carriage.

Aging changes kids, you know.

I've got a sweet little granddaughter who's two and a half. She's a cousin to The Queen and The Princess. When I went on vacation recently I asked the little one what I should bring her. All she wanted was a big, big, big seashell.

Pretty easy, pretty cheap.

That's because she's still at the sweet age. I've warned her father that it won't last. I've warned him that in a little more than a dozen years his life will become a living hell. His sweet little girl and her sweet little sister, just three and a half months old, eventually will become teen-agers. My son and his wife will become suddenly stupid.

They'll dread a lot of things during those teen years, especially shopping.

Trust me on this. I'm experienced.

The Queen and The Princess and I started Sunday at a large store in a strip mall. It carries stuff favored by teens, but I always feel as though store management is convinced that everyone who walks through the door has just one aim: shoplifting.

Security is overly obvious. Too many people are staring and glaring. I just know someone stares into the dressing rooms from above. The place gives me the creeps.

I spent an hour feeling creepy while The Queen looked and touched and held things up to her body. Finally, she narrowed down what suited her royal taste and tried on this and that.

This was good. That wasn't.

She went to look some more. She even looked for a while in the men's department, because apparently teen girls wear some clothing made for teen boys.

Who knew that?

Who knew that sweater coats are back in style? Who knew that fringe on sweaters is fashionable? Who could imagine that a tiny skirt made from about a quarter yard of material would cost that much?

Finally, I paid for her queenly selections, and we were off to the big mall — but not to any stores where I would shop if I were alone.

The Queen favors stores where the clerks are pierced and tattooed and odd music blares from the ceiling. Clothes feature logos of companies unfamiliar to me and come in unfamiliar sizes — right down to zero.

Oh, is size 2 too large? Let me go get you the zero.

That's never happened during my lifetime.

The Queen and The Princess also spent what seemed like days in a store filled with cheap jewelry and glittery nail polish and fuzzy book covers. It's another place where the clerks seem convinced that everyone is on a mission to steal.

I collapsed briefly on a bench in the mall while the royals bought some oversized earrings.

Picking the perfect size ear hoops can work up a royal appetite. We ate pizza in the food court. Five slices and three sodas cost almost 16 bucks. I could have gotten two pies delivered at home for that.

It was just one more expense in an expensive day.

I can hardly wait for Christmas.

A YOUNGER GIRL SOMETIMES
CAN LEAD OLDER ONE

As the mother of sons, I'm used to kids with dirty faces, messy clothes and constant motion. Spending time with my granddaughters is a journey into uncharted territory.

Last weekend, my dad and I joined my son and his daughter at the circus. What amazed me most was the way this 2-year-old watched the show.

She remained in her seat, laughed and clapped with the audience. She tapped her foot in time to the music. She behaved just as I always dreamed my kids would.

They never did, especially not at 2.

Her daddy bought her a balloon — an oversized parrot. She held it all through the show. She took it to my house and then she took it home. Her father said she took it to bed.

Her father and his brother, as I remember, would have been letting go of the string and watching the balloon drift upward. Then they would have lunged and grabbed the string just in the nick of time.

They would have thought they were ever so clever. Of course, sooner or later they would have missed. Sooner or later they would have lost that balloon, and then they would have fussed and hollered and yelled.

But she just held the balloon ever so nicely.

Girls are different, I think.

The same thing occurred to me Sunday when I took her cousin shopping for her 12th birthday. She and her sister always want to go to a mall for their birthdays, so I can spend my money on them.

They have a brother, those two girls. We shop on his birthday, too, but much faster.

Shopping with him reminds me of shopping with my sons. If he likes something, he buys it. He doesn't even try it on.

Girls, well, they're different.

Miss 12-Year-Old meandered around a department store, looking at this and that. Occasionally I showed her something I liked. She'd wrinkle her nose and meander some more.

Eventually, she took a few things into the dressing room. She didn't model them.

She used to, but now that she's 12, I've become totally uncool and she doesn't care for my opinion. She picked the clothes she wanted.

Then we meandered some more. She found a really cool pocketbook. I know it's cool, because she told me.

After we paid, we meandered to one of those stores that sells jewelry and sparkly nail polish and things that hold your toenails apart while you paint them with sparkly polish.

No boy ever goes into one of those stores. No one past 18 goes into one of those stores unless she's shopping with a 12-year-old.

Next she led me to a store that caters to girls her age. She confided that their prices are ridiculously high, but the clothes are very trendy. She bought a pair of pants and two shirts off the sale rack. She's apparently learned something from all those years of shopping with me.

We meandered to a candy store, where you take a plastic bag and scoop a little of this and a little of that into a bag. It's what we would have called penny candy in my day. Now it's $7-a-pound candy.

Her brother or any other boy would have filled that bag in 10 seconds flat. She meandered. Two pieces of this, three of that. It took forever.

I told her I'd treat her to a big bag of candy, so she could share it with her brother and sister. She smiled angelically.

When I took her home, I noticed she had concealed the bag of candy in her inside coat pocket. I don't think she was planning to share.

Come to think of it, maybe girls and boys aren't so different after all.

LITTLE THINGS AMONG
LIFE'S BIGGEST JOYS

At 5, she's busy exploring options.

Sometimes when I stop by her house, she's a fairy. With wings and a wand, she leaps through the air.

The other day, her daddy said, she spent her day as a nurse. She dressed all in white and wore a hat with a red cross that she'd made.

When she's a firefighter, she dresses in red and completes her outfit with black boots and a red plastic hat that the firemen gave her when they visited her nursery school.

She parrots all she's learned about stop, drop and roll and calling 911. She amazes her daddy by glancing skyward and explaining that the sun, you know, is really just a ball of fire and if it should fall, well, we'd all better call 911.

She amazes us every day. Did I know half this much at 5? Did her father? She's so sweet and innocent and yet so terribly bright.

Sometimes I look at her and at the equally sweet and bright little sister who's half her age and my eyes fill with tears. They are, of course, tears of joy, for I feel so astoundingly lucky to have these girls in my life.

An acquaintance became a grandmother for the first time the other day, and I tried to describe the sheer joy that's about to fill her world. But words fail.

She'll have to learn for herself that it's the little things that bring the greatest joy.

To walk in the door and have two beautiful little girls drop what they're doing, tear across the floor and leap into your arms is better than being the guest of honor at a surprise party.

To cuddle in a chair and read "Sleeping Beauty" to a spellbound audience of two beats getting lost alone in the latest best seller.

To walk to the park, as we did one recent Sunday, and listen to a 5-year-old explain why she loves her neighborhood can be the most interesting one-sided conversation of the week.

To watch the little sister's face light up as she glides to the bottom of the slide can be more entertaining than any Hollywood blockbuster.

To witness her giggle is better than attending the symphony.

To go to Friendly's for ice cream and have them insist that they both want to sit next to Granny is better than dining with celebrities in a five-star restaurant.

Just a phone call can improve any day. They'll relate what they've been doing. Then each ends her conversation with, "I love you. Bye."

Oh, and I love them. I want to wrap them in a cocoon to protect them from the evil in the world. At the same time, I want them to feel free as butterflies so they can see and explore and experience all the wonderful things the world holds for them.

I want them to know that it's possible to be a firefighter or a nurse or the president of the United States, and that it's fine to leap like a fairy and eat ice cream and giggle on a sliding board.

But most of all, I want them to know how it feels to love and be loved.

The best I can wish for them is that someday, a long time from now, they experience the love and joy you can only get from being somebody's granny.

From where I'm sitting, life just doesn't get any better.

ISABEL HAS GRANDMA'S NUMBER

She pulled in some air and puffed up her cheeks, aiming at the candles and the large "3" on her cake.

A round of applause greeted her success.

She beamed. Her smile unveiled the deep dimples that dent her face when she's happy or finds something to be funny.

That's often.

Since she's been old enough to laugh, she's displayed an enthusiastic sense of humor. At first she laughed at peek-a-boo and funny faces. Nowadays she prefers silly songs and silly people, like the grandma who tries to slip bits of cracker in her mouth as she flies by on the swing.

And oh, how she loves to swing.

"Higher, higher," she's been saying since she first started parroting words.

She loves to fly high in her grandma's tree and grab the leaves.

When grandma feigns dismay and asks, "What are you doing to my tree?" the dimples appear.

After the third or fourth repetition, they're accompanied by a belly laugh.

What a joy is Isabel.

She is the littlest grandchild. She loves Disney princesses: Snow White, Cinderella and Sleeping Beauty decorated the pink birthday cake that we shared at Knoebel's Amusement Park.

Pink, of course, is her favorite color. She also loves stickers and Hershey Kisses, dressing up in glittery clothes and hats, and sitting in the rocking chair watching DVDs.

Most times, she loves her sister.

As an only child, I've never experienced the whole sibling thing.

But I think it must be tough to be the younger sister.

No matter what you do, someone's already done it. Your sister is the focus of hundreds, maybe thousands, of photographs, the star in hours of videotape.

You're lucky to get half that, along with her hand-me-downs.

As the family marvels at the older sister's accomplishments, something — call it fate or nature or the gods — intervenes to make the little sister special in her own way.

Big sister reads aloud; little sister learns to somersault. Big sister taps out a song on the piano; little sister counts to 20. Big sister stages a puppet show; little sister disarms you with her rendition of "Twinkle, Twinkle, Little Star."

And she's a hugger. When she wraps her arms around your neck and melts into your body, you know you've been hugged.

Isabel's hugs are strong medicine. A rotten day at the office, an argument with some idiot on the phone disappear from thought when you're wrapped in an Isabel hug.

Sweet, her Daddy calls her.

Sweet, she is.

She beamed through most of her special day at Knoebel's as she soared in the sky on the helicopters and "drove" a car around a track.

But hours on the carousel and the bumper cars and splashing in the swimming pool finally wore her down. As her sister sailed down the swimming pool's sliding board for the 98th time, Isabel grew weary.

I left big sister and her parents frolicking in the pool and wrapped a towel around Isabel. She curled up in my lap, newly 3 years old and exhausted.

As Isabel's eyelids fluttered, Granny gazed down at those sweet little cheeks, feeling truly contented.

MARKING A TRIP'S MOMENT

Somewhere between the hills of bed linens and the mountains of towels, I asked myself, "Why did I agree to this?"

Somewhere along Interstate 95, passing another in an endless stream of minivans with spare possessions strapped to the roof, I muttered, "What am I doing here?"

Sometime that first day, with my arms and legs screaming from exhaustion and my hands locked around a grocery cart, I maneuvered around the other shoppers stocking a kitchen for a week and asked myself, "Why am I doing this?"

The preparation is too intense. The trip is too long. The traffic is impossible. Then when we finally arrive, I'm forced to tend to the task of hauling in supplies to feed a dozen people for a week.

Sure, it's a good week, but a black cloud hovers over my head, holding the promise that after seven days we will have to haul all the dirty laundry and trek 500 miles home.

You've really got to love the ocean to tackle this project.

The game plan starts right after Christmas with shopping for the right house and making reservations for a week that suits everyone's schedule. In the spring, I write checks that make my bank account groan.

The pace picks up in the week before vacation as I yank sheets out of the linen closet. How many singles? How many doubles?

Number of inhabitants times towel allowance comes to, man, just a staggering number.

Two or three days before we leave, someone or another will announce, "I'm packed."

That's when I grit my teeth, bite my tongue, and think, "Sure, because all you have to think about is your own clothing. You don't have to remember the washcloths or pack enough shampoo to wash a gaggle of teenagers' hair."

Eventually, I relax. I sit on the porch and watch the ocean. I enjoy the moments.

Early in the week, I was walking with the 4-year-old. We were skirting the waves, looking for shells. I carried her orange pail.

She deposited a few treasures from the sea.

I planted my foot hard in the wet sand and pulled it away. She looked at my footprint, grinned and ground her own small footprint into the sand next to mine. We exchanged a smile and a giggle, then watched as a wave washed away the evidence of our passing.

Life's kind of like that, I thought. Someday, all evidence of our trek will be washed away. Might as well make your mark while you can.

So that's what I was doing there.

KINDERGARTNER: 1ST DAY SEEMS 'VERY LONG'

The Divine Miss M and her entourage walked to the bus stop yesterday morning.

When you're the firstborn child heading toward your first day of kindergarten, it's a first-rate deal.

Miss M was dressing for her premiere performance when I arrived shortly after 7 a.m. For the occasion, she'd selected a black velour jumper with floral trim and a white blouse. She completed her ensemble with Finding Nemo sandals that light up when she walks.

Last-minute dressing decisions are not part of her makeup. We need to pick our outfit in the night, she explained in a serious tone.

She ordered up breakfast, deciding that a peanut butter and jelly sandwich (PBJ to the in-crowd) would do just fine, thank you.

Kindergarten, she said, would be fun. She knew this, she said, because she'd been to Exploring Kindergarten, a program that shows kids around before that first day. It's offered, she explained, because some kids never went to preschool.

To get into kindergarten, she was to wear on her person a tag containing information about her classroom and buses. Her Mommy tied it to a pink ribbon so she could hang it around her neck like the ID badge that Daddy wears to work.

"Wow, that looks great," she told her Mom.

She decided between the purple Powerpuff Girl backpack and her pink Powerpuff Girl backpack. In a few minutes, she changed her mind.

While Mommy whipped up a snack for her backpack, Miss M spent a few quiet moments cuddling with Dad. He was taking this whole kindergarten thing pretty hard.

They revisited an album of her baby pictures. That seemed to comfort him some.

Miss M went onto the porch to pose for pictures. In a few minutes, she was sitting out there alone.

What are you doing? I asked.

Waiting for the school bus, she replied.

Every car, every distant motor prompted her to ask whether the bus was coming.

She'd been on a practice run on the bus and knew the rules, she said.

Please be quiet on the bus, and if you lift up the window, a buzzing will start and the bus driver will come to see what the emergency is.

And just what is good about going to kindergarten? I asked.

You get to meet a lot of kids, make new friends and go out at recess and play, she said. So she was ready, and it was time.

She grabbed her little sister's hand and led the way to the bus stop, followed by Mommy, Daddy, two grandmas and several cameras.

She waited with a few other children, one of them a girl wearing a similar ID badge and destined for the same kindergarten class.

Miss M introduced herself and pulled a pop quiz on her new classmate: Are you excited for school?

Too soon, the big yellow bus rolled to the corner. She climbed on as her entourage waved solemnly.

A tear rolled down my face. Mommy and Daddy blinked hard.

And then she was gone.

But the story doesn't end there. I returned at noon and waited for the big yellow bus to return.

How was it? Inquiring minds wanted to know. Very long, she said.

LEARNING FROM A LITTLE GRAD

For many kids across the region, today is the last day of school, a time to heave a large sigh and start basking in 2 and a half months of freedom.

Today, the Divine Miss M spends her final day in kindergarten.

Perhaps you recall that I was part of her entourage Aug. 30 when Mommy, Daddy, little sister and two grandmas sniffled as they watched her climb on that big yellow bus and ride off to her first day of school.

I thought it only appropriate that we sum up how that year went, so Miss M and I sat down the other day and talked about kindergarten.

Miss M, who tends to be exuberant about most things, proclaimed the year "great."

She showed me marigolds grown from seeds. She and her classmates, she said, stuck the seed in dirt in plastic cups and watched them grow. Then they took them home.

She said she learned about money, how to identify coins and determine their worth.

"Like one penny is worth one," she said.

She knew the alphabet going in, but as her class focused on each of the 26 letters, she enjoyed making things, like a vase for v and a pig for p. Then they colored them, she said.

Surely, I said, the school year had highlights, days that leaped off the calendar pages.

Well, she said, the very best event involved counting the days of school. When they reached the 100th day, they celebrated with a party, "and I love a party," she said.

She also enjoyed those days when it was her turn to be "catch of the day." From her description of the tasks involved, it sounds like a fancy title for teacher's helper.

She liked the assemblies, a trip to a nearby firehouse, a visit to Chocolate World.

And, of course, the other children.

"The whole entire class is my friend," she said.

Friendship is at the core of the advice she would offer someone heading to kindergarten in the fall.

"If you want some friends," she would tell them, "just be nice and be nice in school, too."

She and I recalled her first day at the bus stop, and how one of her classmates seemed reluctant to climb on the yellow bus.

Should that happen to someone else, she advised, "You don't have to be scared because you will get brought back on the bus."

And finally, she advised those going to kindergarten to "just be happy, even though you're not having fun."

As for Miss M, she will miss school, she said, but she's not sad because "I know I'm going to go back to it in first grade."

And she's been gearing up for that.

Her class visited the cafeteria to learn the tricks of fine dining. The menu included pizza, green beans and salad. Then they ate snow cones outside.

"We've been practicing first grade," she said. "We practiced recess."

First-grade recess, she explained, takes you to a different area of the playground where you can play with Hula-Hoops and jump ropes.

As for what lies on the first grade learning horizon, Miss M isn't certain. But she speculated it might be "some more about money."

But then, isn't everything?

THE LIFE AND TIMES OF AN MVP

Six years ago, I spent this day in Philadelphia.

I know this because that's when our family experienced the delivery of a Most Valuable Person.

Yes, the granddaughter with the initials MVP turns 6 today.

We were visiting Sunday when she suggested her birthday as a column topic.

Her chuckling daddy suggested that she ease Granny's burden by doing the column herself. She then took pen in hand to write: "My granddaughter has a big thrill today. It is going to be her birthday!

"I can't wait to come. Her friends all know that they are invited.

"I think this is the best time of the year to have a party for a birthday."

Great job, MVP, but the column needs to stretch to the bottom of the page. So I'm dipping into some old columns to recall these six years ...

When she was 13 months, I baby-sat for a couple of days. Mommy had typed four pages of instructions on what baby ate and when baby slept.

"Of course, baby ate what she wanted when she wanted and slept when she wanted," I wrote. "I guess she didn't read Mommy's note."

She was 2 when four generations attended the circus.

"What amazed me most was the way this 2-year-old watched the show," I wrote. "She remained in her seat, laughed and clapped with the audience. She tapped her foot in time to the music. She behaved just as I always dreamed my kids would.

"Her daddy bought her a balloon — an oversized parrot. She held it all through the show. She took it to my house and then she took it home. Her father said she took it to bed."

My sons, I recalled, "would have been letting go of the string and watching the balloon drift upward. Then they would have lunged and grabbed the string just in the nick of time. ... Sooner or later they would have lost that balloon, and then they would have fussed and hollered. ...

"Girls are different, I think."

When she was two and a half, I asked what I should bring her from my beach vacation.

A "big, big, big seashell," she said.

"That's because she's still at the sweet age," I wrote while recounting a trip to the mall with her teenage cousins. "I've warned her father that it won't last. I've warned him that in a little more than a dozen years his life will become a living hell.

"His sweet little girl and her sweet little sister... eventually will become teenagers. My son and his wife will become suddenly stupid.

"They'll dread a lot of things during those teen years, especially shopping. Trust me on this. I'm experienced."

When she was 3, I was playing with her little sister's toes when MVP glided into the room and said, "This little piggy went to Target ..."

"Ah, the power of advertising," I recorded.

When she was 4, I observed, "After a long day at work, I find a phone conversation with her is the ticket to a brighter mood. She ends our talk with those two magic words, 'Love you.'"

When she was 5, she grabbed her Powerpuff Girl backpack and hiked to the bus stop with Mom, Dad, sister and two grandmas in tow. Most of us were fighting tears.

Grandparents savor such times. The gifts of her first six years whet my heart for those of the next six.

PLUMBING THE DEPTHS OF MY BOOK

Someday I'm going to write a book.

Critics will declare, "She certainly displays a vivid imagination."

When I appear on "Oprah," skeptics will claim I'm another James Frey. They'll suggest I made this stuff up. But I couldn't.

Take the latest chapter from my life. It will be titled "How I came to have a new toilet."

Saturday, I was supervising the activity of the 16-month-old who toddles around my house. He was clutching a hard plastic ball, one of a set of three. Each has something inside that shakes, rattles or rolls.

I heard him turn the corner toward the powder room. It didn't concern me because that door's always shut.

Twenty seconds of silence blasted me out of my chair. After all, this is the same sweet toddler who locked himself in a bathroom a couple of weeks ago, prompting hysteria on both sides of the door, the removal and eventual destruction of a door knob and his mother's swan dive through a window after I used a mighty long screwdriver to pry out a screen — and bend the frame permanently, I might add.

But that's another chapter.

This chapter was made possible because the door that's always shut wasn't.

En route to the powder room, I heard the flush.

When I walked in, the villain still had his pudgy little fingers on the handle. Water swirled in the bowl. The plastic ball had disappeared.

Little guy was wearing what I call his "cheesy" smile — that's the one he flashes when he knows he's doing something off-limits, such as touching the telephone, playing with the computer mouse, or flicking the television on and off.

In an effort to undo what he'd done, I became intimate with the toilet. Even though I plunged my arm into water up to my elbow, I couldn't dislodge the plastic ball.

I could touch it. I could feel it turn. But it had wedged in a bend and it wasn't about to shake loose.

The plumber's reaction was what people like me usually get from people like him. They know we're inept and they want to make sure we know they know.

He expected a two-minute job.

Two hours later, he conceded it was time to buy a toilet.

He'd lugged in one tool after another. He'd assumed 14 yoga positions around the toilet. He'd dismantled the thing and yanked it off the floor. He'd carried it outside, tried to blast the ball out with water pressure, shaken it, turned it upside down and dragged more tools out of the truck.

Now he was admitting defeat, throwing in the towel, hanging up his plunger, so to speak.

We decided to drive to the big, orange store to buy a toilet. But first, he said, he wanted to measure the rough-in distance, just to make sure it was the normal 12 inches.

I nodded like I understood.

I didn't then, but I do now.

Twelve inches represents the standard distance from the wall to the hole in the floor under the toilet.

If the distance deviates from the standard, a toilet's going to cost you more.

You know the punch line, right?

I'm working on my next chapter: "Nothing I own is standard and always costs more to replace."

SISTERS' LOVE KEEPS
FAMILY TIES STRONG

Ask who her best friend is and my teenage granddaughter, without hesitation, names her sister.

I've been thinking a lot about sisters lately.

I have none. No brothers, either.

I envy those who do.

I see my granddaughters chattering and laughing, and I envy their closeness. They're separated by about two and a half years — and a brother born between them. At times, growing up, the brother felt surrounded, overwhelmed, I think.

So did the adults around them. The three, so close in age, were a real handful.

More than once, a driver pulled the car over to the side of the road and threatened the three of them with bodily harm if they didn't stop poking and picking in the back seat.

Now that they are older teens, they tend to get along. The three of them chat, share stories, laugh. But the sisters seem to share a special bond, as well as earrings, scarves and other girlie stuff.

I expect their closeness will continue, the way it did with my mother and her sister. Although miles separated them as adults, the telephone kept them very much a part of each other's lives.

I learned early in life never to disturb my mother when my aunt called. No excuses.

They crossed miles to be together for holidays, birthdays and any special family event, and drew the rest of the family into their circle.

My parents selected my aunt as my godmother, just as her sister and her husband had chosen my mother.

I recognize that sisterly closeness developing in my younger set of granddaughters, who — like their cousins — have about two and a half years between them.

At seven and four and a half, they still shove each other occasionally, and the younger one hasn't completely outgrown the need to avenge some slight by yanking a wad of her sister's hair.

But she's as likely to give her sister a hug.

When I deposited the older sister at her home the other day, the younger girl pointed to a wad of foil on the table. She'd been to a party and brought home two cookies — one for her, one for her sister.

It was a fleeting moment that I found very sweet.

These two little girls would do well to mimic the closeness so evident between their mother and her sister.

My daughter-in-law and her sister are 30-somethings leading busy lives an hour from each other, yet when I see them at family gatherings, the ease of their relationship never fails to snag my attention.

What I envy about them — and all these sisters — is their connection.

A sister, it seems to me, links your present with your past. Who else remembers your childhood doll, your summer vacation, that crazy family reunion?

When you are grown, when your parents gone, a sister validates your memories.

For me, an only child, my early years are stowed in photographs of no interest to anyone but me.

Like my memories, I am their sole keeper.

SHE HOPES HER FULL HOUSE IS
A LAUNCHING PAD

Before my high school class held its one-year reunion, I was married and had a child. Before my second child exited his teens, he had become a father — making me a grandma just before I turned 40.

He fathered three kids in less than four years. For about five years, they all lived with me — mom, dad and three little ones. Then mom and dad went their separate ways and the kids accompanied her on what became a rocky road.

I spent a lot of time with them and tried to let them know if the rocks became boulders, they could always come to me.

A little over two years ago, they did — or at least two of them did.

The middle kid, a boy, was 16; the younger girl was 15 and pregnant.

I told her she had options.

She disagreed. She planned to give birth and keep her baby. In her mind and heart, no other option existed.

From my end, I knew she had chosen the most difficult path.

But a woman who's yakked about choice all her life, when faced with a pregnant 15-year-old, has to put her actions where her mouth has been and support the teen and her choice.

For me, that meant becoming legal guardian to her and her brother. I moved them into my home, enrolled them in cyber school, set up new computers, rearranged rooms and furniture, found health care, helped him obtain a learner's permit and a job, and helped her gather baby necessities.

The paper work, forms, phone calls and correspondence overwhelmed me at times. But we waded through.

The 8-pound baby boy she delivered in November 2004 now tears through the house as a 38-pound toddler, dragging my heart wherever he goes.

Not long after the baby arrived, the oldest of the three grandchildren moved in, too. She had a few months left of high school — in Lancaster — and no driver's license. So we added to our daily stress by finding ways and means to deposit her at school and get her home again.

The day she graduated, won an award and thanked me from the stage made the aggravation worth it — I think.

Once upon a time, my house didn't look too bad. I was no Martha Stewart, but I didn't have to hide if unexpected guests knocked.

Now, walking from the kitchen to answer the front door means stepping around toy trucks and blocks and a blob of something someone slopped on the floor.

The kitchen trash can always seems to be overflowing and some weeks our two recycling bins aren't enough to hold all the soda cans and milk containers.

My grandchildren weren't just sloppy when they arrived, they were oblivious. They truly didn't see all those dishes in the sink or the towels on the bathroom floor.

After two-plus years, their sight has improved somewhat — although it's far from 20/20 — because their ears ache from hearing my complaints.

I can't really say I'm raising my grandchildren. When they arrive at 15, 16 and 18, they're pretty well raised.

I think of my house as more of a launching pad. They'll be going off on their own sooner or later (at least I sincerely hope so), and I'm trying to make sure they are packed for the trip.

Driver's licenses? Check.

High school diplomas? Check.

Work experience? Check.

A sprinkling of common sense? Check.

At least, that's my intent.

The amount of prodding required on my part to get them to accomplish those basic goals sometimes makes me feel as if I want to explode.

Living with my grandchildren means I've lost my privacy, some of my friends, my sense of freedom and a big chunk of my bank account.

Being one of those who sees the glass as half full, I muddle through, convinced that down the road if any one of these three kids becomes a productive citizen, it will all be worth it.

In the meantime, would somebody please grab that half-full glass because the toddler's about to spill it all over the floor.

JUST LOOKING

ACT NOW BEFORE IT'S TOO LATE

What would you do if you woke up tomorrow morning and a doctor said you had to have surgery or you would die?

What would you do if four of the other five people who had taken their chances on that same surgery died within months?

Would you cast your lot with fate or trust a still-developing science?

And once you had settled on the rock or the hard place, what would you do? How would you spend your precious time?

Gov. Robert P. Casey had one short weekend to do what he would do before he put his faith in science.

He spent that weekend with his wife, their kids. What they talked about, how they spent that time belongs within their family circle.

But our minds can wonder and wander. We can imagine. And consider what we would say and do.

We can imagine what Sen. Arlen Specter said and did as he spent his weekend preparing for surgery for a brain tumor.

Knowing something foreign was growing in his head. Spending long hours imagining the worst.

We can assume Specter, like Casey, shared his feelings with his loved ones. Spent precious time with his family.

Even under the best of circumstances, the ties that bind families are tenuous. Family relationships, like relationships of all kinds, require nurturing.

Raising kids is never easy. Being someone's kid is difficult, too.

Wife. Husband. Friend.

Sister. Brother. Grandchild.

Tough. Difficult. Demanding.

All of us have so little time. So much to do.

Work. School.

Exercise. Fun. Extracurricular activities.

Shopping. Cleaning.

Dashing here.

Running there.

Keeping appointments.

So little time to tend to our relationships and our relations.

Then suddenly, tragically, the clock appears to be running out.

What mattered?

It takes losing someone close or almost losing them to discover it wasn't money earned or errands run. It wasn't who had the fanciest house or the newest car. Who finished the report for the boss or balanced the checkbook.

It wasn't whether the loved one sat in the halls of power or cleaned them. Whether she wrote reports or typed them, made decisions or carried them out.

What matters is time. Shared time.

Being there because you want to be.

Letting someone know why you are there. And why you care.

The coincidence of Casey and Specter both in their early 60s and probably the state's two most well-known men undergoing the knife on the same day is something the rest of us couldn't, and shouldn't, ignore.

Their pain and their families' offers us an insight into something that has nothing to do with politics or government, Republicans or Democrats, balanced budgets or tax increases, congressional testimony or passing legislation.

It offers a harsh reminder that none of us has an endless supply of time.

It forces us to consider the question: What would we do?

And gives us a chance to act on the answer, before time runs out.

GOOD NAME ISN'T DEAD, JUST A TOY

Christmas arrived the other day in a toy catalog.

Prominently displayed among such hot dolls of the holiday season as Telephone Tammy and Twist 'N Style Tiffany was My Newborn Nancy.

Imagine that. Nancy.

Right there with Kaitlin Holiday Doll and Talking Katelyn was a doll named Nancy.

A baby doll, who drinks a bottle and sucks her thumb once you insert 3 AA batteries (not included).

Obviously, if there's a newborn Nancy, my name is not as passe as I had assumed. Until I encountered her, the only Nancys of any prominence were — well — has-beens.

There's Nancy Reagan, a shriveled woman, who was old even when she was somebody and living in the White House.

And Nancy Sinatra, whose claims to fame are an antique record about boots made for walking and a dad who walked away from her mama Nancy in favor of women with more exotic names, like Ava and Mia.

Nancy wasn't out of fashion when I was growing up, but it was never as popular as Linda or Donna or Karen. Most of the girls in school had those names, or some play on Mary — Mary Sue, Mary Jo, Mary Ellen.

And in the style of today's Kaitlin, Katelyn, there were always girls named Cathy, or Kathy, or Cathie, or Kathi.

Today's names don't need exotic spellings to be fancy.

The state Department of Health's Division of Health Statistics and Research reports that, for the ninth year in a row, Ashley, given to 1,463 newborns last year, was the most popular name for infant girls.

Ashley. The name of a weak-willed man in my all-time favorite movie and its currently showing TV sequel.

Ashley. Name of 85 more baby girls than runner-up Jessica.

Coming in third was Emily, followed by Samantha, Sarah, Amanda, Brittany and Nicole. Rachel made a first appearance at number nine and knocked Megan out of contention.

Rounding out the list was 10th-place Lauren, name of 849 newborns and a '40s movie star who married Humphrey Bogart.

Humphrey. Now there's a name you don't hear any more.

Not like Michael, which continues to top the list of boys' names, much to my son's dismay. Many years ago, when he was in kindergarten, four of the eight boys in his class were Michael.

The 2,724 boys blessed with Michael last year also seem destined to have something in common with a lot of elementary school pals.

Michael, Matthew and Christopher were one, two and three for 12 consecutive years. That changed in '93, when Christopher was knocked down a peg by Tyler.

Coming in fifth was Ryan, followed by Nicholas, Joshua, Zachary, Joseph and Andrew.

Zachary, name of 1,413 boys born last year, made a stunning leap from 14th to eighth place, knocking John out of the top 10.

John and Mary, which topped the list in 1960, are now as stale as week-old popcorn.

With Zachary on the fast track, 30 years from now, instead of "Do you, John, take Mary?" we'll hear, "Do you, Zachary, take Ashley?"

Of course, with this new doll, don't count Nancy out just yet.

While Pennsylvania parents named only 40 babies Nancy last year, this doll could be the start of something big.

Why, by next year's Christmas catalog, My Newborn Nancy could have grown into a Barbie-size phenomenon with her own cars, phones and clothes enough to share with her friends, Karen and Donna and Linda.

MICROWAVE'S, COOK'S
GOOSE BOTH COOKED

Having confided my crisis of the day to a friend, I wait for sympathy.

Instead, she laughs.

My microwave has died, leaving me without access to most of the food in my kitchen.

And my friend is laughing.

It isn't the news of the death that tickles her funny bone. Instead, it is my inability to prepare my favorite treat.

Without that microwave I am helpless to console myself with my favorite comfort food — ice cream.

For a decade, in five homes, that microwave has stood ready. When the time is right, when I'm bored or deserving of a treat, I go to my freezer, dish out a serving of ice cream (actually, it's non-fat yogurt, but if I call it ice cream, it tastes like ice cream), and pop the bowl into the microwave.

Seventeen seconds later, it's perfect.

Soft, but not runny. Ready to slide onto my spoon, into my mouth.

But my microwave has died and I'm denied.

And laughter rings through the phone.

Although we talk daily, I apparently had never shared my culinary secret. Now that I have, my friend laughs.

I sulk.

I stare at the lifeless appliance, remembering how I resisted. I never really wanted it. But others insisted. Raved. Said acquiring it would revolutionize my life.

They were right.

A microwave is as necessary to life, as I know it, as a bank machine. I became so dependent that my vocabulary changed. I no longer cooked dinner; I nuked it.

Friends call me "queen of the microwave." I shrug.

It's not that I can't cook, I tell them. It's that I prefer not to.

As evidence of my ability to cook, should I choose to, I point to the home where I grew up, and its kitchen filled with cookbooks and recipes neatly typed on index cards and covered lovingly in plastic (to protect against spills). In that home, preparations for the evening meal began early in the day. Still do.

But despite my proper upbringing, I rely on a microwave.

Now I wonder how long I can live without one.

In my kitchen, with my microwave dead, I open the freezer door and realize I can't prepare most of the food stacked inside.

The directions taunt me: Microwave 6 minutes.

My microwave was so perfect it turned the food itself. No pausing after 3 minutes to shift the carton.

Microwave 4 minutes. Then serve.

Tonight, that's impossible.

Currently all the microwave is serving up is the time. And that's off by six hours and 32 minutes.

I know it's time to say goodbye. To pull the plug and haul it to the basement to await a proper burial with its dead compatriots — the air conditioner that doesn't cool and the fan that no longer turns.

Never again will I stand beside it, listening intently for the pop-pop-pop of a bag of corn. Never will it thaw another burger or sizzle a piece of bacon. Never again will it stretch last night's gourmet restaurant meal into tonight's dinner.

Its untimely death leaves me depressed.

And until I recover enough to shop for its replacement, my life will be changed.

Life without a microwave means standing in front of a stove. More dishes to wash. Pots. Pans.

Hard ice cream.

And a friend guaranteed to stop laughing the first time she tries my recipe for ice cream.

February 23, 1994

PACKING TOUGH: JUST "THE STUFF"

Memories in sterling silver rest in the bottom of a wooden box.

When I pick them up, tiny charms dangle from a thick chain and their meanings rattle my brain.

A mask of "Tragedy," a reference to participation in a high school play.

A "no parking" sign, received with pride when I became a licensed driver.

A radio, a class ring, a cap and gown.

Ancient history.

Thoughts of high school bring a smile.

The smile decides the charm bracelet's fate.

It stays.

The decision to keep a bracelet I'll never wear again is but a momentary deviation from my mission.

I'm being brutal — trying to, anyway. Preparing to move, I have vowed not to pack, lug and unpack anything that isn't essential.

My motto: "Don't need it, don't want it."

I study shelves full of textbooks, ones I've been packing, lugging, unpacking and never using for more than two decades.

Who still has all her English literature textbooks from high school?

Not me. Not this week, anyhow.

I got brutal with them. Said, holy cow, if I haven't opened even one of them in the four and half years I've lived under this roof, why would I expect to need one of them next month, or even next year?

Anyway, I told myself, it's not like the library doesn't have Chaucer and Keats on its shelves if it comes to that.

So they're gone, the high school lit books. College texts, too.

Delegated to the rummage pile with more clothing than any one woman could possibly wear in one lifetime unless she happens to be Dolly Parton or Liz Taylor.

I call my friend Karen.

"Where did I get all this?" I complain.

She laughs. I laugh.

We both know. It was all those Saturdays we spent together. And I do mean spent.

All those Saturday shopping sprees left me with bushels of baskets, shelves filled with shells and closets of clothes.

Clothes too big or too small, too old or too unstylish present no challenge. I confine them to the rummage heap with no more thought than a pirate in a late-night movie commands someone to walk the plank.

But with some things I can't be brutal — essentials, like my collection of wooden fish or my decorator tins.

So I find myself with a huge box marked "baskets" and smaller ones designated "sea shells" and "fish."

Tins, well, they fill two large boxes.

As I stack the boxes containing tins among the ever-growing piles, I realize a lot of the other boxes are marked "stuff."

"Stuff from my room."

"Stuff from the kitchen."

"Dining room stuff."

Stuff is essential, but never practical.

It's not sheets or pillows or dishes or tablecloths.

Stuff is what makes a house a home, what defines the space inside four walls as Nancy's home.

Stuff generally has little or no purpose. But like a 30-year-old charm bracelet, stuff evokes such pleasurable feelings that its owner casts aside vows of brutality and packs it, stacks it and hauls it, knowing full well that stuff isn't the kind of thing you can locate on a library shelf.

MIDDLETOWN TO
HARRISBURG VIA HONDURAS

Honduras is a Central American country that borders the Caribbean Sea.

Harrisburg is a Pennsylvania city that borders the Susquehanna River.

They would seem to have little in common, except that both begin with "H."

Because the two places would not be easily confused, I had to wonder why a letter someone mailed me from Middletown went to Honduras.

In February, I was scheduled to speak to a class at Penn State Harrisburg. The professor wrote me a letter outlining the time and location of the class, where to park and other pertinent details.

The letter was postmarked Feb. 6 in Harrisburg. Six days later, it was postmarked again in Honduras.

Then, it fell into a black hole.

On April 23, I found it in my mailbox at The Patriot-News. On the front of the envelope someone had stamped "Extraviado a Honduras," which, our resident Spanish expert tells me, means "misplaced, stranded or lost in Honduras."

That explains where the letter had been since Feb. 12. But I still wondered how it got to Honduras in the first place. So I called the post office.

The folks over there were appalled and astounded. They wanted to see the envelope, so I faxed them a copy. Then they wanted to see it up close and personal, and they thought it would be nifty if I brought it over. That way, they could show me around.

You can't tour the postal facility on Crooked Hill Road in Susquehanna Twp. without being impressed.

Between 4 million and 5 million pieces of mail are processed there on an average day, most by some innovative machinery.

Huge sorters find the stamp on each letter, cancel it and apply the Harrisburg postmark. Machines read the bar codes on letters, or put bar codes on letters that don't have them, then sort the letters into the right pile. A brand new robot nicknamed "Big Bird" because of its size and color reads the labels on trays of mail, picks them up and stacks them in the appropriate cart.

But how, I still wanted to know, did a letter destined for a newspaper office wind up in a country that produces bananas and coffee?

This is their educated guess: When the professor wrote my address on the envelope, she used five lines: name, title, company, street address, then city and state. The fifth line, which lacked the zip code, skirted the bottom of the envelope. That bounced the letter out of the automated machinery to one of the letter-sorting machines operated by real people.

But "Harrisburg, PA" may have been too low even for the human machine operator, who probably intended to send it to something called nixies, a pile of letters that must be sorted by hand because the addresses are difficult to read.

The code for nixies is one digit different from the code for international mail, which may have started the missive on its path to Central America.

It's no big deal, really, that the letter from Middletown arrived a couple of months late. I had bronchitis the week I was to go to the class, so I never needed the information.

It's just kind of irritating that my letter spent a couple of months in a warm country bordering the Caribbean, while I spent the cold spring along the Susquehanna.

UNIFORM STILL GIVING FITS
TO EX-SCHOOLGIRL

Everybody's talking about uniforms in school. To me, they were simply part of high school life.

For four years, I was one drop of water in a sea of navy skirts, white blouses and navy vests that bore a school emblem on the left side, over what, I assume, is the approximate location of one's heart.

They were made of some mysterious material that got thinner every time you washed it. By senior year, most of the skirts resembled blue mosquito netting.

This caused great concern to the nuns who ran the establishment. Their role in life was to keep us pure and prevent any of us from causing an obscene thought to enter the minds of our male classmates — a pretty tough task in a building holding almost 1,000 teen boys.

Anyhow, as the uniforms got thinner, the chances of one of the boys seeing through them and possibly even glimpsing the outline of a girl's legs increased substantially. The only preventive measure, short of demanding that a girl's parents purchase new uniforms, was to ensure that all the young ladies wore proper slips under their uniforms.

If you aren't an aging baby boomer, this word could puzzle you: pettipants.

Pettipants, popular for a time in the '60s, were half a slip with legs — silky culottes you wore under your clothes. They drove the nuns crazy. We all wore them.

Pettipants under a thinning uniform skirt could allow the boys to see the outline of your legs, or at least the outline of the legs of your pettipants.

Periodically, one or two nuns would haul a classroom full of girls out into the hall and make us stand in front of a window with our legs apart.

Sisters showed no mercy to girls wearing pettipants. They were sent home to change, or their mothers called to bring them a proper slip.

Pettipants patrol took place at the same time the nuns did hemline inspection.

Uniforms had to cover your knees. To ensure compliance, we girls had to kneel on the floor in the hallway. If your skirt didn't touch the floor, it was too short.

Growth was no excuse. Neither was uniform shrinkage. Knees had to be covered. Period.

Of course, most of us simply rolled over the waistband of our uniform skirts whenever we weren't kneeling.

The other obsession the nuns had with the uniforms involved sweaters.

Occasionally, it got cold in the sprawling ancient building that housed our school. For instance, every year from October to April. To ward off pneumonia, girls would wear cardigan sweaters. That sent some of the nuns into apoplexy.

Sweaters, you see, can cling to the body, creating the possibility that a couple of those 1,000 teen boys would notice that their classmates had breasts. This was definitely not acceptable.

Better we girls should freeze.

Perhaps it was being cold for the better part of four years that made us detest those uniforms. Maybe it was just being part of that sea of blue. But uniform hatred increased as graduation grew nearer. We dreamed of the day we would burn them in a huge bonfire and never again allow anyone to tell us what to wear.

Now, 30 years after that fire, I look in my closet a lot of mornings, sigh at the selection, and wish life were still that simple.

THERE'S A TIME AND A PLACE ...

Let me start by saying I don't hate kids. In fact, some of my favorite people are under the age of 12. I love them because they are honest, funny and eager to learn.

But just as you wouldn't wear cut-off jeans to a black-tie dinner, you shouldn't take kids to adult places. Their insistence on doing so is one thing I don't understand about a lot of parents today.

Last week at a Caribbean resort, parents with their tots in tow left me shaking my head. A band blasted island tunes most of the night and recorded music pulsed throughout the day. Poolside events included limbo contests, volleyball competitions and slightly off-color comments delivered by a series of perpetually cheerful entertainment directors.

For a lot of the crowd, no event was complete without booze. Waitresses hustled to deliver drinks to sunbathers. Hotel guests stood three deep around the bars from midmorning to the early hours of the next day.

Why would you bring tots to a place like that?

Sitting at breakfast one morning, I watched a mother wrestle a broken glass out of her kid's hand. The little boy, no more than 2 and apparently accustomed to a plastic cup, had slammed the glass on the table, breaking off the stem.

The mother shrieked, drawing the attention of most of the dining room and apparently of the tot's older brother, who looked about 4. As soon as the glass had been removed safely from his brother's hand, he threw a hunk of toast on the floor, beginning a five-minute stand-off with his mother.

She requested that he pick up the toast. He jumped out of his chair and stood with his back to the wall, grinning. Her requesting turned to insisting. His grinning became a mocking laugh.

Eventually, grabbing the back of his shirt, she guided him to the toast on the floor. He picked it up, threw it on the table and returned to his seat, laughing.

She spent the next few minutes telling him what a good boy he was.

Yeah, right.

A little later, down on the beach, two women and four tots sat behind me. One of the tots had to, as he put it, wee-wee. The rest room was approximately 100 feet away. Mom instructed him to go down to the water and take care of business.

Made me want to dive right in.

During the week, I listened to a shrieking kid in a classy restaurant where dinner for two carried a $100 check. I watched another tot fall asleep face down on the table at a Caribbean buffet.

Both incidents happened at 8:30 p.m. No wonder one kid was incredibly cranky and the other excessively tired. They should have been home in bed, not sitting in rooms full of adults.

And what about the woman whose tot kept rushing up and knocking over the wooden horses being used in a pseudo horse race in the bar?

She obviously thought her kid was adorable, such a spirited little guy. Four or five times she pulled him away from the horses he had knocked down, looking around and smiling with pride.

The folks who had wagered money on the race didn't smile back. They knew a kid doesn't belong in a bar any more than he belongs in a restaurant at 8:30 at night.

Now, if somebody could only convince the parents.

ONCE AGAIN REASON TAKES
A BACK SEAT

Let's just make things simple:

Let's take newborn children and put them in a plastic bubble to live in climate-controlled, germ-free comfort until age 12 or 15.

Parents can wait on the children, delivering whatever they need to thrive, protecting them from secondhand smoke and other forms of pollution, insuring against injury in a car or bicycle accident, or being traumatized for life by a swat on the butt.

Let's treat kids like they treat cows in India.

In fact, with all the bicycle helmets, child safety seats, arm pads, knee pads and hysteria whenever a kid gets a well-deserved swat, I think they've already gained cowlike status.

In the latest bout of insanity, the National Transportation Safety Board wants to force kids under 13 into the back seat.

If this dumb suggestion becomes law — and you can bet in our kid-worshiping society it will — it will be a boon only to the manufacturers of minivans.

As law, the transportation board's suggestion would force anyone with three kids or more to buy one of those station wagons of the '90s just to haul the kids to soccer practice, ballet, play groups, Scouts, ice skating, gymnastics and all the other scheduled events that take up the time of the average spoiled kid these days.

As any parent knows, three children cannot sit in the back seat of a car for more than 37 seconds before someone yells, "Mom, he pinched me."

Forcing all the kids into the back seat would require parents to buy minivans simply to spread the kids around, limiting chance encounters of siblings.

Minivans, if I may digress, are without doubt the ugliest and stupidest vehicles on the road. (Don't bother to call me; I don't care if you like yours.)

As the driver of a "normal" vehicle, I hate them because when I am behind one I can't see anything ahead of me. Can't tell if the light is about to turn red. Can't read the signs that tell me what intersection I'm approaching. Can't see anything but a rounded blob that usually has a bumper sticker proclaiming the driver's child is an honor student somewhere.

Even worse is finding myself parked next to a minivan or — horror of horrors — sandwiched between two of them at Wal-Mart or the grocery store.

Ever try to back out of a parking space when a minivan is parked next to yours? It is impossible to see if anything is coming. A four-wheel drive truck with tires the size of New Jersey may be barreling down the row headed straight for the rear of your car, and you wouldn't know it.

Even worse is arriving at your normal vehicle in a parking lot just as a minivan family is getting into their sliding-side-door van, which is parked next to yours.

You wait and wait to open your door while everyone climbs in, finds a seat, buckles up, and puts the youngest child in fortress-type protective gear.

I waited so long outside the video store one day that my new-release movie transformed itself into a two-evening rental.

During that wait, I had time to wonder how I got to this ripe old age. I rode in the front seat, didn't wear a seat belt, rode my bike without a helmet, got the occasional spanking, and sat in rooms with friends of my parents who smoked.

Maybe I should see a lawyer. Maybe I can make a case for child abuse.

IN THE OCEAN, SHE
FINDS BIT OF BUOYANCY

MYRTLE BEACH, S.C. — In my earliest memory of the ocean, I am standing hip-deep, fighting the undertow. I'm not afraid, because my Daddy — so tall and so strong — is clenching my hand.

Maybe the relationship began with the confidence he gave me, but the ocean is like an old friend and every visit feels like coming home. Simply hearing it and smelling it makes me feel welcome.

Like a friend, the ocean has moods.

Sometimes the waves pound, like a prizefighter pummeling an opponent. Sometimes they tease the shore gently, like a lover stealing that first kiss.

Whatever its mood, I find its rhythm hypnotic, drawing me to the water's edge by day, lulling me to sleep at night.

As I write this, it is Sunday. A sun day. About 65 degrees. A few hearty souls don bathing suits, grab lounges and offer their bodies to the tanning god.

Dozens prefer just to walk the shore.

The ocean here is a dull gray/brown, the same gray/brown the Atlantic paints beaches from Maine to Florida. It may lack the sparkling color found on beaches in the Caribbean or Hawaii, but it delivers the same treasures.

And so they walk, folks in their sneakers, T-shirts and jeans, heads down, ever alert, seeking that perfect shell to slip into a pocket or a plastic bag.

The beach is a kaleidoscope of sparkling shells, each unique: A tiny blue shell the size of a fingernail. An egg-sized shell decorated with orange and brown stripes.

The prized conchs are elusive. The perfect ones are plucked from the shore at first light. Even the damaged ones, their twisting interiors exposed, are a source of fascination.

Sea gulls, like sentinels, patrol the beach, waddling occasionally into the surf on webbed feet and matchstick legs.

They seem always to be waiting for something. The next wave. The next meal. The next guy with a bread crust.

Like us, the gulls cannot mark the beach permanently. Someone named Aaron tried today, carefully printing the five letters of his name in the dampness left behind by the exiting tide.

Aaron's mark is temporary. The tides will take it before sunset, just as they will erase the footprints of the folks from New York and Connecticut and Maine who came here seeking relief.

The tides will take the shells, too, delivering a new batch tomorrow. Perhaps they also will hide a treasure for the man who works the water's edge with a metal detector.

They promise nothing, except to wipe away all signs of men and sea gulls, serenade me gently through the night, and be there always, fresh and clean and welcoming.

Sitting along the shore, I recall some of the best times of my life: Skimming waves on an air mattress. Watching the surprise in a child's eyes the first time the surf tickles his toes. Admiring the strength of a son-become-man as he dives confidently into a wave. Sharing girl-talk for hours on two lounges in the sand. Watching palm trees sway in the breeze.

I learned to love the ocean as a child. I continue to love it because no matter how much we change and our world reshapes itself, the ocean remains a constant, its waves forever rolling onto a beach.

January 2, 1997

SUM TIMES, THINGS
JUST DON'T ADD UP

Painful is the word that best describes the process of getting change in some stores these days.

You know. You've been there; you've done that.

You walk in a store, pick up a couple of items and hand a clerk a $10 bill for a purchase that totals $6.34. She looks at the bill, she looks at the cash register. The machine is telling her to give you $3.66 back, and she just can't figure out what to do next.

Experience has taught you that if you try to help, it will only confuse her. So you stand there, biting your tongue.

She digs out three ones, then tries to figure out just what combination of coins from the drawer will add up to 66 cents.

Seconds tick by. People in line start shifting from one foot to the other. Finally, using fingers and toes and some basic knowledge she dimly recalls from second grade, the clerk dumps into your hand three ones, two quarters, a dime, a nickel and a penny, all wadded together.

End of transaction; next, please.

Doesn't anybody understand basic math or courtesy any more?

I'm not blaming teachers. I know they try. I know it for a fact because I spent several hours with a 7-year-old recently and her idea of "fun things we can do in the car" involved me grilling her with math questions.

She was studying money, she said, and she wanted me to ask which coins she would need to reach amounts under one dollar. And she knew all the answers.

So what happens between the ages of 7 and 17, which is the age most of these store clerks appear to be? Does some hormonal change at puberty wipe out everything basic they ever learned? Does listening to too much rock music kill brain cells? Or maybe everything they've learned seeps out through all those holes they put in their ears, noses, navels and other body parts.

I feel qualified to criticize because I've been there and done that.

For a lot of years in high school and college, I pushed cash register keys in a grocery store.

That was, of course, in the dark ages, before computers and scanners and universal pricing codes. We actually had to punch in the price of every item our customers bought. Then we had to deduct the value of any coupons they had, announce the total, take their money and figure out how much change we owed them.

For example, if Mrs. Smith's bill totaled $16.19, that's all the knowledge the cash register shared. If Mrs. Smith handed over a $20 bill, we had to figure out that we owed her $3.81.

We were required to count the change into her hand, a custom that apparently died a quiet death some years ago.

It went like this: Mrs. Smith would hold out her hand, palm up. We would count, starting with the total of her purchase, $16.19. We would place a penny in her palm and say "$16.20," then a nickel and say "$16.25." Add three quarters, one at a time, $16.50, $16.75, $17. Then, individually count out three ones, $18, $19, $20.

That allowed Mrs. Smith to see that she was getting the proper change and to put that change into her wallet in some orderly fashion.

While she did that, we thanked her for her business.

Quaint, weren't we?

STAY-AT-HOME VACATION
HAS LOT GOING FOR IT

Talk about a great vacation!

Last week brought me to a place with all the comforts of home.

All around were plenty of places to go and things to do. Lots of shopping, movies, restaurants. And when I wanted to relax, I had a deck to sit on and a comfortable sofa where I could curl up with a book.

Best of all, staying there didn't strain my checking account.

You see, I spent my vacation at home.

Until now, I had always thought a person had to go somewhere if she had vacation. A week off required me to get in the car and drive to the shore, hop on a plane and head to an island, indulge myself on a cruise ship, visit a foreign country or explore some corner of the United States.

All of those things are wonderful experiences, and all of them are things I hope to do again. But a lot of times I find I return from a trip needing a vacation. There's something about traveling that wears me out.

Lately, something about life in general wears me out. It's always so busy. A lot of times I'd like to go shopping or catch a movie. I intend to visit a friend or eat in a new restaurant. But once the workday ends, I've lost the motivation and the energy.

That's why spending the week at home seemed like a perfect idea. I could do all the things I lack the time and energy to do during a normal workweek. I could do as much or as little as I wanted and not feel guilty because, after all, I was on vacation.

Before my vacation started, co-workers asked where I was going. When I said "home," I got strange looks.

Some thought that home meant a place where I grew up. Others seemed to think I was being flip. But I was sincere when I said I was looking forward to the experience.

And once it began, I relished it.

I confess that a couple of rainy days I stayed in my jammies until lunchtime. That came about because I slept late, gave the daily newspaper the leisurely treatment usually reserved for a Sunday edition and daydreamed a bit.

A couple of nights I stayed up really late. What kept me up were books — three novels read for sheer enjoyment, rather than for redeeming social value. When you're on vacation, it's not necessary to put down a good book until you've turned the final page.

In between sleeping late and staying up late, I spent time with a couple of girlfriends I don't see enough. I visited my parents. I took the munchkins to a kid-friendly restaurant. I dined in a grown-up restaurant where I hadn't eaten before. I browsed in a couple of stores I hadn't visited in ages. I had long telephone conversations with relatives and friends. I went shopping for flowers and dug in my garden. I sipped peanut-butter milk shakes two consecutive nights. I went to yard sales.

I fantasized about retirement. This is what it must be like, I thought. Retirement is about lots of free time to explore and enjoy.

I counted the years, decided retirement was too far off and bought a lottery ticket, hoping to cut the time.

The $2 I won didn't do anything to hasten retirement, but it helped me to buy a couple of things at a yard sale.

I brought home my yard sale treasures and decided to put them away another day. Next time I looked at them, I opted to take a nap. Later, I considered putting them in their proper place, but a rerun of a favorite TV show was about to start.

It's like that when you vacation at home. You can do a little. You can do a lot.

You can do what you want. It's the ideal vacation.

LIKE BEAUTY, TV'S STATUS
IN BEHOLDER'S EYE

Television fascinates me. No, not what's on it, but the way people react to it.

Have you ever been someplace when a TV news or weather person walks in? Everyone looks, pretends they aren't looking and whispers to the people around them. The fact that a person makes his or her living staring into a TV camera seems to bestow special status.

Two recent experiences got me thinking about this. First, someone at The Patriot-News corralled me into doing a TV commercial. Actually, it wasn't a commercial. It was one of those public service "good cause" things.

The paper and other media were collecting canned goods at malls for the food bank. I was in a commercial with a TV gal and a radio guy, asking people to take food items to the mall.

I confess right here that they had to shoot my portion about 85 times. But the technicians finally got something they could live with.

Soon people started telling me, "I saw you on TV." People always say this breathlessly.

There you are, the real flesh and blood thing, standing right in front of them, and they are impressed that they saw you on a 27-inch box in their living room.

Even the munchkins were impressed. The 10-year-old called me at work to say she and her mother had just seen me on the tube.

"I screamed, 'That's my Granny,'" she said.

Apparently, this put me temporarily in the category of "cool."

The second TV experience wasn't mine, but I witnessed it repeatedly last week.

About a year ago, my older son appeared on "Jeopardy." He won a trip for four to California. We went last week — my son, his wife, my father and I. It was my son's way of saying "thank you" for a bit of help we've given him here and there.

He's had a busy year, you see. He graduated from law school and became a first-time dad. Important stuff.

But what do you think impresses people?

"You were on 'Jeopardy'? Oh my gosh. I watch it every night. Oh, you must be very smart. Oh my heavens. Hey, Bob, come here. He was on 'Jeopardy.' Won this trip. We watch it every night, don't we, Bob?"

Lawyers. Oh, they're a dime a dozen.

Dads. Even the best of them — which he is — are standard fare.

But "Jeopardy" contestants? Wow. That's something special.

In fact, my son thinks TV is what got him on "Jeopardy." People who audition for the game are asked to write down some quirky or unusual thing about their lives so that Alex can say, "So, Jason, I understand you've collected and framed a copy of every Elvis Presley record ever made," or "Well, Helen, they tell me you've traced your family back to Noah."

My son wrote that his only prior TV appearance had been on "Percy Platypus." For those with short-term memories, Percy originated at WGAL, Channel 8. Percy was a puppet, and the audience generally consisted of Scouts and other groups, which is how my son got there.

The "Jeopardy" folks apparently found this impressive. They were wowed by his six seconds on local TV.

The impact of TV works two ways. Apparently an appearance, however brief, imparts a fleeting celebrity that you can reactivate by telling people about it.

On the other hand, if you get up close and personal with those who appear regularly on TV, you can score points. For example, if you see weatherman Chuck Rhodes in the grocery store, you can impress your co-workers by letting them know that you and Chuck briefly breathed the same air. If you talked to him, you score even more points.

In fact, as I was telling Chuck, just the other day...

December 14, 2000

HOW TO OPEN GIFT FROM
'GREATEST GENERATION'

We lost an uncle last week, my many cousins and I did.

He was flamboyant, loved big cars, sharp clothes, his family and Atlantic City. He called us, each one of the female cousins, "My beautiful niece," and could be counted on to pinch your cheek and squeeze you in a bear hug.

In New Jersey last weekend, at the wake and the funeral, we talked about losing his generation. He was 76.

The cousins have seen our parents and aunts and uncles slipping away.

We don't want to lose them. So we've vowed that in the year to come we will make an effort to gather them more often.

We're going to pick a day soon after the holidays and get them together for lunch at a midway location. We're going to let them talk, and we're going to listen. Because we still have so very much to learn from them.

I share the thought because, all around us, we are losing The Greatest Generation. They are the people who grew up during the Depression, survived World War II and reared us, The Spoiled Generation.

We watched them last weekend, knowing that they had grown up poorer than we could imagine. They don't talk about it much, but we know that food was scarce and money even more elusive.

As a result of that hardship, they waste nothing. They clean their plates. If a restaurant serves them too much, they take it home and eat it tomorrow. They save everything.

My 80-year-old aunt went up to my thirtysomething son Sunday and handed him a note she had stashed away for more than 20 years. He was 13 when he wrote it.

The note thanked her for a card and money. (At the end of the line, he drew a card and some money.) He wrote that he was going to use it to buy Puma sneakers. (He drew the sneakers.) He said he'd use any leftover money to take his brother and me to McDonald's. (He drew the Golden Arches.)

What she handed him was a glimpse into his past. She held a piece of it that he couldn't get anywhere else. Returning that note was a gift far more precious than the original.

Those are the things her generation has a lock on — stories and memories that flavor life.

That same aunt has been a godsend to me as I sort through photographs in my mother's trunk. Mom told me at some point — probably more than once — who was who in the photos and when and where the pictures were taken.

I paid no attention. Perhaps I figured I had all the time in the world to look at those photos with Mom.

Well, I didn't.

Now I rely on my aunt to fill in the gaps.

I'm thankful that at 80 she's still as sharp as those Depression-era hunger pangs must have been.

I know it's a busy season. We're all busy in every season.

Still, here's my advice: Don't be too busy to listen to the stories. Sit down with the photos and your parents, grandparents or other relatives and let their memories flow.

Their stories will make you richer in a way that has nothing to do with money.

WANNA SELL TO ME?
TIDY THOSE TOILETS

We've been Christmas shopping at my house. A lot.

In an effort to support local businesses and workers, we've been patronizing area stores and malls instead of buying over the Internet.

That could change. If I shop from my home computer, at least there's a relatively clean bathroom nearby.

Yes, this is a column about bathrooms. Filthy bathrooms. Out-of-order bathrooms. Crowded bathrooms. Bathrooms without necessary supplies.

Some have accused me of being obsessed with bathrooms because, over the years, I've attacked the condition of public rest rooms in several places. But I defend those critiques.

If a store owner or a restaurant or mall or amusement facility wants my hard-earned money, the management should supply a relatively clean, working rest room.

That's not what I found last weekend.

During our shopping extravaganza, we stopped for dinner Saturday night. Food was good. Service was OK. Rest room was passable. Then all of a sudden I found myself standing at the sink with dripping hands and no means to dry them. The paper-towel holder on the wall was empty. The rest room didn't contain one of those half-baked hot-air driers.

Thankfully, I was wearing jeans. In a pinch, they're pretty absorbent.

Saturday night is probably a restaurant's busiest time. Shouldn't somebody's job description include: Check the rest rooms periodically to make sure they are clean and contain adequate supplies?

The next day we traveled to that foreign territory across the Susquehanna. Yes, we went shopping on the West Shore.

Our destination was a major department store that once had a home in a mall on the East Shore but doesn't anymore.

We shopped. It was crowded. It was hot. I decided to take a rest-room break. A half dozen other women had made the same decision and were waiting in line.

The rest room had five stalls. Two had out-of-order signs, one was too disgustingly dirty to use.

I shrugged and decided not to wait behind six other women for the privilege of using one of two functioning facilities in an otherwise repugnant room.

We left and drove to a discount store whose name prominently features a letter of the alphabet.

We filled a cart. I followed a large sign to the rest room. Two stalls, one out of order, a line for the other.

No, thanks.

We headed to the cash registers (they have plenty of those and they all seem to work), paid for the cart-load of stuff, drove back across the river and home to our relatively clean bathroom.

Sure, they got me. Despite the lack of adequate rest rooms, I spent my money in those stores.

But I'll think again before I return. Same with the restaurant. The food was good, but whoever runs the place lacks good sense, or good manners.

So don't criticize me if I finish my Christmas shopping on the Internet. I can find some of the same products at pretty much the same prices.

Best of all, the rest room's the next room. It works, it's relatively clean and there's no waiting.

IT'S TIME TO QUIET OUR
FEARS, MOVE ON

When you have a little one around the house, the dangerous stuff goes. Furniture with sharp corners, out the door. Cleaning products, under lock and key. Knickknacks that could shatter and cut tiny fingers, off to a higher place.

No matter how diligent the parents, however, kids get hurt.

You can belt them in seats, wedge helmets on their heads and fill a cart at Babies "R" Us with items to childproof your home, but you're never going to prevent every scrape and bump.

The world's kind of like that, too.

In the past year, Americans have acted like overanxious parents. We've hauled in the high-tech equipment, put security firmly in place and tried to ensure that not one more American gets killed or even hurt. But deep down inside, we know someone's going to get scraped, bumped or worse somewhere, sometime, somehow.

Just as there is no foolproof means of protecting a kid from everything in the big, bad world, there is no foolproof method of foiling every big, bad nut intent on sending himself to "heaven" with a suicide bomb.

In no way do I mean to diminish American efforts of the past year. I feel reassured when I pass Three Mile Island and see armed guards. I'm glad Tom Ridge is doing what he does, even if I haven't committed the color code to memory.

I suppose it's wise to store potassium iodide pills and to have turned the front of the state Capitol into a bunker. I guess it's necessary to check bags at football games and certainly at airports.

But I don't think for a minute that all this security can prevent the next ugly incident.

And I detest the second-guessing. Over the past year, we've heard claims that the FBI knew this or that and didn't act. Some say that people in high places ignored warnings of terrorist activity.

People bash those in authority for failing to be clairvoyant.

Bad stuff happens, and it's useless to blame someone.

When a kid falls off a swing or a tricycle, there's always someone alleging the parents shouldn't have pushed so high or so hard. Grandma asks Grandpa why somebody wasn't watching the child more closely.

When a toddler trips and falls, the neighbors might say he should have been wearing shoes, or he should have been barefoot. The parent should have been closer or held the kid's hand.

It's that old story of 20-20 hindsight.

None of us will ever feel safe again. We've seen too much, read too much, felt too much pain. You didn't have to know anyone in the World Trade Center or the Pentagon or on Flight 93 to have been profoundly devastated by the events of a year ago.

But we've mourned for a year, and it's time to move on.

Parents who worry to excess don't allow themselves to enjoy their child running in the grass or climbing in the playground or zooming past on a bike.

People who focus on fear of what we can't prevent have no time to enjoy their lives and liberty.

And if we fail to do that, we've let the bad guys win.

LET'S GET MANNERS ON A ROLL

That chewing sound you hear is me eating my words.

Chomp, chomp, chomp.

Yes, I am the woman who wrote that minivans "are without doubt the ugliest and stupidest vehicles on the road. ...

"As the driver of a 'normal' vehicle," I wrote, "I hate them because, when I am behind one, I can't see anything ahead of me. Can't tell if the light is about to turn red. Can't read the signs that tell me what intersection I'm approaching. Can't see anything but a rounded blob that usually has a bumper sticker proclaiming the driver's child is an honor student somewhere."

That was June 12, 1997.

This is now.

Guess who's driving a minivan?

Chomp, chomp, chomp.

Yes, that's me you see sitting high behind the wheel of a red Ford Windstar. It has tinted windows and shiny wheels. Friends tell me it's pretty sporty for a minivan.

Yeah, right.

Like George Will in a Speedo.

Let me tell you why I'm rolling along in this vehicle. Chomp, chomp, chomp.

I have an excuse, really.

You see, my dad's been rolling along in an electric wheelchair, and we needed a vehicle to hold the wheelchair. It was Pop's money that bought the van. I'm just the driver. Honest. Chomp, chomp, chomp.

While I'm digesting my 5-year-old words, I also feel I must signal you that this van-and-wheelchair saga is about to take a more serious turn.

In recent months, pushing a wheelchair that isn't electric, I've experienced the best and worst of people and places.

I've seen folks stop what they're doing and pause, to hold a door or help to push a big man up a steep hill.

I've also seen doors slammed in our faces and delivery trucks parked across three handicapped spaces so those who needed them couldn't use them.

I've tried to enter businesses and been stymied by steps or grass or narrow doors.

Most distressing to me is the attitudes some people adopt. They seem to think that a person in a wheelchair has lost his mind.

Twice — in doctors' offices, of all places — I've been asked whether my father is capable of filling out a form.

My standard reply is, "His legs don't work; his brain does."

Rude, true, but it gets the point across.

Pop isn't the only one who gets that treatment.

Patrick Patterson, a community organizer for the Center for Independent Living of Central Pennsylvania in Camp Hill, has endured plenty of it since he began using a wheelchair after an accident in 1984.

"They speak to the person that's with you like you don't know anything at all," he said.

Patterson says the treatment stems from a lack of education. One of the many things the center does is to train employees and other groups to better understand those with disabilities.

The point to remember, Patterson said, is "we're still people. We still think. We still have to pay bills. We still go to work."

What he wants others to know when they encounter someone in a wheelchair is simply this: "I'm still me. I just roll around."

Now those are some words worth chewing on for a while.

YOU HAVE TO GET UP EARLY TO BEAT THIS BARGAIN HUNTER

Thursday's a good day for those of us with an addiction to yard sales.

That's the day when most people start advertising.

So Thursday, I grab the paper and a glass of Diet Coke, prop up my feet and peruse the ads.

They're divided, you know, into Yard Sales East and Yard Sales West. Being an East Shore resident, I always check the sales on my side of the river first. But I'm not averse to crossing the river to buy someone else's junk. (I wonder, though. On certain parts of the West Shore, would that be junque?)

What I'm looking for is convenience. I like lots of yard sales in one place so I can get out of my car and walk. It's great if I can park, loop a block, return with my treasures and then loop a block in the other direction.

That happens less than I would like. Too often, people place ads for development sales — probably after inviting everyone in the development to participate — but when I get there, I discover one house with a sale on this block and one on the next block and two way, way up the street.

Another thing that hampers walking is having nowhere to walk. It's surprising how many developments don't have sidewalks.

Then there's the whole hill thing. I don't mind walking up a little incline, but a lot of developments are built on streets that look like something out of the Alps.

After getting ideas Thursday, I get serious Friday. I get my newspaper, check for new ads, pick up a pencil and circle where I want to go. I gather a lot of change and a bunch of $1 bills.

Saturday, I try not to be an early bird. I've held yard sales, and nothing is worse than people picking at your stuff while you're still trying to get it situated.

I'm also not much for haggling. I figure if you put a price on something, that's what you want.

But I do like to see the prices. Nothing is more frustrating than having to ask, "How much is this?" "How much is this?"

If pressed to name my favorite development sale, I can list a few.

But my all-time favorite is Old Reliance in Lower Swatara. It generally has lots of participants, the opportunity to walk, and plenty of food. Best of all, it has someone I know and she lets me use her place for a potty break.

That's yard sale heaven.

...and one for the buyers

Plenty of my treasures started life belonging to someone else.

Take, for example, the blue cracked-glass ball. It serves no functional purpose, but it sure is pretty.

It hangs in my kitchen window where I can admire it several times a day.

The first time I saw it — early one Saturday — it was hanging on a metal hook on a table at the edge of some guy's lawn.

"How much?" I asked, in my best "don't care if I buy it or not" voice.

He looked at his teen-age son, who shrugged.

"A buck," Pop said.

"Tee-hee-hee," I thought. Gotcha.

At least $25. That's what I figure the cracked-glass ball would have cost in a gift shop.

Sure, I love it for itself, but part of my affection comes from knowing what I paid for it.

It was a bargain, and I sure love a bargain.

That's why I love yard sales.

Let me say up front that I don't like the hours. Who decided that yard sales should be held really early Saturday mornings? I hate getting up early, particularly on Saturday.

But if the weather's fair and a whole neighborhood's participating, the lure of bargains gets the better of me, and I drag myself out of bed.

Part of the strategy of yard-sale shopping is being open-minded.

Sometimes I'll look at something and really like it. Then I stop and ask myself, "But where would I put it?"

The idea is not to worry about that. Sooner or later, I'll come up with someplace. If I don't, I'll just share.

My friend, Karen, and I have been doing that for years.

She bought a wooden shelf last year at a yard sale. One day not too long ago I was at her house, and she asked if I wanted it.

She simply had no place to put it.

It looks terrific on my porch.

No money changed hands. After all, she has some yard-sale treasures in her place that my house outgrew, including a nice wicker piece she uses to store towels.

So, you see, it all works out.

It pays to be open-minded not just about use, but also about colors.

My porch holds a couple of wicker tables I picked up at a sale once upon a time. I forget what color they were. They're blue now.

I'm wicked with spray paint. It's great stuff for making those yard sale purchases match your decor.

Just don't try to paint in the wind.

When I go to sales, I hunt for all kinds of stuff. I'll buy almost any picture frame. Sooner or later, a kid's picture winds up in it.

I also buy a lot of kitchen stuff that I use only occasionally.

One favorite item is a soup tureen that I bought almost a decade ago. My mother fell in love with it, so I gave it to her. She kept it on her kitchen counter and hid O'Henry candy bars in it (to keep them from the grubby paws of her grandchildren and great-grands).

After she passed away, I took it back. I often look at it and smile. Occasionally, I even put soup in it.

Like the soup tureen, my favorite crystal vase came from the home of newlyweds discarding some of the wedding gifts that were cluttering up their closets.

Some of this prime stuff comes in the original boxes. Young couples' homes are also great places to stock up on stuff for the grandkids.

I buy age-appropriate toys, keep them around for visits and don't feel guilty about getting rid of them when the kids outgrow them.

In the meantime, I store them in a cute wicker chest I picked up, you know, at a yard sale.

OSWALD KILLED A WHOLE
LOT OF INNOCENCE, TOO

It's probably not unusual, but I was pretty self-centered in high school.

My world revolved around school and social activities. Sitting in class and hearing the loudspeaker broadcast that the president and vice president had been shot, I assumed it was the president and vice president of the student council.

You've heard what they say about the word "assume."

I wrapped my head around the truth within minutes. John Fitzgerald Kennedy, our hero, our hope, had been shot.

Kennedy, the first Roman Catholic president, was considered pretty special in my Catholic high school.

We didn't know then what we would learn in later years. We assumed he was what he appeared to be: the perfect husband, the perfect dad. He symbolized the man every girl in my Catholic school wanted to marry. He was rich, good looking, a war hero, personable, religious.

The words of the announcement had barely faded that Friday when the nuns pulled out the rosary beads. We prayed, but soon learned Kennedy was dead.

We heard that announcement on the loudspeaker, too. Forty years ago, classrooms didn't have televisions, or even radios. Someone in the office broadcast what they wanted us to know. In the vice president's case, the announcement proved to be wrong. He was very much alive and well.

They sent us home early, I believe. I remember a lot of crying, on the streets, in our homes, on television.

Until Kennedy, presidents always had seemed to be really old men. Truman and Eisenhower, I know now, were in their early 60s when they became president. Both seemed so dreadfully old.

Kennedy, born in the 20th century, was dynamic in a novel way. He had that sophisticated wife and those adorable children and that huge Irish Catholic family.

I saw him once. He was campaigning, and his motorcade passed near my house. We lined the street and waved. We imagined when he waved back that he was looking directly at us.

Now he was gone. His wife was a widow. His children had no father.

I was sad. But in my self-centered high school way, I also was devastated. They canceled all the dances for Friday night. Saturday, too. Teenage social life disappeared for an entire weekend.

With little else to do, families sat glued to their TV sets. The TV, black and white, was kept in the living room. Kids didn't have TVs in their rooms. Parents didn't either. Everyone sat together, spellbound.

I couldn't imagine then, naive teen that I was, that some people hated Kennedy. I learned about hatred in the days that followed. I hadn't encountered much prejudice until then. I didn't know there were people who hated the Irish, people who hated Catholics, people who just hated.

That weekend, a lot of us learned to hate. We directed our hate at Lee Harvey Oswald, assassin. We learned he'd lived in Russia, for Pete's sake. No one lived in Russia except God-hating communists.

At least that's what they had taught us.

People speculated about how Oswald got into that awful country. More importantly, they wondered how he got out.

Then, we saw him die.

I was sitting on the living-room floor, intermittently watching television, reading the Sunday funnies. I looked up just as Jack Ruby walked up to Oswald. I saw the shot, Oswald's awful grimace, the absolute confusion that followed.

In one short weekend, our hero died in Dallas, and we saw the accused fatally shot on TV on a Sunday morning.

For my generation, the weekend was a milestone. It marked the end of innocence.

GOODBYE, BANK; HELLO, COMCAST!

I divorced my bank the other day.

It was a no-fault split: The bank didn't contest.

You'd think after a 10-year relationship, it might have wanted to reconcile. But no.

I admit that I was to blame for the initial friction between us. I was distracted. I lost interest and overlooked my bank account's needs. Before long, I was pulling out more than I had put in.

The bank fired off a nasty letter. Not only that, but it snatched $30, shoving me even further into the hole. Our relationship was going bankrupt.

I thought it was unreasonable, and it quickly became a matter of principle. I use direct deposit. Money dumps into my account every Monday night. To charge me $30 on a Monday afternoon was pretty low. At least I thought so.

Then, it happened again. As I said, I was distracted. I was at fault. But after 10 years without a transgression, I expected a little slack.

Finally, I sat down with a nice man who straightened everything out. I vowed to be faithful to the bottom line. He promised to erase those nasty fees.

He didn't hold up his end of the bargain.

Then the bank sent a nasty letter claiming I hadn't made a monthly payment on a loan and it wanted the money. Now.

But it had been paid. In fact, the loan had been paid in full.

Did the bank give me $30 for its mistake? I don't think so.

I confronted the bank the other day. It has a new name now, which is at least the third during our relationship. I said I was breaking it off, that I'd committed to another, that I was tired of being treated cruelly.

OK, a man said, sign here. He cut up my ATM card. Barely said goodbye. Moved on to another customer.

I wouldn't have stayed with that bank even if he had begged, but a girl does like to feel wanted. Some small effort to win me back would have been nice.

Perhaps the bank could take a few lessons from the cable company. Now there's a place that's learned how to treat a lady.

In the past, the cable company has had other names. Back then, I would have bet that all cable company employees were required to graduate from a course called "How to Be Rude and Really Tick Off the Customers."

Of course, this implies that any of them spoke to customers. I'd have sworn then that the cable company had one phone line and it was busy 23 hours and 55 minutes a day.

On the off chance you could schedule someone to come to your home, you had to stay on the premises for three days because the cable company couldn't pin down a date, let alone the arrival time.

For these reasons, I wasn't too thrilled the other day when I had to call about fuzzy reception. I picked up a magazine and a soda and settled into a comfortable chair before I dialed. I figured I'd read while music played in my ear.

I dialed. I pushed in the answers to two or three questions. The phone rang once and a person answered. And not just any person — a polite person. She told me she was sorry I was experiencing problems. She said it sounded like something at the pole. She said she'd send someone the next day and no one needed to be home. If the problem wasn't resolved, she said, I should call back. She told me to have a nice day and a great weekend. Even thanked me for being a customer.

Color me flabbergasted.

The next day the cable guy showed up and fixed the problem. He called my house and left a message. He said if I wasn't satisfied, I should call and he'd return.

Now, that's how you treat a lady.

Comcast, you're my new love. I envision a long, happy relationship.

ONE WAY TO ENSURE LESS WASTE

Although my father has passed away, he's left behind a very enthusiastic pen pal.

I thought, perhaps, the pen pal had peaked the day that 16 letters with the same return address arrived in the mailbox. Lo and behold, a few days later, I opened the box and found 18 more.

All of these letters, from Highmark Blue Cross Blue Shield in Pittsburgh, regard my dad's supplemental medical insurance.

Like most folks past 65, my dad relied on Medicare to pay most of his medical bills. But he paid a premium every month to Highmark for a policy that would pay the remaining 20 percent.

I have to be honest here and tell you that I encouraged him to buy the supplemental insurance through his former employer. He had it only for a year or so. Trust me, Highmark lost a bundle on him.

But I think the company also is losing a bundle with the system it uses to process mail. The postage on each of the letters sent to Pop represents 27.8 cents. I don't know what Highmark pays for its letterhead and envelopes, but I'm going to round off the cost of a letter at 30 cents — for convenience sake.

Just one day's shipment to Pop represented a $5.40 expenditure. Inside each letter is one explanation of who paid what to whom.

Here's an example: A patient is in the hospital and his physician calls in a specialist — we'll call him Dr. Knowalot. He stops by, says hello and looks over the patient. As Dr. Knowalot leaves, he orders some test or other.

For sharing five minutes of his valuable time and knowledge, Dr. Knowalot bills the patient $100. Medicare pays the bulk, and Highmark puts out the difference, so the bottom line is zero. The cost to Pop is nothing.

Highmark sends a letter telling us that.

Repeat this with numerous specialists and dozens of tests and procedures and you've generated hundreds of letters postmarked from Highmark to alert us that my dad didn't owe anybody anything.

Now I'm no business major, but it seems to me Highmark could devise a more efficient way to tell a subscriber to keep his checkbook in the drawer. I suggested as much to Karen Early, director of public relations for the company.

What I didn't know was that the state (didn't you just know that government would be involved in this somehow?) requires timely notification of payment of medical claims.

Highmark's churning computer can't stockpile bills from two or three or four docs and then every week or two spit out its payment records on one sheet of paper. Doing that would thwart government regulations.

Every claim from every doctor and every specialist and every test has to be handled as it's received.

"This is the most efficient option," Early said.

Perhaps.

But to me — the person opening two or five or 16 or 18 envelopes every day — it seems terribly inefficient. And it makes me wonder whether all those letters at 30 cents a pop might be a teeny, tiny bit responsible for the high cost of medical insurance.

BOOZE, SEX: WHAT TO
TELL A COLLEGIAN

If I had a daughter of college age, I'd sit her down and chat.

First, I'd show her the article from last week's newspaper about the Dickinson College student accused of having sex with a woman who drank herself into a stupor at a fraternity. She downed beer and shots. For dessert, she smoked marijuana.

After 4 a.m., the freshman said, she couldn't remember anything. When she awoke, her underwear was missing.

Next, I'd tell my daughter the article was similar to several I saw while teaching at Penn State University last semester.

The names and locations change, but the basic story goes like this: Woman drinks, passes out on a couch or bed and wakes up to discover she's been raped.

Finally, I would tell my daughter that no woman deserves to be raped, no matter how dumb her conduct.

That said, if you walk into the woods during hunting season without an orange vest, you might get shot. Likewise, if you pass out cold in front of a bunch of college guys with raging hormones, you make yourself another kind of target.

You might get raped. You shouldn't, but you might.

For many students — and I don't assume Penn State is the exception — heavy drinking is as much a part of college as attending classes.

Penn State students revere Joe Paterno. But they'd feed him to a volcano before they'd give up drinking.

That impression comes from reading the student newspaper, talking to students and profs, and just soaking up the atmosphere in Happy Valley.

It's an impression backed by a survey, reported in the student newspaper in 2003, that 83 percent of students said they drink.

In other words, you'd have to stop five students walking across campus to find one who doesn't.

Among those who imbibe, 58 percent said they down five or more at a sitting. I don't begrudge the kids a drink — but five?

That cloud over Mount Nittany is inhibition floating away.

Parents, send your daughters off with a bit of real-world wisdom: Not everyone is nice. Some men rape.

Rapists aren't necessarily figures lurking in the shadows with a stocking obscuring their face. Sometimes rapists are cute and personable fraternity boys or football players.

Don't fall for that nice guy facade. Keep your wits about you. Don't drink yourself into a lifetime of bad memories.

Now, if I had a son of college age, I'd sit him down and have a chat, too. First, I'd show him the article from last week's newspaper about the Dickinson College student accused of having sex with a woman who drank herself into a stupor at a fraternity house.

Then, I'd tell him that the article was similar to several I saw while teaching at Penn State last semester.

Finally, I would explain that no means no and that the inability to say yes is the same as saying no.

So if some young lady passes out — no matter how tempting — he cannot view her as a slab of raw meat tossed into a tiger cage.

If he does, I would tell him, he is committing a crime. And when he is caught, he will go to prison.

A prison term, I would tell him, is guaranteed to create its own lifetime of bad memories.

Sex, I would assure him, just ain't worth it.

WARNING: HOLIDAY
TALE MIGHT OFFEND

This is a seasonal story about a little girl named Susie who ...

Wait, wait. Unless they're Amish, no one today names their kid Susie.

OK. This is a story about a little girl named Ashley who's sitting in the room she shares with her sister.

No, no, no. Children don't share rooms with their siblings. Parents produce two kids. Homes come with five bedrooms. Each kid is entitled to her own room — preferably with bath.

OK. This is a story about a little girl named Ashley who's sitting in her room, writing a list: "One Disney Princess 13-inch color TV, one interactive Furby with voice recognition, one Disney Princess doll, one Dora the Explorer Talking Kitchen ..."

As she writes, Ashley begins to sing, "We wish you a merry Christmas, we wish you a merry Christmas. We wish you a merry Christmas and a happy New Year."

Ashley's mommy, sitting at her desktop computer ... Wait. Wrong again. Mommies aren't tied to desktops. Ashley's mommy relies on a laptop so she can catch up with correspondence and check in with the office while sitting at her kids' soccer practice or dance classes.

All right. Ashley's mommy, catching up on correspondence on her laptop, suddenly stops and gasps. She stands, walks to Ashley's room and — respecting her daughter's privacy — knocks.

"Come in, Mommy," Ashley says.

"May I speak with you?" Ashley's mommy asks.

"Yes, Mommy."

"Ashley, that song you were singing upset Mommy."

"Why, Mommy?"

"Because, Ashley, not everyone celebrates Christmas. Some of your little friends' feelings might be hurt if you were to wish them a merry Christmas."

"Like who, Mommy?"

"Well, I don't know, Ashley, but we certainly can't take the chance that someone, somewhere might be offended by your song."

"I don't care, Mommy. I'm writing my list for Santa. I can't wait for Christmas and I'm going to sing my song if I want to."

"If you insist on upsetting me, Ashley, Mommy is going to smack your bottom ..."

Halt. Wait. Child abuse alert. Parents never, under any circumstances, smack their children on the bottom or anywhere else. They reason. They count. They put them in time-out.

Right. Right.

Ashley's mommy says, "I'm afraid that if you continue to sing that song, you will force Mommy to make you stay here in your room with only your Barbies, Little Ponies, DVDs, Harry Potter books, Leap Frog learning system and Bratz dolls to keep you company."

"Fine. I'll stay," Ashley says as she resumes singing, "We wish you a merry Christmas."

As the author of this piece, maybe I'm steeped in outmoded ideas, or as immature as a 7-year-old. Like Ashley, I don't get the flap over wishing someone a merry Christmas.

People who celebrate some other holiday, or ignore holidays altogether, can sing whatever song they like, wish us whatever they like and put up any decorations that strike their fancy.

Since I've got no beef with them, I'd appreciate the same slack.

I'm out of here now, taking time off to celebrate Christmas.

Shocking, simply shocking.

December 8, 2005

DISNEY'S THE PLACE FOR PRINCESSES

Last week I spent all my time in Disney World.

Plenty of folks have suggested that I didn't have to fly to Florida to see Goofy, Dumbo and a Mickey Mouse operation. Just a short walk to the Capitol would have accomplished the same thing.

The difference is that Disney World's wackiness is intentional.

Anyway, a while back the son and his wife invited me to join them and their two little princesses for a week in Disney World. I really didn't know what to expect; I'd been there years ago — Epcot was under construction — and only for a brief visit.

This was going to be a totally Disney experience — stay in a Disney resort and spend the entire time on Disney property.

Of course I was going. A week anywhere with the princesses is a treasure.

By happenstance, my cousin and her hubby went to Disney World in September, and she offered me the benefit of her recent experience.

Her primary advice consisted of reminding me repeatedly to buy the best walking shoes I could find.

I did, but I still hoofed my way to several blisters.

The amount of walking involved is incredible.

But I walked my way into becoming an unofficial Disney expert, or at least someone willing to offer advice. This isn't the travel section, but I'm willing to share:

- If you have an opportunity, go.

But read up on everything and book special events long before you leave for the airport. (I didn't; fortunately, my daughter-in-law did.)

• No, you don't need kids to enjoy Disney. Had I been alone, I could have spent several days perusing the "countries" in Epcot, sampling the food and shopping.

Even without kids, I would have enjoyed the parades, the fireworks and the Christmas decorations. I might have skipped the "Beauty and the Beast" Broadway-style show at MGM or the Mickey Mouse nighttime performance of "Fantasmic," which would have been my loss, because both were outstanding.

• No, your kids aren't too old. If they're teens, you probably don't want to book meals with Disney characters, but they'll still find plenty of activities to love.

If they don't — if they're bored — they've got to be brain dead.

During our week, we ate breakfast with Mickey Mouse at the Contemporary Resort, lunch with Cinderella at her castle in the Magic Kingdom, lunch with Winnie the Pooh in the Crystal Palace, and dinner with the Disney princesses at a Norwegian restaurant in Epcot.

If you want to see awe on the faces of 4- and 6-year-old girls, that's the ticket.

• Yes, your kids may be too young. Pushing a fussy infant through the parks didn't look like fun, though apparently, a lot of parents disagree with me.

• Is everything orchestrated in Disney?

Yup, but I've never experienced a more well-oiled machine. We kept searching for flaws, to no avail.

The bus driver who delivered us to the Orlando airport reported that Disney World employs 70,000 people. Every employee we encountered was pleasant and smiling and seemed to be happy.

Try matching that in the Capitol.

OLD FRIENDS GROW
OLDER, AND SPECIAL

Back in the '70s, a couple of guys wrote a book called, "What Really Happened to the Class of '65?"

Thirty years after the book, I can tell you what happened.

They got old; that's what happened.

I went to my class reunion Saturday night. At first glance, I figured the place was hosting more than one party. All these old people were ambling through the parking lot.

Then I realized they were my classmates.

Geez. We used to be so young and so hip. We danced. Goodness, how we danced. Jitterbug, stroll, cha-cha, limbo. Friday nights. Saturday nights. After the football games.

Fast forward 40 years and I'm listening to one of the girls who was nearest and dearest to me praise the two artificial knees that enabled her to toss out her cane.

Another claimed that every time she looks in the mirror she asks, "Is that you, Mom?"

Parents dominated the conversation for a while. A lot of us have lost parents, and because we once were close, most of us knew one another's parents. So, it was with sadness that we learned how many are gone.

We shared stories of cancer and Alzheimer's and nursing homes and the physical pain that wallops you when you realize that you are now the oldest generation in your family.

But we also traded positive tales. Successful kids. Happy marriages.

And grandchildren. Any mention of grandchildren lit up most faces.

Most of us seem to have some, and all of us seem to enjoy them.

Some classmates are retired now, especially the cops and teachers.

Some are on second or third careers. Some left town and came back.

Some moved decades ago, but flew from Boston or Florida to reminisce.

Of course, the conversation eventually turned to what one fellow called the "defining moment of our generation." And so, one by one, those at our table related where we were when the public address system rocked our world with the news that JFK had been shot.

We fast-forwarded to Vietnam, who went, who didn't, how they fared.

As we reminisced, we decided we early boomers were special — sons and daughters of men who fought back the enemy and the women who kept the home fires burning. We grew up prosperous, in the suburbs, better-educated, better-cared-for than previous generations, exploring a world unimaginable to them.

The topics weren't all so serious. We table-hopped and ate and drank and hugged and laughed — a lot.

Then, too soon, it was time to stroll back to the parking lot.

We exchanged e-mails and promised to stay in touch. Some will; most won't.

But five years from now, we'll gather again. I'm convinced we will.

We'll arrive with a few more artificial knees and hips and other parts, so we might amble a bit more slowly across the parking lot. But I'm sure most of us will show up.

Maybe we're deceiving ourselves. Maybe the Class of '65 wasn't special. Maybe we're no different from the Class of '55 or those who followed in '75 or '85.

But for a few brief years we shared something that sure felt special, and that lures us to rekindle those feelings every five years.

May 19, 2005

WOMEN'S SLAYINGS ELUDE SOLUTIONS

When I heard Tuesday afternoon about another woman shot dead by a man she knew, I felt sickened.

I've read too many stories that sound the same: Enraged man with gun kills woman, kills self. Enraged man with gun kills woman, goes to jail for decades.

Always, in the stories, it's not a stranger, but a man jilted or suspicious or otherwise warped who pulls the trigger.

The stories pull me back to a time and place long ago and not so far away. Once upon a time a man stalked me. It's not an experience a woman forgets, or can easily describe.

I recall it as a series of flashbacks. Lifting one slat on the blinds ever so slightly to peer into the night. Wondering if the wind — or something else — is causing the rustling in the bushes outside. Terrified to take a shower because the running water masks sounds outside the door.

Eventually, his lurking broke my spirit. I moved in with a girlfriend.

The flashbacks include a freeze frame of the two of us squatting on her kitchen floor, trying to determine the color and model of a car driving by repeatedly in the dark.

The simplest tasks become complicated when you fear someone is watching. Driving to the minimart after sundown is out of the question.

In daylight, your eyes dart in six directions. Your stomach churns. Your head pounds. He steals your freedom to live your life and compromises your health.

Society has made tremendous strides in the years since fear gripped my life. Cell phones offer a level of protection. Summoning the police takes three digits, not seven. Caller ID identifies a stalker. Cops take threats seriously. Judges issue protection from abuse orders. Domestic violence groups offer advice and support.

But no protection amounts to much if a man is intent.

It's a lesson proved by the shooting deaths of Kim Keefer of Lower Allen Twp. on Tuesday, Alice Torres of Lebanon last week, Betty Jane Waltermeyer of Fredericksburg in November.

It's a lesson learned from 157 Pennsylvania women who were victims of domestic violence in 2002.

I hate bullies. Men who stalk women are bullies.

I also hate guns.

I've heard all the arguments about people, not guns, being responsible for the deaths of so many women. I've listened as gun enthusiasts run down an endless list of women killed with bats and knives and rocks.

But a stalker with access to a gun can become a murderer too quickly for my taste.

I won't debate gun control. The Constitution gives you that right.

For my part, I won't have guns in my home — now or ever.

Yes, I acknowledge that men can be victims of domestic violence and that women sometimes kill people with guns.

It simply doesn't happen enough to cause more than a blip in the statistics.

Too many men terrorize women. Too many men kill women. I've read too many stories. Every one sickens me.

But even now, after hundreds of stories and dozens of years of flashbacks, I don't know what to do about it.

MIKE'S ALIVE, WELL, BUT ANN'S GONER

Finally, I have proof.

Often, when I'm in a roomful of mature women, I encounter another Nancy or two. And then I say, "Did you ever notice that all women named Nancy are of a certain age?"

People just don't name their kids Nancy anymore.

The proof comes from this neat Web site, babynamewizard.com. You type in a name and it produces a graphic that shows how many people in the United States gave their child that name in any given year.

Nancy looks like a mountain climber's dream, with the peak in the 1940s, when the name soared to seventh in popularity.

Apparently, that had something to do with Frank Sinatra, his daughter, Nancy, and a song, "Nancy With the Laughing Face," which Sinatra recorded in 1944.

Nancy has fallen into the foothills now. My high school girlfriends, Karen, Donna and Linda, landed there, too, after peaking in the '40s and '50s.

Nancy, I'm sad to say, is included in a lineup of "old standbys expected to drop off the list altogether," along with Ann, Carol, Janet and Joyce — all girls I knew in high school.

Their prom dates — Donald, Gene, Gerald, Glenn and Ray — are headed for obscurity, too.

Nancy and her classmates don't make the grade with today's parents who demand names that are creative, not comfortable, according to babynamewizard.com.

Our only hope is to await revival, like Hazel, a name apparently hip again with a "z" right in the middle.

Also ripe for revival, they say, are Alice, Jane, June, Marian, Ruth and Carl, Frederick, Lawrence, Hugh, Stuart.

If Jane can come back, why not Nancy?

After all, almost no one named their child Madeline in the 1950s, '60s and '70s, when it slumped to 448th in popularity. By 2003, my 6-year-old granddaughter's name had bounced back to 60th, making her quite trendy.

Same goes for her sister, Isabel, born in 2001. Her name died off in the 1940s but surged 50 years later, jumping from 460th on the 1980s popularity list to 82nd in 2003.

Similarly, parents of boys have rediscovered Zachary well enough to make it No. 20 on the popularity list. It didn't reach the top 1,000 in the 1940s, but today, the Web site says, it's "the epitome of biblical cool."

What remained cool through the '50s, '60s, '70s, '80s and '90s was naming your son Michael.

I did it. So did a zillion others.

Michael shows up as this huge blue blob on the babynamewizard. com site — No. 1 from the 1950s through 1990s. That explains why if you stand in any workplace and yell, "Hey, Mike," half the guys in the room will look up.

By 2003, Michael had dropped a notch to No. 2. Still, it will be a lot of years before you can yell that name without turning a lot of heads.

What's hot in the immediate future, according to the Web site, includes Asher, Decian, Emmett, Hudson and Otto for boys, and Ainsley, Annalise, Willow, Susannah and Estella for girls.

I'll confess that some of those names make me wrinkle my nose. But I'm comfy, not creative — and almost obsolete — so what do I know?

CLEANING UP HAS BECOME
TOO COMPLEX

My mother's house was spotless.

Always.

I was thinking about that the other day as I walked along the supermarket aisle that stocks cleaning supplies.

My mother scrubbed and polished and shined everything using just a few staples: Top Job, Ajax cleanser, Pledge and Windex. She probably kept a few other tricks in her bag, such as oven cleaner and silver polish, but the basic four got her through most weeks.

She had a dry mop for wood floors and a wet mop for her kitchen and bath. She tossed the dirty mops in the washing machine and hung them in the sun to dry.

Looking up and down the supermarket aisle, I decided life today offers too many choices.

Take Windex. My mother's was always blue. Now I have to choose between blue and a reddish-purple they call Mountain Berry.

And do I want the original runny stuff or no-drip?

Do I plan to use Windex only on my glass, or do I want the new Multi Task variety for lots of surfaces? And if I do, should I get vinegar, orange or sparkling lime?

Or would my life improve if I bought the Multi Task Vinegar Wipes? Or the Dry Microfiber Cloths?

All choices change if I want to clean the windows from outside, because then I should grab the green bottle that attaches to the hose.

Complicating life further is my addiction to Swiffer. I got hooked because I loved that little jingle on the commercial.

Although I bought in, they didn't convince me with that "stop cleaning, start Swiffering" stuff. I don't care what they call it; when you're moving around dirt, you're cleaning.

Anyhow, I started with the Swiffer duster, which is pretty neat since it extends to high places and acts somewhat like a magnet for dust.

Then I bought the mop-like thing that uses wet pads to clean the floors. Next I added the Swiffer Wet Jet, which has a bottle of cleaning stuff attached to the handle — choose from multipurpose, wood cleaner or antibacterial with a citrus scent — and a different sort of pad you stick on the mop.

Most recently I picked up a Swiffer Carpet Flick, which uses a sticky pad to grab crumbs and other unwanted gook from the rugs.

I rearranged the garage to create enough space to hang all the cleaning equipment and store the various sticky items and pads. Of course, I always seem to be out of the Carpet Flick thingies when the rug is crumby, and I can't find the wet pads when I want to mop the floor.

And, I have to be careful not to confuse those pads with the pads that attach to my new Mr. Clean Magic Reach, a handy tool that's supposed to make cleaning the bathroom easy — once you figure out how to snap all the pieces together.

Magic Reach uses two types of pads: the Scrubbing Tub/Shower Pads and the Mopping Floor/Multipurpose Pads, sold separately.

If I use Mr. Clean on the bathroom floor, I don't need the Swiffer mop there, although I will still need it in the kitchen. I have to load up with so many different pads, no room remains in the grocery cart for food.

Like I said, life offers too many choices. I think I'll go do something simple — like vote.

March 7, 2006

CLOSER LOOK IS NEEDED
ON JUSTICES' EXPENSES

Dear Boss,

I'm attaching this memo to my expense voucher to prevent you from flying out of your office, fists shaking, to pepper me with questions.

As Desi used to say on the "I Love Lucy," show, "Let me 'splain."

At first glance, a few items on my voucher might look, well, a little iffy and maybe even a little pricey. But if you hear me out, I believe you'll find everything I've submitted is a legitimate expense.

I've taken a cue from the state Supreme Court justices. I read in our Sunday paper — in an article by Jan Murphy — that taxpayers reimbursed the justices for expenses totaling $53,473 over six months.

Of course, my total doesn't come anywhere near that. But then my salary doesn't reside on the same plateau as theirs either.

Judges are paid $155,782 a year. The chief justice pulls in $160,000 and change. And cars. Taxpayers shell out for their cars— something you've never done for me.

Still, Chief Justice Ralph Cappy is demanding more.

But I digress.

Russell Nigro — the first person ever booted off the high court by the voters — submitted a bill for a $318 dinner just before he stepped down.

After seeing that, surely you can't get upset at my restaurant bill.

Nigro said he dined with law clerks, lawyers and judges and discussed court business.

So if I treated a few reporters and editors to a meal while we gossiped — I mean discussed newsroom business — shouldn't my $178 tab be covered?

And if you're wondering about the $43 for picture frames, well, Justice Max Baer paid $80 for a print for a wall in his office and Justice Ronald Castille was reimbursed $173 for framing two photos of the justices.

Granted, I don't have any walls since I don't have an office, but I've got the cutest darn grandchildren, and I found these adorable frames on sale. They look great on my desk. In fact, drop over and I'll show you.

And speaking of grandkids, you'll note I paid one of them $75 to drive me across the river. But it was a legitimate venture.

Justice Sandra Schultz Newman paid $170 for a driver to Hershey, where she made a presentation. There I was, invited into the wilds of Cumberland County to speak to a civic group, and I was a little tired and a bit stressed, so I asked the kid, "Will you drive me?"

Why shouldn't he get paid like anyone else?

While I was over there, still dragging, I felt thirsty, so I sent the kid into the mini-mart for a Powerade energy drink. I figured if Cappy could charge us $2.50 for a Powerade while attending a conference at the Hotel Hershey, I could too.

On the way back, I told the kid to take the turnpike, so I'm seeking reimbursement of the 75-cent toll. I'm following the lead of Justice J. Michael Eakin, who was reimbursed $5 for tolls to travel to Newman's husband's funeral.

Surely you can't argue with my logic. I'm in tune with the supremes— and I'm not talking Diana Ross.

Who could be more trustworthy, more honorable than a justice of the state Supreme Court?

I'm not asking you for anything they haven't taken from the taxpayers, so surely it's OK. Right, boss?

A PATIENT'S PATIENCE GROWS SHORT

Years ago, when my kids were tots, my family doctor was a grandmotherly type. She and her husband shared office space and didn't schedule appointments. They simply set office hours. You went in and took your chances.

Many times I spent hours waiting, trying to tame two rambunctious boys in a room full of people with runny noses and hacking coughs.

My mother urged me repeatedly to go elsewhere, but I loved my doctor and thought her brand of medicine was worth the wait.

Fast forward to yesterday.

I changed my way of thinking many years ago. I want a doctor who sets a meeting time, and I don't want to be stood up.

Recently, I've had constant pain in my arm. I diagnosed the problem as tendinitis. My family doctor agreed. We tried a prescription. It still hurt. So she shipped me off to a specialist.

I won't say where I went, but it's the kind of place with a lot of people arriving with casts or on crutches.

When I arrived a few minutes early for my 9:30 appointment, I was ordered to take a chair and wait for my name to be called.

From behind the desk, office staff occasionally bellowed a name. No privacy in this place.

By 9:44, they still hadn't called mine.

Finally, at 9:53, I heard my name. So did everyone else.

I went to the desk and signed a bunch of legal stuff about privacy—which I found rather funny — and my duty to pay what my insurance doesn't.

Then I was handed a clipboard and told to return to my chair and fill out a medical history.

I completed my task at 10:04 and decided to peruse a magazine. The choices included the Aug. 22 Time, the Nov. 14 Sports Illustrated, a year-old House and Garden and a current Field and Stream.

Instead, I reread my medical history. "Do you smoke?" "Do you drink?"

Better, I thought, to inquire if you have ever stood up in the middle of a packed waiting room and shouted obscenities.

Things picked up at 10:40.

Seventy minutes after my scheduled rendezvous, they bellowed my name again.

I was moved to a chair in a hallway, grabbed for a couple of X-rays and returned to the hallway with a promise I'd be called shortly.

I didn't believe it.

Then boom, boom, boom.

I was whisked to an examining room, the doc arrived, confirmed my diagnosis, gave me a shot and a prescription, and sent me packing. I was driving out of the parking lot at 11:04.

I have no complaint about him or my medical treatment.

What I resent is being treated as if my time isn't important. When I whined, a staff member explained that they see a lot of patients.

I suggested they see fewer.

She also explained that in their practice, they face emergencies every day.

I mentioned they might plan for them if they are that routine.

She said if it bothers me that much, I should tell the doctor.

I said I would.

I think you should, too.

Maybe if enough of us needle them, the doctors will feel our pain.

VISITORS LEAVE TOKENS OF
LIFE AT FLIGHT 93 SITE

At first glance, it's puzzling.

The temporary memorial to Flight 93 consists of hundreds of items left by some of the 150,000 people who find their way to the remote Somerset County location every year.

Many are baseball-style caps. Among those hanging on the 40-foot fence yesterday were caps from New York; the Orlando Fire Department; the United Mine Workers, Steamfitters and Plumbers 85 of Saginaw, Mich.; and Stiney's 3 Oaks Tavern in Tiffin, Ohio.

The fence that serves as the linchpin of the memorial also holds license plates, including one from American Legion Post 184 in West Fairview and the Ebenezer Fire Company in North Lebanon Twp.

Nearby is a license plate that belonged to Colleen Fraser, one of the 33 passengers who died when Flight 93 crashed in a field just beyond this memorial three years ago this morning.

"Colleen loved to drive. It's important to me" to have the license plate on the fence, said her sister, Christine Fraser of New Jersey.

"When I come here, I feel closer to my sister. I do consider that her cemetery," Christine Fraser said, scanning the large green field in the distance.

She doesn't find the bits and pieces left behind by visitors to be unusual or strange.

"They go to their car and get whatever. It really is important for people to leave something here," Fraser said.

They leave rosary beads and artificial flowers, key rings and wind chimes. More than 100 emblems from veterans and fire companies and police departments hung on a board attached to the fence yesterday.

Among the other items were two Matchbox fire engines, a foot-high Sponge Bob doll and a plastic dinosaur. Nearby were seashells, a small mirror with a purple handle and a pair of dice.

Items eventually are removed, cleaned, cataloged and stored by the Somerset Historical and Genealogical Center. Eventually they will go to the National Park Service.

Jerry Bingham of Wildwood, Fla., finds emotional comfort in the collection.

He lost his son, Mark Bingham, 31, when Flight 93 crashed. He and his wife, Karen, lost two rooms of their house when a tree crashed through his roof during Hurricane Frances last week.

Neighbors patched their roof and protected the house from the elements so Jerry and Karen could travel north for ceremonies at the memorial today. Gov. Ed Rendell will place a wreath. The National Park Service will launch a design competition for a permanent memorial on the site.

A year from today, the park service expects to unveil the winning design.

Joanne M. Hanley, superintendent of the Flight 93 National Memorial, makes no predictions about the form the permanent memorial will take. But she anticipates a fence will be part of it.

"The American public wants a place to go and leave a tribute," she said.

Even in November, December and January, the coldest months of the past year, people from 41 states and 17 countries visited the site, she said.

Bingham said people want to honor the heroes of Flight 93. Because of the actions of the 33 passengers and seven crew members, the plane crashed here, in a reclaimed strip mine, rather than in Washington, D.C., as the hijackers had planned.

"That's why this story has to be told," Bingham said. "I think everybody thinks they belong to this place, and rightly so. This is our country," he said.

And so they leave behind a pair of red, white and blue sneakers, a golf ball, a Vokswagen emblem or a Harley-Davidson key ring.

"Some little token, some bit of respect," Bingham said. "I think that's great. That shows that America is still hanging together."

PUPILS SAFE, BUT DO THEY FEEL SECURE?

Back to school in 2004 is a study in moldy classrooms, banned bellies and peanut butter-free lunchrooms.

It's a different world.

When I was a kid, security meant knowing your mother was waiting at home with milk and cookies. Today, it involves metal detectors, ID cards and cameras scanning the doorways.

You have to wonder how any of us survived childhood.

Mold was something mom cut off bread. Never, until recently, did I hear of a classroom contaminated with the stuff. I never encountered a classmate allergic to peanut butter, or to wheat.

We ate what they dished up in the cafeteria, while adults stood over us and demanded we clean our plates.

Kids were starving in China.

I remember one kid whose mother tried to protect him from germs by wrapping his lunch money in a cloth handkerchief. Every day, the lunchroom lady unwrapped his coins and dropped them into the cash register. Every day, kids teased him.

Back then, we didn't have anti-bullying assemblies.

We wrote with No. 2 pencils and chewed the yellow exteriors. We sniffed the purple ink on mimeographed papers and, innocently, inhaled glue fumes in the air during art class. If we were lucky, the teacher might select us to go outside and clap the erasers to clean out the chalk dust. I assume we inhaled that, too.

A few years ago, most midstate school districts borrowed huge sums to remove asbestos. I don't know when the asbestos went in, but it's a good bet we survived that, too.

We learned reading and writing in classrooms with 50-plus students.

We spilled out onto a macadam playground at recess, played dodge ball and occasionally tripped over a classmate and skinned our knees.

Crowding was commonplace for the baby boomers.

For over a year, I rode a school bus on which all the seats were filled. Those of us who boarded late stood in the aisle for the four-mile ride.

If I complained, my father, a child of the Depression, would tell me that I was lucky to have a bus to ride. Then he'd describe walking a couple of miles to high school in all sorts of weather.

He didn't own a winter coat or shoes more sturdy than canvas sneakers.

My aunt — now a spry 84 — was reminiscing recently about her introduction to high school. Because she had skipped a couple of grades, she was only 11.

No one was concerned with the social impact of her leaping ahead. There were no conferences with counselors or personality tests to complete.

She simply climbed on a streetcar and traveled to a strange town and a new school and searched the halls until she found her name on a homeroom list on a classroom door.

Today, she and I noted, schools offer kindergarten orientation and middle school tours and high school parent nights so no child wanders into the unknown.

Children today are sheltered and pampered and wrapped in cocoons. Their environments are stripped of anything harmful and the outside world is locked out of their schools, along with the peanut butter.

We had no such protection. Danger lurked around us, and yet, I truly believe we felt a security that's missing in childhood today.

PHOTOS PUT FOCUS ON AFFLUENCE

If you're in my age bracket, or even a decade or two younger, you probably remember the ritual involved in posing for your high school senior picture.

For girls, it meant putting on a black sweater and a string of pearls, teasing your hair into place, sitting on a stool and smiling.

For guys, it was much the same except they wore a coat and tie, and slicked instead of teased.

Several weeks later, you got a packet of proofs and decided which of the black-and-white pictures should smile from the yearbook.

Your parents — and maybe your grandparents — would get a 5-by-7 or 8-by-10. You gave classmates wallet-sized photos. On the back, you'd write pledges to be friends forever.

Flash forward to 2004.

Recently, I went with my granddaughter Tiffany to view the pictures she'd posed for a few weeks earlier. The photographer sat us down in a small room and cued up a digital slide show. A huge Tiffany appeared on the screen as Pink's "Get the Party Started" spurted from the speakers.

There was Tiffany in black-and-white, in color, in a skirt, in pants, in the city, in a field, hugging a tree, sitting on a stoop.

Tiffany with a red background, Tiffany with a zebra background, Tiffany by a window, Tiffany with her head tilted.

The choices were dizzying.

Not to worry. The photographer provided pencils and tablets and took us through the show again. We could write down the numbers of the possibilities, view them again and again and start whittling.

His packages allowed us to select four poses or more in sizes ranging from wall poster to postage stamp.

If we were so inclined, we could even buy the slide show. Imagine sitting home night after night watching giant Tiffanys click across the big-screen TV.

When did senior pictures shift from pearls to fields of clover?

About a decade ago, said Aura Hill, who served as the yearbook adviser at Palmyra Area High School for more than a couple of decades. She's a year from retirement and recently passed the torch.

Senior pictures, she said, have become "big, big, big business."

Seniors display their hobbies in their photos. They might pose on a motorcycle or a horse, change clothes between photos, follow the photographer to several locations.

Palmyra and many other schools limit students to head and shoulder poses for their "official" yearbook photo. But many parents buy "grad ads" saluting their graduating seniors. If they're willing to pay, they can feature one or more of the personal photos in the ad.

Photos go to grandma and the aunts and so on. Friends get the wallets, which often have the student's name printed in gold script.

The point, I'd like to think, is that today's seniors are urged to be individuals. They don't have to conform, the way we did in our black sweaters and pearls.

I'm afraid, though, that it has more to do with affluence. Parents today are willing to spend much, much more on their kids than our parents could or would.

Hill cautioned that senior pictures are only the beginning of an expensive year.

"It takes so much money just for a kid to get out of school," she said.

ISN'T IT REALLY ABOUT
OUR GROWING APPETITES?

My parents landed in the suburbs early.

In 1953, they handed over a $1 down payment, signed a GI mortgage and moved into their dream home.

Their dream was a rancher — three bedrooms, one bath, with a small section at the end of the living room called a dining area.

When it became apparent that I would be their only child, they transformed one bedroom into a dining room. Over the years they added a porch and a patio. Mom created a little sewing room at one end of the basement. Dad hung his tools on peg board at the other end.

They adopted suburban life, growing tomatoes, planting flowers, grilling steaks. A power mower cut the grass.

The house was my mother's pride and joy. She cleaned it and polished it and kept it neat as a pin. We used to tease her by claiming the rooms had shrunk significantly over the years because she put so many coats of paint on the walls.

When my mother died and my father sold the house in 1999, not many families were interested in two bedrooms, one bath — even if they were recently painted and neat as a pin. The eventual buyer was a young, single woman.

As I drive through Colonial Park with its neat rows of small brick houses, I think about my parents' neighborhood. Call it early suburbs, where the neighbor's so close you can hear his kid practicing the piano — if you can squeeze a piano into the living room.

But tolerating the neighbor's noise, getting by with two or three bedrooms and one bath, are as dated as saddle shoes. Drive through Hampden Twp. or South Hanover and you'll find yards so large people couldn't shout loudly enough to get the attention of folks next door.

The yard engulfs a home with a minimum of four bedrooms, three baths. The kitchen is larger than the little house on the prairie and features an "island" the size of your car. The entry hall would hold my parents' dining room, and — naturally — has a cathedral ceiling.

The yard demands a riding mower or weekly visits by a lawn service.

A friend remarked recently that the only time she sees her neighbors is when they ride their mowers. Children don't play outside; adults don't leave their screened porches.

"Why do they have all that yard if they don't use it?" she asked.

"Bigger is better" is the motto of today's suburbs.

If a house in Camp Hill or Colonial Park seems cramped, a developer will build you a larger one. Of course, he'll have to build it farther from the city on what used to be someone's farm.

Once upon a time in the suburbs, my friends shared a bedroom with a sister or two. Today, kids expect their own room and their own bath.

Once upon a time, I watched TV with my parents in the living room. In my home now, we have six — or is it seven — televisions.

As people haul their TVs and DVDs and CDs and PCs farther and farther from the city, stores follow. Where developers go, minimarts blossom. Soon we demand a liquor store and a supermarket and a Blockbuster.

There goes another farm.

Kmart isn't enough; we want Wal-Mart and Target and Home Depot and Kohl's and Circuit City, and one of those huge bookstores where you can relax with a double skim cappuccino.

We blame sprawl on a growing population, but I wonder if it isn't really about our growing appetites.

The stores follow us farther and farther into the suburbs for good reason.

Once upon a time, a bumper sticker read, "He who dies with the most toys wins."

First we buy the toys. Then we buy houses large enough to hold all our stuff.

Or is it the other way around?

PENNIES SPURNED BY FOOLS
WITHOUT MONEY TO BURN

A house is not a home.

Once again, I found myself last week standing in an empty house in Lancaster assessing the work needed to make the place livable.

I don't want to own this house, but I do. It's a long story. Since I haven't been able to sell it, I offer it for rent.

Despite some city officials' claims about people who live in one place and own property in another, I'm not a slumlord.

The house has a new roof, new paint. I have a property manager.

Together we keep it attractive enough to be tempting in case somebody — anybody — wants to buy.

The tenants in my place always seem to be people who can't get a mortgage for one reason or another. The first had dirty credit and was trying to clean it up. She didn't improve her status when she moved without notice, leaving a $1,000 water bill and a dog behind.

Another couple had been through a bankruptcy. For a while they were intent on buying, and made — with my OK — improvements to a couple of rooms.

When they changed their minds and moved, my claw-foot bathtub disappeared.

When this last tenant left, my son filled a pickup twice with the stuff she had abandoned. Guess who paid to dump it.

Besides the two truckloads of downright junk, she also left a futon, a youth bed frame, a bicycle and a folding crib — still in the box.

Guess she didn't need them.

That's what I don't get. If you aren't exactly living at the top rung, wouldn't it be smart to value the things around you? For the price of an ad, somebody might give you a couple of bucks for the stuff.

To me, pennies have come to symbolize a refusal to recognize the value of things. I walked through the house last week picking up pennies. Six or seven here. Two or three there. When I got home, 40-plus pennies jingled in my pocket.

This wasn't the first time. Other tenants, other times had left pennies scattered like so many crumbs.

Granted, there isn't a lot to be had for a penny. Even 40 pennies won't do much for you in a mini-mart. But if you put those 40 with 40 more and then 40 more...

I scare myself. I'm starting to sound like someone who grew up in the Depression.

You want to hear about the value of a penny, talk to one of those folks. They don't stand around and debate when they spy one on the ground.

Younger folks are another story. Some will bend down if the penny's heads-up — good luck, they say.

Others won't pick one up, heads or tails, because it's dirty and might have been walked on — or worse.

I dare say they wouldn't think twice about germs if it were a $20 bill.

A lot of people just don't think a penny's worth their time.

Pennies have become so devalued that they're discarded in dishes at check-out counters, awaiting someone whose bill totals, say, $12.02.

My appreciation of the copper-colored coin goes back to the days of standing in the corner store selecting one of these and one of those, and some that sold two for a penny.

If you had a dime, you'd leave with a little brown bag half full of goodies. Then it was off to the playground to savor Mary Janes, wax lips and shoestring licorice.

Maybe it's the memories of those sweet days on the playground that make me willing to pick up my tenants' pennies. Maybe it's the lessons learned from my Depression-era relatives. Maybe I'm just thrifty.

All I know is I was plenty mad as I walked from room to room last week.

In a moment of deja vu, I realized that people who don't appreciate the value of a penny don't value much else either.

SLIPPING INTO CLASS — THE HARD WAY

At 8 a.m. Jan. 13, I was lying face down on Atherton Street. As waves of humiliation and pain washed over me, I considered staying there permanently. But it was cold. Bone-chilling, mind-numbing cold. Slowly, I eased up. Everything hurt.

The worst injury seemed to be to my psyche, so I continued on my way.

I was supposed to be standing at 8 a.m. in front of a class of aspiring journalists.

Somebody figured that I've learned something about the newspaper business these past 25 years and it was time to share it. So I'm on loan to Penn State for a semester.

I think it's going to be a long 16 weeks.

I'd only been in State College twice before. Whoever laid out the town of State College might have had a serious drinking problem. Streets bend around corners and everything is either uphill or downhill.

I had a map showing where I was supposed to park. No matter which way I turned that map, I couldn't figure out how to get to the parking lot.

I'd allowed plenty of time. I'm staying two miles from campus and gave myself 45 minutes.

In that time, I toured State College from one end to the other four times, made U-turns, even went though a red light that I didn't see until it was too late.

I felt like Lewis or Clark.

When a stranger suggested the parking lot might be nearby, I rejoiced. It was almost 8, but I thought I could make it.

So, yeah, I was hurrying back to my car, but I swear the curb looked smooth.

Then I was on my face.

This is a young person's gig. I've walked more in 10 days than in the past 10 months.

When I realized at 8 a.m. on Jan. 13 how far I had to walk to my classroom, I thought things couldn't get any worse.

Then it snowed.

After classes, I drove back to my apartment — downhill, uphill, downhill, uphill. I gripped the steering wheel so hard, I think I left imprints.

All night, it kept snowing. But I set the alarm determined not to be tardy twice. I walked outside, misjudged the steps and landed on my knees. My pocketbook flew in one direction, my briefcase in the other.

Fortunately, my second fall of the week was cushioned by seven inches of snow.

I'll admit it. I'm a spoiled suburban queen. If it looks like snow, I park in the garage. My husband clears the driveway with a snowblower. The plow arrives promptly.

Now I was on my own, standing in the dark in the snow in the bitter cold with sore knees, brushing snow off my van in a parking lot that hadn't seen a plow yet.

What in the world am I doing here?

I know, it's going to get warm eventually. Spring will come to Happy Valley. If I don't break any major bones before then, I'll be explaining to my students why newspapering is a little bit of heaven.

In the college newspaper the other day, I saw an ad beckoning students to spend a semester in Hawaii. Now that's the kind of place a tired, old newspaper person should go to share all the stuff she's picked up over 25 years.

Aloha!

COLLEGIANS SEEM WELL CONNECTED

It's spring break. Do you know where the college students are?

If they're like the students I'm teaching at Penn State University, they're south of here.

Florida seems to be the destination of choice. And why not? It's 78 degrees in Fort Lauderdale this week. You don't have to be on the dean's list to figure that beats our flurry of 40s.

I'm teaching journalism at Penn State this semester, on loan from The Patriot-News. Along the way, I'm learning a lot about this current crop of college kids.

It's been a long, cold, snowy winter. For weeks, the students have been encased in fleece and boots. Not surprisingly, they were counting the days until spring break.

One young man was anticipating the drive to Florida in a Winnebago with friends. He didn't seem a bit fazed by galloping gasoline prices.

Another had plans to fly to the Bahamas. Half a dozen or so were jetting to various destinations in Florida. One was trekking through England. Another would be cruising the Caribbean.

Me? I was headed to a week at my desk at The Patriot-News. So, sure, I was learning to be envious of the younger generation.

I don't want to say that all collegians are privileged. For everyone going to Florida, there was one heading for mom's home cooking in Scranton, Wilkes-Barre or Pittsburgh. For every one planning to bask on the beach, there was one who would be pounding the pavement looking for a summer job.

Still, I can't help thinking about the dozens, maybe hundreds of articles I've read over the years lamenting the high cost of a college education. Learning costs plenty, but plenty of kids have enough spare change to frolic for a week in the sun. Plenty also have the wherewithal to spend a semester abroad.

The majority of my students are sophomores. As I sat with them individually last week discussing their futures, many described plans for a semester elsewhere. England is popular, but some are contemplating Germany, Italy or Australia.

Penn State, I've discovered, offers 130 programs in 49 countries.

I'm not sure I can name 49 countries.

The other thing I've learned since January is that no matter where collegians spend their time, they are never out of touch. Almost all of them have cell phones and they talk on them almost all the time.

They walk around campus conversing. Not with each other, though. When they walk in groups of two or three, they are engaged in two or three very separate conversations.

They arrive in class folding up their phones, and walk out of the classroom two hours later checking their messages.

It's as if the entire campus is caught up in some ringing, vibrating, chatting, text-messaging frenzy.

This week, as they're spread out from Nassau to Nantucket, I'll bet they're still chatting, comparing their good times.

When we return to campus next week, perhaps they'll share a bit with me so I can envision the blue waters and white sand. Then I'll describe my week in the real world.

It's a world that will be theirs soon enough.

NOT BUYING THE HOSTILITY
TO WAL-MART

When the kid sprinted out of the basement, the clock was inching toward 10 p.m. His sister looked up and burst out laughing.

"We have to go to Wal-Mart — now," he said.

Seems the 17-year-old had been buzzing his hair when the clippers died in mid-cut. Half his head was shorn.

I pulled on some shoes while he hid his semi-cut under a cap, and we headed for Wal-Mart.

I confess: I sometimes shop at Wal-Mart. It's not my favorite place— it's too large for my taste — but where else do you go at 10 p.m. when the clippers quit?

Frankly, I don't understand the horrified gasp that follows every announcement of a new Wal-Mart.

North Cornwall Twp. ended an 11-hour hearing last week with a long list of people still awaiting their turn to insist that allowing a Wal-Mart on Cornwall Road is akin to being invaded by Attila the Hun.

It's not as if Wal-Mart is asking to plop a store in some pristine cornfield. It has selected a Lebanon County site behind Foodland, down the road from Kmart in an area that's also home to Lowe's, a shopping center, a strip mall and a slew of smaller stores and restaurants.

Of course, the protests in Lebanon County aren't nearly as hilarious as the opposition to a Wal-Mart on Route 22 in Dauphin County.

You know Route 22—malls, strip malls, restaurants, Kmart, Ollie's, Target, movie theaters, banks, supermarkets, Borders, outdoor outfitters, car dealers.

The idea that Wal-Mart would be a blight on Route 22 is hysterically preposterous.

But that hasn't stopped people from trying to block it.

The issues they raise are always the same: traffic and those poor mom-and-pop stores that will be driven out of business by big, bad, ugly Wal-Mart.

Wal-Mart, I contend, doesn't create traffic. If people want to shop, they're going to hit the roads to somewhere. Whether that somewhere is Wal-Mart or Toys "R" Us isn't putting more cars on the road.

And if discounts at Wal-Mart don't drive mom and pop out of business, discounts at Target or Circuit City will.

Frankly, I think a lot of the Wal-Mart opposition arises from an effort to be trendy.

Nobody wants to admit a kinship with the moms in the commercials who tell us — usually with a slight Southern drawl — that they just couldn't stay home and raise the kids and make it to all their sporting events if it weren't for one-stop shopping and the bargains they find at Wal-Mart.

Think about it. When was the last time you admired something and its owner admitted buying it at Wal-Mart?

Nah, we'd rather align ourselves with the trendy moms who sip coffee from Starbucks and meander through The Shoppes at Susquehanna Marketplace.

It's funny, though.

When the kid's clippers went kaput at 10 p.m. on a freezing weeknight, the parking lot at Wal-Mart was crowded.

Fact is, it's always crowded.

Somebody's shopping there. Maybe they don't admit it, but a whole lot of somebodies are shopping there.

March 31, 2005

COPY EDITOR ADDED POLISH TO PROSE

If this column doesn't read well, it's because I couldn't give it to Doug Dohne for polishing.

You can't ask a guy to polish his own praise.

For a long time, I've considered Doug to be my personal copy editor. I'm not alone. Plenty of others considered him theirs because Doug has always treated everyone's work with TLC.

Doug retired yesterday, gone to the fishing hole, and I live in terror that readers are going to realize that I have no talent. It's been Doug who's made me look good all these years.

A copy editor's job is to take a reporter's or columnist's writing and make sure it is right: Is everything spelled correctly? Does it read well? Does it make sense?

It's been Doug who has taken my prose — which is OK — and shined it until it gleamed.

Sometimes I speak in public — to senior citizens, mostly. I tell them I took a twisted path to this career, but I wound up being a columnist because of my parents and the nuns. My parents encouraged learning; the nuns insisted on proper grammar and usage.

Then I tell them about Doug. I tell them he combines qualities of both. He is very learned, as well as an expert on grammar, spelling and punctuation. He understands shades of meanings. He'll tell me, "The word you used sounds OK, but here's one that's better."

And he's always right.

I have to confess, I often read his polished version and think, "I wish I had written it that way."

By reading those polished versions, I've increased my bank of knowledge over the years. I spend more time on my writing these days because I'm always trying to compose something that reads as if Doug had polished it.

I'm not there yet, but I keep trying.

Doug is a gentleman. He'd never say, "Nancy, you sure stunk up my computer with this column."

But we've worked together so long, I know when he thinks a column sucks.

Generally, he'll say something like, "You had a hard time writing that one, huh?"

That's when I know we should skip the readers and just line birdcages with my latest creation.

As I've mentioned, Doug is a gentleman. But he's also a gentle man who never rants or raves.

Despite his low-key nature, he can't hide his pride and pleasure when he talks about the things he loves: his wife, Kay; his array of kids and grandkids; fishing; hunting.

His face lights up at the mention of any of those topics. But he glows like a 200-watt bulb when sharing a story that combines more than one of those ingredients, such as taking a grandson fishing or going to the beach with Kay and a truckload of grandkids.

While Doug shares so much with his family, he still finds time to teach a Sunday school class, sing in the choir and tutor every Wednesday at a program on Allison Hill.

He's been an asset to the community as well as to a couple of generations of newspaper folks.

My sincere wish is that this gentle man, this gentleman, this friend, enjoys his retirement.

But I'm not alone in saying I shall miss his polish.

AUTOMATED VOICES PUSH THEIR LUCK

Living, breathing telephone operators are as rare as dial phones.

We've grown accustomed to automated voices and demands to push buttons that eventually lead to violins playing hit songs from the 1970s.

We've let the big phone companies, medical insurers and companies that link us to the Internet sap our lives while we hold, please, for the next available operator.

Here's a true story:

I got a letter last week from the insurance company that protects a house I own in case of fire or other catastrophe. The big insurance company was threatening to cancel my little policy for nonpayment.

This raised my blood pressure 40 points because part of my mortgage goes to an escrow account so the big mortgage company can earn interest until it gives my money to the big insurance company.

So I called an 800 number.

An automated voice asked if I speak English.

Yes, I indicated. This is America, a fact I would like to share with the bank that asks that question every time I use its ATM.

Next, the automated voice directed me to pound in my account number. That reminded me of the big phone company, which always asks me to type in my phone number. Don't they have Caller ID?

Anyway, this big mortgage company offered the standard slop. I could obtain my account balance by pounding one digit or apply for a new mortgage with another or refinance with a third.

Eventually, the automated voice led me to a number that was supposed to deliver me to a customer service representative.

Instead, it brought music and another automated voice that reminded me repeatedly that the big mortgage company appreciates my business and knows I am busy and would connect me to the next available representative lickity-split.

The voice lied.

Much later, when I reached a real person, she asked my problem — and my account number. I explained that her company had neglected to pay my insurance, and if my house burned down it was their ash.

She asked if I had sent them a bill. Yes, I said, two months in a row to the address for the "Insurance Department" as indicated on the back of this month's mortgage statement.

Oh, she said. They closed that department a while ago. That address is no longer good.

Why, I inquired, is the address still on the mortgage statement?

She admitted that the big mortgage company probably should print new forms. But she suggested my blood pressure was rising without reason. The big insurance company wasn't threatening to cancel my policy until the end of May. Even though the payment was due in early April, the big mortgage company had plenty of time to send a check.

I explained that the letter in my hand was addressed to me and said something like, "Dear Deadbeat, Pay up, you no good sleaze."

I noted that I treasure my credit rating and prefer not to receive such letters.

She said I didn't have to get snippy. She promised the big mortgage company would take care of it.

Sure. But just to be safe, until further notice, cooking, smoking and candles are banned from the premises.

LACK OF CLASS TEACHES A BAD LESSON

Time to wrap up the school year with a little fun.

Sometimes the fun involves a male teacher dressing like a woman and shaving his legs during an assembly.

Or maybe, for fun, he shaves his head.

Fun can be two teachers climbing into padded sumo wrestler suits and doing battle as students watch.

A teacher might get his ear pierced during an assembly, parachute out of an airplane or take whipped cream pies in the face, all in fun.

Usually this buffoonery is tied to achievement.

Students must read a ton of books or donate a ton of canned goods or raise a ton of money for some worthy cause before teachers make fools of themselves.

Good intentions, all right, but what are we teaching kids with these so-called rewards?

It seems to me that kids ought to respect their teachers. How does taking a cream pie in the face engender respect?

When I was a kid, the world paused on Tuesday nights so people could watch Milton Berle, who'd say or do just about anything for a laugh. Sometimes, for a laugh, Uncle Miltie would wear a dress.

He was funny, I suppose, but I'm not sure anyone respected him come Wednesday morning.

That's how it is with teachers.

How can you respect someone who acts sillier than the class clown?

Once upon a time, a thick line divided students and teachers.

Teachers didn't act like students, or dress like them, either. And they certainly didn't engage in stunts to amuse the student body.

I'm not sure when the line began to shrivel.

One thing is certain: None of my teachers ever tried to be amusing.

It was clear to us that teachers existed to make sure we learned something. Period.

Now I hear about teachers wrestling in Jell-O, eating worms during an assembly, camping on a roof or kissing a pig, and I wonder where they draw the line these days — if a line even exists.

Or I pass a school and realize that the people strolling out wearing jeans and sneakers are the teachers.

I just can't learn to feel comfortable with that.

Unless it's the end-of-year picnic, teachers in jeans and sneakers just don't send the right message.

Neither do teachers with pie on their faces or Jell-O between their toes.

Education should be serious business, and teachers should dress and act the part, right up to the first day of summer vacation.

And nurses, too

While I'm at it, let me take a shot at nurses.

When I'm in the hospital — either as visitor or patient — I want to be able to tell at a glance who is the custodian and who is the nurse.

More than once I've requested medicine from someone only to learn she's in the room to mop the floor.

Who can tell when everyone's wearing scrub tops decorated with puppies or ducks and dashing from place to place in sneakers or clogs?

Whatever happened to professionals looking professional?

NOWADAYS, WE'RE ALL BORN TO BLOG

No matter how old I get, I hope never to become stuck several decades in the past.

I talk to people all the time who don't have computers and who claim they don't know anything about "that dot-com stuff."

Just the other day, I was telling a group of people how the computer has revolutionized my work life. Once upon a time, I left my desk occasionally. Sometimes I'd stroll over to the really big dictionary to look up a word that wasn't in my desk dictionary. A couple of times a day I'd walk back to our library to search our photo files. I'd get up and check something in the Pennsylvania Manual or the out-of-town telephone books.

Not anymore.

I can do all of that and then some without ever leaving my desk. The computer has changed everything about the way I work and a lot of what I do at home.

Most times, the computer is my friend. Then something happens to make me think we're barely acquaintances. Maybe, just maybe, technology is a swiftly moving river and I'm treading water.

For quite a while now, my son's been after me to start a blog. At first I figured he was just being a nudge. He has a blog. His wife has a blog.

Her blog makes me laugh. Turns out she's quite the comedian.

He's a bit too smart for me. His blog, for the most part, is about books I haven't read, music I haven't heard and movies I haven't seen, with a smattering of politics and sports — two subjects that make me yawn.

As bloggers, they certainly aren't alone. Recently, I went to a convention of newspaper columnists and all anyone talked about was blogs. How often they blog, why they blog, who reads their blogs.

Now I guess I ought to pause here for those of you unfamiliar with "that dot-com stuff."

A "blog" is a Web log. You take anything you think or feel and toss it at the world. People blog about themselves and their lives. Some write exclusively about politics. There are right-wing blogs and left-wing blogs, as well as sports blogs, movie blogs, blogs for new moms and blogs for people who like to cook. There are so many blogs you couldn't possibly read them all.

Suppose you're a Phillies fan brimming with knowledge (or at least opinions) about players, stats and trades. You could write a Phillies blog. Then, you link your blog to other phanatics.

Using links, readers can bounce from one blog to the next. That's how some people spend their leisure time (and work time, too, if the boss isn't looking).

Most of the columnists I encountered blog between their printed columns. It's quite a time commitment.

If I had a blog, I could have told the world Monday that I have a beautiful new grandson.

Instead, using the technology I know, I took photos of him with my digital camera, drove home, downloaded them in my computer and e-mailed them to a few folks.

Pretty slick.

A few minutes later, my son walked in holding something in his palm. He stuck whatever it was into my computer, sat down, stroked the keyboard a few times and showed me the result: On his first day of life, my grandson had a blog.

The blog includes his time of birth, his weight, photos and even video of him stretching and crying. (Yes, it has sound too.) You can watch a slideshow as he meets his big sisters for the first time.

I view it over and over, beaming, but stunned. The Technology River is moving faster than I imagined. I see rapids ahead.

I'm getting a sinking feeling.

September 26, 2006

BOLDFACE NAMES LEAVE ME BLANK

While I was idling on vacation, I picked up my cousin's People magazine and reinforced what I already knew: I am totally not hip.

All told, I couldn't identify more than a handful of People's people.

I recognized Mariska Hargitay because of my addiction to "Law & Order." And, I know who Gwyneth Paltrow is. Know who their mothers are, too.

But most of the so-called celebrities stymied me. Megan Mullally? Ludacris? Jeremy London and Melissa Cunningham? Who are these people, and why should I care?

Meanwhile, I was besieged by almost hourly news updates regarding the death of Anna Nicole Smith's son. While my heart breaks for any mother who loses a child, this was simply TMI — too much information.

What makes Anna Nicole Smith noteworthy? She married well and sued often. But her son's death affects me because ...?

And who, pray tell, is Lindsay Lohan? I went to People's Web site last week, trying once again to find a familiar face, and found Lindsay splat in the center of the page with a bandaged hand and a T-shirt that covered only one of two shoulders.

But she must be hot, because the top story under "breaking news" was "Lindsay & Harry: It's Over."

I didn't know it had begun.

And who's Harry?

And there was more news about Lindsay. One of the teases promised to lead me to "Lindsay Lohan's Mom Drama."

Well, didn't I find out that that Lindsay, now "living clean" (What, she didn't use to bathe?), threw a party for her mom's 44th birthday. But it turned ugly. Mom picked a fight and Lindsay stormed out of a chi-chi New York restaurant, but only after telling her mother to go to the place the nuns used to call h-e-double hockey sticks.

How's that for a birthday greeting to your mother? If this is how the clean Lindsay acts, how rude was she during her dirty phase?

Oh, and how about this: Designer Giorgio Armani (heard of his clothes; don't own any) said anorexia isn't fashionable.

Won't that send Nicole Richie dashing into Dairy Queen?

Whatever he thinks about anorexia, I doubt Armani designs anything for the Lane Bryant woman.

Oh, and how about this headline: Jessica — Simpson, I suppose since that's who's in the photo — dodged an awkward-ex moment. She ran into former flame Adam Levine in Los Angeles but dodged a meeting with John Mayer in Texas.

Who? I thought Jessica's ex was Nick. Isn't he the husband she cooed over on that awful show my granddaughters used to watch?

From glimpses of that show, I became familiar with Jessica. She's blond, considers herself a singer and has beaucoup bucks. Oh, and she's really, really dumb. The dimmest bulb in the chandelier. Two cans shy of a six-pack.

Her husband, I recall, had good abs.

I ended my little trip through the world of the glitterati with a photo display.

There was David Charvet, formerly of "Baywatch," running on the beach at Malibu with a pregnant Brooke Burke, host of "Rock Star: Supernova."

I'm two for two on recognizing that couple; three for three if you count her show; four for four if you count ever watching his show.

People gushed that Charvet and Burke, who are expecting their first child together, a girl, announced their engagement in August.

The nuns would have called that closing the barn door after the horse has escaped.

But hey, I am totally not hip, so what do I know?

TO WOMAN HIT IN CAR: CALL FOR HELP

If you are the blonde who was a front-seat passenger in a silver car eastbound on Union Deposit Road near Progress Avenue about 9:30 a.m. Monday, you are not alone.

I saw what he did to you. I saw the driver smack you in the face twice as he waited for the light to turn green.

At first I doubted my eyes. Maybe he was snuggling, leaning over to give you a quick hug.

Then he swung a third time. That's when I saw your face.

My long-range eyesight is good. I can read signs from a great distance, even though I can no longer decipher directions on a box right in front of my face.

I was far enough away to see the pain on your face. He hurt you.

You reminded me — I hate to say — of a whipped puppy. You looked afraid and very, very sad.

I panicked. I wanted to do something. But what? I was traveling in the opposite direction. I considered a U-turn to follow you and call the cops.

But I wasn't in the turning lane and there was a median.

I decided to sit tight and catch the license plate number as you passed, call 911. Police cruise that strip all day. They would find you, help you.

But the car behind you was too close. I couldn't see the plate.

And besides, everyone started moving and I went with the flow.

So I'm ashamed to say I didn't do anything. I drove to work.

But the memory of your face went with me.

I wish now I had jumped out of my car, right there in the middle of Union Deposit Road, and started yelling and waving my arms. Maybe other people saw what he did. Maybe they would have jumped out of their cars. Maybe all of us could have run up to the car and ordered him to stop hurting you.

I wonder if he would have listened.

While I was still considering what to do, and just before I drove away, some little part of me — the part that reads too much and watches too many cop shows on TV — wondered if he had a gun. If I yelled at him, maybe he would have shot me and you — and then what good would I have done you?

I was a coward. I let you down.

I want to forget the incident, but I see your face when I close my eyes. I feel your fear. I see the man in the knit hat smacking you — once, twice, three times.

You tried to cover your face. You hunkered down, tried to make yourself small, to fend off the blows.

Please don't let him treat you like that. You deserve better.

Don't let him break you down. Don't believe him when he calls you stupid and ugly and worthless.

You are none of those things.

That's what men like him say. They want you to believe you are nothing so you remain under their control.

If he's apologized and said you made him do it, don't believe that either. Men like him always blame others for their faults.

If he's said he won't do it again, he's lying. He will. I know you know that in your heart.

I'm sorry I let you down. But there are people who won't. Call 800-799-SAFE from anywhere in the state.

People will help you. They will tell you how to be safe.

If you're in Cumberland or Perry counties, call Domestic Violence Services at 800-852-2102.

On the East Shore, call the YWCA of Greater Harrisburg at 800-654-1211.

People in all these places want you to be safe. So do I.

So, see, you are not alone.

Please call.

November 28, 2006

MIDNIGHT AT OUTLETS TESTS METTLE

We consider ourselves pioneers, my granddaughter and I.

When they launched shopping at midnight after Thanksgiving at The Outlets at Hershey, we joined the throngs clamoring to spend in uncharted territory.

For some, shopping at midnight might seem surreal. But as a night owl, I find it more appealing than being jolted from bed at 4 a.m. to save a few bucks at Wal-Mart or Target.

Frankly, I didn't expect much from our expedition. I figured the oldest granddaughter (affectionately known as "The Queen" or Elizabeth for her, shall we say, imperial ways) and I would join a small band of hardy souls, unearth a gift or two and chart a course home.

I don't think the folks who run the outlets expected much, either.

In fact, one of them told a reporter Saturday, "When we first started thinking of doing this, people said we were crazy and that not enough people would come out."

He didn't have a clue. Neither did we. And whoever scheduled the cashiers really was in the dark.

The Queen and I sailed with different intentions. When I hear Hershey outlets, I think Liz Claiborne. Her focus was a Coach purse.

What we shared was a desire to reward ourselves first.

Driving to Hershey, I was surprised by the number of fellow travelers. The Queen declared they were shoppers; I suspected they were sleepy-eyed employees who had pulled the midnight shift.

She was right.

We arrived 20 minutes before midnight and secured one of the few remaining parking spaces. She forged a path toward the Coach store, where 100-plus people waited in line.

I don't want to demean anyone's products, but I don't get the whole idea of a purse that costs the equivalent of a television set.

When the doors opened, the crowd surged inside, grabbing pricey purses as if they were gold bars free for the taking. The Queen made her selection and indicated her intention to wait in line to pay.

I opted for breathing.

The last time I remember feeling that claustrophobic, I was standing at the jewelry counter at Macy's in New York City on a Saturday afternoon right before Christmas.

Once I regained my equilibrium, I discovered Liz had opted out of midnight shopping. So I cooled my heels — and the rest of me — on the sidewalk while she waited one hour and 20 minutes to pay for her purse.

Waiting on her highness allowed me plenty of opportunity to survey the crowd. Young. Collegiate, I'd say. Lots of jeans and cell phones.

When Elizabeth emerged with her purse, we walked the square that is the outlets. We considered Aeropostale, Carter's and The Children's Place, but lines of Coach proportions inching toward the cash registers changed our course.

So, we headed home, past cars parked helter-skelter on the grass and in neighboring lots.

With the maiden voyage history, I offer three predictions:

Do I think the outlets will open at midnight next year?

Oh, yes.

Do I think other stores will follow suit?

Definitely.

Should more employees expect to work at midnight?

If you're in retail, mark your calendar now.

Finally, I'll share my royal reward: The day after our adventure, Elizabeth proclaimed me an extraordinary grandma, heralded for my uncommon willingness to explore new territory despite advanced age.

HOLIDAYS

December 20, 1989

TRADITION CAN BE SYMBOL OF LIFE
RATHER THAN RITUAL AFTER LOSS

Traditions and Christmas. The two go together like mistletoe and kisses.

On Christmas cards and Christmas commercials we see the traditional family celebrating their traditional Christmas: Mom and Dad are smiling with pride as Sis and Junior unwrap just what they ordered from Santa.

Hovering in the background are a gray-haired Grandma and a balding Grandpa and the family pet, usually bedecked with a Christmas ribbon. 'Tis the season to be jolly.

It's also the season to be depressed. Those of us whose families don't fit the traditional Christmas mold can feel like yesterday's discarded wrapping paper.

Consider the case of the newly divorced. Last year may have resembled a Christmas card. This year the days leading up to Dec. 25 are an endless series of negotiations over who gets the kids when and who buys them what. The children are bounced from mom to dad then over to grandma's where tension is as thick as taffy whenever the absent parent's name is mentioned.

If divorce is a problem for the kids, it's no easier on the adults.

Once upon a time a newly separated mother spent the early part of Christmas day eating turkey and unwrapping gifts with her kids and their grandparents. Then it was time for the kids to move on, to dad and another set of grandparents. The mother, who initiated the separation from her emotionally abusive husband, spent the rest of the day crying alone and wondering why she found pain instead of relief.

Even coping with holiday preparations can open a Pandora's box of painful memories.

A woman who separated this year said she found those painful memories in the box marked "Christmas tree decorations." She and her missing husband had bought many of them together and received others as gifts. What had meaning last year can't be displayed publicly this year. The decorations with meaning stay packed away like the feelings in the woman's heart.

But those feelings are hard to suppress any time a stocking is missing from the mantle.

The family that always spent Christmas at grandma's may find itself adrift the first year she is gone.

The teens who rolled their eyes at grandpa's corny jokes miss the laughter they shared with the guardian of silly Christmas stories.

Every day someone loses a mother, father, sister, brother, husband, wife or, worst of all, a child. Each loss chips away at our Christmas traditions, leaving us feeling like the jagged edge of a broken Christmas ball.

In this holiday season we need to remember that traditions are molded, not cast in stone. Just as they can expand to include a new child or a new spouse, they can survive a loss.

The traditions that bring us joy and peace can ebb and flow with changes in our lives — and they should.

Those who face change this year may find their holidays different, but different doesn't have to be bad. We become better people simply by forging ahead with the determination to create something new.

And in establishing our new traditions, we may find that the best times come while we're creating them.

NON-TILTING TREE IS
JUST PURRRRRFECT

Yes, Virginia, there is a Christmas tree in my house.

Why? Because I want one.

That's the answer I gave my son rather firmly, I must say when he asked why a mature (my word, not his) single person would go to all the bother.

I say you don't have to be walking through life with somebody to enjoy what life has to offer.

So, I did my thing. I went to the tree place and told the man the tree could be no taller than me, recalling all the years I'd said that and all the trees that brushed my eight-foot ceilings.

He held up this one and that. If the one I picked were a person, we would have been staring eye to eye.

The tree and I arrived home just as my son showed up. (We mothers really do have good timing!)

He did the unloading, grumbling about single people and trees, retrieved the stand from the basement and started stuffing the trunk in the stand.

That's when I took over.

Every mature adult knows you've got to saw a few branches off the bottom to get the tree to stand straight. So I grabbed my garden pruner. Pretty soon the tree and I were ready.

Tree in the stand, fasten the bolts. Instant Christmas.

Next came the fun part, digging through the box filled with lights and ornaments.

Reminiscing about the ornament a kid made in first grade and another crafted by a friend, I had slipped into nostalgia when I spied him: that cat.

This lousy no-name black cat has been living in my house for going on six months now. A friend of my son's got him for his wife. When he stopped to show me, I told him their dog would surely eat that little cat.

He reflected for a moment and asked if I wanted a pet.

I said no way, but told him if fangs appeared, he should bring the cat back.

Within an hour the thing was living in my house. He's still there. Still nameless, since I firmly believe that naming a cat implies you intend to keep it.

So there was this nameless thing disturbing my Christmas mood and staring at my Christmas tree. I think he had a gleam in his eye.

I glared, telling him in my most authoritative voice that he'd better keep his mitts off my tree.

Next morning he had declared war.

The tree was listing to the right severely. Ornaments were strewn about. Water was spilled out of the stand. And tannenbaum's nameless nemesis was purring and stretching on the tree skirt.

Trying to right a fully decorated tree is a lot more difficult than putting it in the stand in the first place. For one thing, you can't lay it on its side.

Instead, I slid under the tree, putting my body on top of all those prickly dried up needles that had fallen off overnight. I turned the bolts on the tree stand this way and that. Slid out, stood up and eyed the tree.

Still listing.

Back under the tree. Back on the prickly needles. Back across the room to look.

Finally, frustration.

I looked at that miserable black cat and realized I could spend an hour straightening that tree and the next morning I'd be back in the same boat listing. Or I could do something unattractive, but practical.

So I got a roll of green wire, nails and a hammer and I fixed that tree so it was perfectly vertical. No matter what that rotten cat does, the tree isn't going to tilt.

Now we're both happy. Hope you are, too.

Merry Christmas.

CONFESSIONS OF CHRISTMAS
CRAFTS KLUTZ

Deck the halls with boughs of holly?

Not if I gotta make them, by golly.

'Tis the season when my insecurities leap to the forefront. When my inadequacies flow like Santa's beard. Everywhere I go, people are sewing, quilting, needlepointing, painting, glueing and creating the most wonderful holiday crafts.

Take City Island, for example.

Walking through the doors of the big white tent is like stepping into a crafters' wonderland. Adorable tree ornaments. Clever magnets. Seasonal pillows. Decorated trees. Hand-dipped candles.

Where do these people find the ideas and the talent for such creations?

It's the same thing in every firehall, church and high school gymnasium. Hundreds of colorful crafts, whipped up with seemingly no effort by dozens of crafty souls.

For someone who finds replacing a button challenging, this whole holiday craft scene is overwhelming. And now, I find, it has sunk its tentacles into the most unlikely of places.

Take my best buddy, the gal I've shopped with, laughed with, cried with and shared secrets with for more than 30 years. The gal I thought I knew better than anyone else.

Suddenly, she's got talent.

Last Christmas Eve she arrived at my house with this wonderful lighted table-top Christmas tree decorated with dozens of tiny ornaments.

A gift I really loved.

Then, she spent the next few minutes telling me and all the others how she had made it — even made some of the tiny ornaments that she had painstakingly hung with a glue gun.

And I thought I knew her.

Thanksgiving, she produced another one for my mother.

Tit for tat, I guess, since a couple of years ago my mother gave her one of the dozens of framed needlepoint creations she's whipped up in her "spare time."

Now Mom, who's had a needle in her hand for as long as I can remember, has enlisted the family munchkins in making miniature lampshades from pins and beads. They're festive, really quite cute, and they're being fashioned by folks as young as 7.

In fact, as I discovered quite by accident the other day, little people are heavily involved in this craft scene.

You see, I needed to go into one of those big craft supermarkets, a place where people buy the fixings for all the clever things I keep admiring at craft shows.

Don't ask why I was there.

Just let me say that I felt as if I had just stepped off the Starship Enterprise into a totally alien world.

Mothers and daughters were selecting patterns for sweat shirts they were going to stitch. Grandmas and grandsons were buying birdhouses and the ingredients to paint and decorate them. People were toting beads and bows and scraps of material that they apparently would take home and transform into something grand.

I was slinking through the store like a spy behind enemy lines, hoping I wouldn't be detected. I had visions of an army of crafters, grabbing me, ridiculing me, making me the object of public scorn.

"Look at her, she's helpless," someone might yell. "She can't wield a needle or string a bead. She doesn't know a crochet hook from a fishhook. She decorates her house with items she BUYS."

But wait, I thought, as I escaped into the parking lot. I do buy.

Which is why they need me and all the other Christmas klutzes.

When we deck our halls with boughs of holly, it lines their crafty pockets, by golly.

FAST-BREAK MEMORY IN SLOW-MO

Some holidays are memorable.

For years to come, we might remember baby's first Christmas or the year Johnny got his big-boy bike. Perhaps we recall that difficult first holiday without Grandma or the year piling snowed canceled our trip home.

At my house, memorable holidays generally are linked to near-disasters.

One holiday during the '90s, I started an oven fire while roasting a turkey. My son threw baking soda on the flames, averting tragedy, but not before those flames burned memories into the munchkins' minds.

Every time I put a turkey in the oven now, it's the same old thing.

"Granny, don't set the oven on fire," they warn. Or, "Granny, we'll keep the fire extinguisher handy."

We're raising a generation of comedians.

Christmas just past will be remembered as the year of the maple syrup disaster.

Among the gifts given to my Dad was a bottle of pure maple syrup. This wasn't the ersatz stuff you buy in the grocery store next to the pancake mix. This was thick syrup, boiled down from sap tapped right out of the trees.

Pop put the syrup next to a jar of plum jam on one of those tray tables people use in the living room when they eat a snack.

A couple of hours later, most of us were sitting around the dining room table. Two of the tiniest munchkins were watching cartoons in Pop's living room. All of a sudden, one munchkin's chair bumped the tray table, and the maple syrup and the plum jam went sailing through the air. It was one of those slow-motion experiences. A collision was imminent and no one could stop it.

Somewhere in midair, the jam hit the maple syrup and the maple syrup bottle shattered onto the rug. (The jam landed intact. I can't explain why.)

Hundreds of tiny pieces of glass slathered in thick, rich maple syrup oozed across the rug.

Adults jumped up, intent on dual missions: cleanup and policing.

Removing tiny shards of glass and a bottle's worth of maple syrup requires the use of a wet/dry sweeper and a rug shampooer. We had appliances to grab and solutions to mix.

Keeping the munchkins out of harm's way was a different part of the equation.

At one point in the cleanup (I was the wet/dry vac person), I glanced at the munchkin who had bumped the tray table. He was uncharacteristically quiet for a 4-year-old.

I stopped the vacuuming operation and positioned myself at his eye level. I explained that the Christmas catastrophe was an accident plain and simple. It wasn't his fault and no one blamed him.

When others echoed that thought, he brightened.

As I returned to vacuuming, I realized that our holiday disasters can be viewed as shining examples of how families operate.

The year of the burning turkey, while my son grabbed the baking soda, their mother spirited the munchkins outside to safety, shouting, "My kids, my kids, my kids!"

That repeated phrase of concern spoke volumes about relationships and families and what's important in life.

I'm hoping the munchkins will learn a lesson from the year of the maple syrup.

Oh, they'll probably laugh when they recall the jar and the bottle sailing in slow motion through the air. They'll snicker when they envision thick syrup oozing across the rug.

But I hope they also will remember how a really big mess became a minor inconvenience because a family pitched in and worked toward a common goal.

OUR HEIRLOOMS GIVE
CHRISTMAS ITS REAL SHINE

Can't you just feel it? It's Christmas. It's all around us.

Look at the tree, the decorations, the gifts.

Check out the tablecloth, the Christmas glasses, the ho-ho-ho plates.

This most special day has morphed into an industry. It's not enough anymore to hang your stocking with care. You have to bedeck the whole house.

Guests entering the perfect holiday home walk by the twinkling decorations to wipe their feet on a snowman or chubby Santa. Holiday doormats are as much a decorating must as an outdoor wreath.

The table, of course, will display everything Christmas, from the tablecloth to the centerpiece to the salt and pepper shakers. In my house, we drink from Christmas glasses and reach into a ceramic Santa cookie jar. The crackers have their own ceramic sleigh.

We've resisted the urge to buy a set of Christmas silverware, although numerous patterns are available.

Actually, we've stifled the urge to buy a lot of this stuff. Much of it we inherited.

Some families store heirlooms in safe deposit boxes. Ours are kept 50 weeks a year in the attic, although I confess that some don't make it downstairs anymore.

Left behind are boxes of Norman Rockwell and Campbell soup ornaments. There's simply no more room on the tree.

My mother was born a Campbell, which explains one box. Norman Rockwell I can't explain.

I also can't explain the 20-year-old Holly Hobbie Christmas plate or the Danbury Mint silver bells — one per year.

I thought I might get rich selling my heirlooms on eBay, but I looked at what similar items were bringing and decided it wasn't worth my time.

I do drag Mrs. Claus down the steps. She's about 3 feet tall, has an electric candle in her hand and moves — after I remember to plug her in. She was a gift to my mother years ago. I feel compelled to stay in step with this tradition.

For the same reason, I drag the iron across the Christmas runners and dutifully drape them across my tables. It's also why a Christmas flag flies in front of my house.

I really can't explain the rest of this stuff. We have Christmas tea towels and hot plates and oven mitts. We even own a Christmas apron, although no one in my house wears an apron. I think you have to cook to do that.

Christmas hand towels hang in our bathrooms, and I think if I look around, I can locate a Christmas bath mat set.

We haven't bought Christmas toilet paper, although I've seen it for sale on the Internet. One place was selling HO HO toilet paper for $30 for six rolls. They described it as a bargain.

The ad said "no returns," but I'm not going there.

If you wanted to jazz up the HO HO toilet paper, an eBay seller was offering a toilet-tissue holder that plays a medley of carols as it turns. It was a bit cheaper than the HO HO paper, but I resisted the temptation.

It's enough, I think, that my sofa sports Christmas pillows and a Christmas afghan. Maybe if you cuddle up with them, visions of sugarplums will boogie in your bean. I don't know because I've been so busy dragging out the Christmas items that I haven't had time to cuddle.

Digging to the bottom of the biggest storage box, I retrieved the Christmas magnets and stuck them on the refrigerator. But I sent the Santa Claus doorknob cover home with my granddaughter.

After all, a person should share her heirlooms.

DECEMBER LEAVES US, WELL, SPENT

December weighs us down. I think that's because it's always headed someplace else.

Today is Dec. 2, but who has time to enjoy it? It means there are just 23 shopping days until Christmas — if you count today. And you have to; you have to make every day count when you have this much to do.

We have to buy the cards and sign them and find Aunt Martha's address and dash to the post office for stamps.

We need to select a tree or drag the artificial number out of the attic, drop it into the stand, straighten the branches and string the lights.

Of course, half of the lights won't work, so we either have to fiddle with them or throw up our hands and drive to the store to buy more.

Then we string more lights outside. They won't work either, and it's back to the store again.

Don't you get tired just thinking about December?

Just look at that shopping list.

Mine includes teenagers whose only request is for something green with a picture of a dead president.

I feel obligated, however, to hand them something to unwrap. So I must make my way through the mall, into one of those stores where music blares and the clerks wear size 2 jeans and toss their hair back over their shoulders every 12 seconds.

They'll show me something with too little material and too high a price. I'll sigh a lot and pull out my credit card because I just don't have time to look elsewhere. And where would I look? And what would I — a grandma, for heaven's sake — know about fashion anyway?

This time of year also requires that I visit the toy store with the backward letter. You know the one. It's the size of a supermarket, its aisles jammed with carts spilling over with bicycles and scooters and Barbie playhouses. About three-quarters of the carts hold a screaming kid who wants Elmo or Winnie the Pooh or Barbie NOW.

I've learned through earsplitting experience to visit the backward letter store as close to midnight as possible. By then, most of the screaming tots have gone home, and I can shop in relative peace.

In fact, that's my philosophy for most of my Christmas shopping.

Most stores stay open until 11 or later, so I hit them after everyone else has pooped out for the day.

I prepare by napping while everyone else shops.

I've also learned over the years to keep a list of what I've bought for each person. That prevents embarrassing Christmas Day gaffes, like a pile of six gifts for one kid and just two for another.

Kids notice those things.

Kids also notice if you try to eliminate a holiday tradition.

I've been trying for a couple of years to forgo stockings, but the kids — OK, it's not the kids, it's the teens — beg me not to stop.

Filling stockings is time-consuming and expensive. The 5-year-old is thrilled to find a pack of gum in her stocking; the 15-year-old wants perfume and cosmetics and CDs.

Oh, what the heck. It's only time and money. In December, when you have so little anyway, what's a tad less?

REAL FEAST IS OF FRIEND AND FAMILY

It's hard to avoid the trite as we rendezvous again in this spot on Thanksgiving.

Family and friends, food on the table. We're thankful. Yeah. Yeah. Yeah.

You're looking for more. I know it.

I've searched. I've pondered. I've come up short.

I'd love to write something funny, such as, "Yes, it is a tragic but statistical fact that every Thanksgiving, undercooked turkeys claim the lives of an estimated 53 billion Americans (source: Dan Rather). Sometimes the cause is deadly bacteria; sometimes — in cases of extreme undercooking — the turkey actually springs up from the carving platter and pecks the would-be carver to death."

Dave Barry beat me to it in his column last Sunday.

I'd love to be a stargazer and write, "Born today, you are a versatile individual, and you're not likely to be known for doing only one thing or pursuing only one line of endeavor. You are the type to explore so many opportunities and options in your lifetime that you're sure to turn from many activities with ease and eagerness."

Unfortunately, Stella Wilder sees that, not me.

Perhaps I could be profound: "You might think that Indians won't be in a party mood come Turkey Day.

"After all, given the historical record of how the founders of this country treated the first people of this land, it does not take much cultural sensitivity to understand why some Indians don't celebrate Thanksgiving.

"But there are those myself included who choose to find something to be thankful about during this season.

"We are still here."

Those thoughtful words come not from me, but from Mark Anthony Rolo, a Wisconsin Ojibwe.

In desperation, I searched our archives wondering if I had been funny or prophetic or profound on Thanksgivings past.

I unearthed stories of the season. Senior citizens giving thanks. Serious shoppers studying the ads in preparation for Black Friday. Hunters packing the SUV. Football. Food.

What struck me were the changes in and around my life. In my early days as a columnist, I slept in, showered, dressed and drove to my parents' for the feast.

With Mom around, I could be irresponsible in the kitchen. Heck, I could be absent.

After we lost my mother, getting food to the table became my task. The real work began the night before and resumed in the early a.m.

Call those the grueling years.

Then we lost my Dad. My son and daughter-in-law left the big city. Dinner was reborn in their new home on the West Shore.

Now, in my relaxed years, I bake the bird and truck it across the river where the side dishes wait.

Like the location of our meal, those sitting around the table have changed with the years. We've lost a generation. We've gained a new one.

I've metamorphosed.

I'm more interested in the latest project crafted in kindergarten than the floats in the Thanksgiving Day parade. I'd rather snuggle with a 3-year-old than eat another piece of pie. If I can cuddle a baby or hang out with a teen, I'll forgo the traditional after-dinner nap.

In the end, it's trite but true. Today is about family and friends. Enjoy them while you can.

April 8, 2007

EASTER LEAVES BUNNIES FAR BEHIND

When I was a kid, Easter meant a straw basket, a large chocolate bunny, a few jelly beans, a couple of yellow Peeps and hard-boiled eggs that smelled like vinegar.

My dad would break off pieces of my bunny, all the while sharing sad tales of growing up poor without candy in the Depression. My mom would break off a piece here and there and recall the World War II years when sugar rationing made it difficult to get candy.

About the only thing that distinguished my Easter basket from those of my friends was whether the bunny was hollow or solid chocolate.

What the Easter bunny delivers today is tailor-made for little Jacob or Emily. I couldn't believe the selection of goodies I found while visiting Target and Party City last week.

First let me say, I thought I was pretty hip on what the preschool crowd likes. I can sing the theme songs from the shows "Bob the Builder" and "Thomas the Tank Engine and Friends." So imagine my surprise when the first basket I encountered was actually a baglike item with grasslike sides decorated with pictures of something called the Backyardigans.

A quick trip to the Internet taught me that "The Backyardigans" is a Nick Jr. show aimed at kids ages 2 to 5 and featuring five preschool friends named (are you ready for this?) Uniqua, Pablo, Tyrone, Tasha and Austin.

After that quintet, it was time to seek out something I recognized.

How about a Disney princess basket, fuzzy pink and resembling an upside-down crown? Or Dora the Explorer? Party City had those and baskets shaped like fuzzy animals, butterflies or balls — football or soccer.

For the lazy basket filler, the store offered Easter basket kits featuring either SpongeBob SquarePants with pink ears or Dora the Explorer. The whole shebang was wrapped in plastic so you could drop SpongeBob and his Krabby Patties or Dora and her microwave popcorn right into the basket of your choice.

Of course, for the more adventurous, candy, like baskets, can suit just about any wee one's fancy.

Take Peeps. I remember them as yellow. Target was selling pink, blue, green, a ghastly orange-red, purple and something called cocoa Peeps.

I suppose the orange-red might have worked well in the Spider-Man basket, which had to be — hands down — the worst excuse for an Easter basket on this, or any, planet.

Although, I suppose if you're an 8-year-old boy ...

Speaking of boys that age, Target also had Superman and Shrek baskets, and, yes, Shrek's face was green. Boys also might have liked what looked like a basketball or soccer net with the appropriate ball built into the handle.

For young ladies who can't get enough princesses (I know a couple of those), Target offered Disney princess baskets filled with princess gear, including a crown and a gaudy ring. For the ambitious young gal, the lovely gardener basket delivered a straw hat, watering can and trowel along with a small bit of sweet stuff.

I also saw a basket filled with Play-Doh, which is something you might buy if the contents weren't going to be opened in your own house.

Baskets could be filled with a variety of goodies, from a mesh bag full of foil-covered gold coins — something that was available when I was a kid — to a similar product featuring sports balls rather than coins. You could also pick up a Hot Wheels hollow racing bunny — a product that doesn't make much sense when you think about it — or a Thomas the Tank Engine die-cast model. Its only connection to Easter seemed to be the egg-shaped cardboard backing.

Finally, I took a look at the stuff you could buy to color eggs.

I'm pretty darn sure my mom never used anything other than food coloring and vinegar to dye eggs, but I suppose that's old-fashioned.

Had I wanted, in Party City I could have bought Dunk an Egg, Stamp and Color for eggs, Egg Coloring Racers, the Eggstreme Sports egg decorating kit, Noah's Ark Dye Kit (again, I couldn't connect the dots to figure what Noah had to do with eggs and dye), or some sort of puff paint that makes eggs look like they're covered with fur (which I think happens naturally if you leave them in the refrigerator for a couple of months).

Target also offered Hello Kitty egg dye and stuff to tie-dye eggs or make them look like marble.

Perhaps my favorite — although I didn't buy — was the Wonka Egg Hunt Family Fun, which, the box claimed, lets you decorate eggs to look like members of your family.

Just imagine the arguments that could stir up around the holiday dinner table.

WORRYWARTS ARE
DEFACING HALLOWEEN

Once upon a time, Halloween was a treat.

As kids, we'd put on a sheet with a couple of holes cut out at the eyes or grab a pointy black hat and broom and head out to collect candy from the neighbors.

Making our way through the neighborhood, we'd pass ghosts and goblins and witches and try to figure out if they were kids who sat on the other side of the classroom or the noisy boys from the back of the school bus.

Once in a while, the bad kids smashed a pumpkin in the street or soaped a grouchy neighbor's windows. But nobody ever told us that by dressing as witches or ghosts or goblins we were in danger of being tricked into Satanism or pagan rituals.

Suddenly, it's the '90s and Halloween is becoming another victim of society's paranoia.

In some midstate schools, teachers are abandoning the traditional Halloween parties and telling the kids to leave their costumes at home. Instead, they celebrate the fall harvest.

Corn is good. Apples are healthy. Witches and ghosts are politically incorrect.

In at least one Lancaster County school district, principals have banned witches and ghosts as decorations or as the subject of instructional materials.

No Shakespearean "Double, double toil and trouble." No "Fire burn and caldron bubble." Macbeth is out, another victim of a few loud members of the religious right.

These folks insist on emphasizing Halloween's link to the Celts and Druids, people who surely had some weird practices like human sacrifice but who weren't exactly living in enlightened times.

No one will argue their claim that Halloween has its roots in the Celtic tribes who inhabited Scotland, Ireland and Wales before the Middle Ages. But they are also the source of a lot of our Christmas traditions. Decorated trees got their start because they thought their gods lived in evergreens. Mistletoe was the focus of a solemn ceremony for the Druids, the unholy priests of the Celtic tribes.

Maybe next our present-day worrywarts will want to dim the Christmas lights or outlaw mistletoe because they might lead their neighbors to devil worship.

For the moment, however, they are content to suggest that a kid who dresses like a witch for one night of merriment could topple into a Satanic cult.

Their attack on Halloween as we knew it is bolstered by another group — the overprotective parents of the '90s who are terrified that their precious offspring will have their psyches permanently handicapped if they pass a miniature Freddy Krueger in the street.

Together they are trying to spoil something that has been a treat for generations of kids.

What was good about Halloween when we were kids were the mystery and the pretense. Who was that masked stranger? Did good or evil lurk behind that mask? For one magic night we could be anything we wanted to be. The poorest kid in the neighborhood could be a princess. The sweetest child could be a witch. The powerless could be Superman.

In the streets we faced our fears. We cringed when a devil approached, but we knew we had to plod past him if we wanted the treat at the next doorstep.

We didn't realize it then — we were too busy having fun — but Halloween's biggest treat was what it taught us about life.

Unfortunately, too many kids today have their treats spoiled by parents whose determination to protect them from anything or anybody different or strange prevents the youngsters from tasting life.

OK, MEN, GET OUT THERE
AND ROMANCE 'EM!

Gentlemen, tomorrow is the day.

How you play tomorrow may determine the tenor of your weekend. Will it be the thrill of victory or the agony of defeat?

Tomorrow, of course, is Valentine's Day, a very special day for the lady in your life.

Trust me on this.

Women expect a gift on Christmas and require that you remember their birthdays and pertinent anniversaries, but Valentine's Day is another kind of game.

Putting it into language you men can understand, birthdays and anniversaries are the playoffs; Valentine's Day is the Super Bowl. Failure to run with the ball could result in severe penalties.

To women, the competition on Feb. 14 is as intense as in any bowl game.

If one gal in the office gets a delivery from a flower shop, it sets the pace for every other woman. If your lady is the only one without a vase full of flowers on her desk, she will cry foul.

If her sister or best friend gets a 2-pound box of chocolates, she expects you to tie the score.

Women put great stock in romance. Don't groan. It's as inborn as the color of their eyes. If you want to win at the game of love, you've got to learn to live up to her romantic expectations, even if you can manage it only once a year.

She feeds her expectations with a steady dose of movies or novels. On more than one occasion, you must have seen her cry during a movie. And, you've probably asked what's wrong. Then, she has sighed and told you, "You wouldn't understand."

Well, let me help you figure it out.

Romance makes her cry because she craves it in her life.

OK. Maybe you still don't get it. So follow this, play by play:

Go to a store. Select a card.

This is very important: The card must have hearts or flowers or Cupids on it. It must use the word "sweetheart," or "honey" or "darling." Bigger cards are better.

Buy the card. Under the message inside, write the word "Love," followed by a comma and your name.

Now comes the hard part.

Continue shopping. Select a present.

Flowers are good (unless she has allergies). Chocolate in heart-shaped boxes is good (unless she is on a diet). Perfume is good (see flowers for the disclaimer). Anything from Victoria's Secret is good (so long as your intent is to make her feel good, not you). Jewelry is very good (diamonds upgrade it to excellent).

Delivering the gift in front of others is like going for two points after the touchdown and making it. This lets the world know that she is truly cherished.

This late in the game, you may need some creativity. Think of it like a Hail Mary. If the florist is overworked and can't deliver tomorrow, drop a bouquet at her office yourself.

If you call every restaurant within a 30-mile radius and find them all booked, make an end run.

Tell her instead of going out among all those people, you've planned a romantic dinner for two at home. Then either learn how to cook (and do dishes) or stop at the nearest Chinese restaurant for takeout. (No, pizza won't do. I know it's Italian, but it simply isn't romantic.)

That's all it takes. Really.

Now, if you lose the game tomorrow, you have only yourself to blame.

You have been coached.

FROM CUPID'S LIPS TO YOUR EARS, GUYS

Quite a few women have requested that I repeat last year's Valentine's column.

It explained, some of you may recall, why Valentine's Day is important to women. It was directed at men. It was simple. It spelled things out specifically. Women said it worked.

A gal who works in this building credited me when she got a heart-shaped diamond necklace. Women called to report they had received flowers. Even I got a dozen red roses.

So, in an attempt to aid the helpless, I'm going to go over the rules of the game again, briefly and simply so men can understand.

It's important, guys, that you pay attention and act quickly because Valentine's Day is Saturday. Yes, this week. The day after tomorrow.

First of all, I've heard from numerous sources that restaurants are booked Saturday. A lot of them are booked Friday, too. Somewhere, I'm sure, there is a restaurant with an empty table. You better call now, this minute, if you intend to find it.

If restaurants are filled and your honey won't be thrilled with eating under the Golden Arches, what's left? Take-out food is an option; so long as it's not pizza. As I explained last year, pizza may be Italian, but it's not romantic. You have to trust me on that.

You could cook, but most of you won't. So here's a suggestion: Go to one of the local farmer's markets. Most are open Saturday. Buy some prepared food. Go to the nearest State Store. Buy a bottle of wine.

Chill the wine in the refrigerator. Heat the food in the oven or microwave. Serve the food on real plates, not paper. Pour the wine into wineglasses, not plastic. Light a candle or two.

Instant romance. Trust me on that, too.

But, failing to follow through could douse the flame.

This may shock some men: When you serve food on real dishes or wine in real glasses, someone has to wash them. Or at least rinse them and put them in the dishwasher.

If you cook (or reheat) and expect someone else to clean up, romance will wilt like yesterday's lettuce. Trust me.

If you are scared off by the cooking thing or are, frankly, too lazy to do the dishes, get to a store — fast.

You need a gift. Don't expect to call a florist tomorrow and arrange for delivery. It's probably too late, baby. You can do flower pick up, but you better get there early.

That leaves the mall. These hints gleaned from last year's column should get you through: Chocolate looks good in heart-shaped boxes, but she really won't appreciate it unless she is the one woman in North America who isn't on a diet.

Perfume is good so long as she isn't allergic and it isn't cheap. Unless the price on the box makes you suck air, don't bother to buy it.

Victoria's Secret is good if you can keep your mind focused on what she likes, not what you would like her to like.

Jewelry is good. Diamonds are excellent.

Now here's the part you guys never get: Whatever you are doing to make Valentine's Day special, it isn't complete without a card.

You may be whisking her to Paris on the Concorde for the weekend, but if she doesn't get a card you will hear about it. Not now. Someday.

When you least expect it, she will remind you that on Valentine's Day 1998, you didn't buy her a card. She will describe in detail the card her sister or her best friend got — that it had hearts on the cover or a poem inside.

She will spew this information in your face, making you feel like a cad. She will feel hurt. You will feel bad.

Save both of you the aggravation. Buy a card. Do it now. A big card. A flowery card. A romantic card.

Romance, brothers, is in the cards.

READY GUYS? BIG GAME ALMOST HERE

Like many greeting cards, this column consists largely of recycled materials.

It's pitched to men, so the women might want to snag it and tape it to their guy's shaving mirror.

The topic is Valentine's Day. It's urgent because tomorrow is Feb. 14.

Gentlemen, how you play tomorrow might determine the outcome of the upcoming three-day weekend. Will it be the thrill of victory or the agony of defeat? Have a game plan?

As I told you fellows back in '97, women require a gift on Christmas and expect you to remember their birthdays and pertinent anniversaries, but Valentine's Day introduces another kind of game.

Think of birthdays and anniversaries as the playoffs. Valentine's Day is the Super Bowl.

If you are naive enough to imagine no competition exists, you're wrong.

If one gal in the office is on the receiving end from a flower shop, she sets the pace for every other woman. If your lady remains the only one without such a reception, she will cry foul.

If a 2-pound box of chocolates is handed off to her sister or best friend, she anticipates you will tie the score.

Whatever you buy — and you must pick up something — women require that it be accompanied by a card. Men sometimes foolishly think that cards are designed only to be mailed to those a continent away. No. No. No.

A card is to Valentine's Day what a ticket is to a football fan.

If you've booked three days in a romantic bed and breakfast but didn't get her a card, you'll hear about it. Not now, but someday.

Hand the card to her. Put it on the table next to her cereal bowl. Tape it to her purse.

But don't go home without one.

In the card store, you will find hundreds of selections. This is very important: The card you choose must have hearts or flowers or cupids on it. It must use the word "sweetheart," "honey" or "darling." Bigger cards — like running up the score — are better.

After you purchase the card, open it and write the word "Love," followed by a comma, then your name.

Card-buying is the warm-up, like calisthenics. The grueling part comes if you've been sitting on the sidelines and have no gift in your mental lineup.

It's tomorrow, fellows. You wouldn't expect to get into the Super Bowl without buying a ticket in advance, would you?

OK, it's late, but you aren't locked out of the stadium yet.

Flowers are good (unless she has allergies). This late in the game— the two-minute warning is coming up — delivery is out of the question. You'll have to stop at the florist's, stand in line for Mike the flower guy at Third and Locust, dash into the Broad Street Market or one of the suburban supermarkets. Attach a helium balloon, preferably heart-shaped, and score an extra point.

Chocolate is good (unless she is on a diet). Perfume is good (but ditto the allergy disclaimer). Anything from Victoria's Secret is good — so long as your intent is to make her (not you) feel good. Jewelry is good. Diamonds are excellent.

Completing delivery of the gift in front of others is like making a two-point conversion. This lets the crowd know she is truly cherished.

If your gal is on a diet and allergic to flowers and your wallet lacks the pizzazz to purchase diamonds, don't punt and don't panic: A loss is not inevitable.

I can coach. Really.

"My Big Fat Greek Wedding" was released on video and DVD this week. It's a funny, funny chick flick. If you buy her a copy, she'll think you're sensitive and possess a great sense of humor. She'll think you truly understand her. Really.

If you truly want to score, pick up Chinese and catch the movie with her. But, remember: Snooze on the couch during the show and you lose. Game over. Really.

TAKE A TIP FROM A KID ABOUT DAD

It was more than a Kodak moment. I wanted to bronze it.

She soared through the air on my backyard swing last weekend, her daddy pushing her higher and higher, her giggles echoing off the trees.

"I love you, Dad," she hollered to my son. "You're the best!"

She was laughing. He was smiling. I was beaming.

Little can compare to hearing your favorite 4-year-old describe your son as the perfect dad.

For those who keep track of such things, only 24 shopping days remain until Father's Day.

I was reminded that it's looming by a slew of news releases that arrived this week with suggestions for Father's Day gifts that stretch beyond the shirt and tie.

In fact, some of them stretch beyond the imagination.

The "Grow Your Own Furniture Kit"? That's an acorn with an instruction booklet.

The "Racquet Zapper"? An electronic bug zapper shaped like a tennis racquet.

I wouldn't be the first to point out that a lot of Father's Day gift ideas are downright insulting. They seem to equate pop with the family pet. Pat him on the head occasionally, and he'll be content relaxing in his easy chair with the remote control and a beer, oblivious to what the family's doing around him.

He's like the man in the commercial who — after a whirlwind of breakfast table activity — looks up from his newspaper and asks his wife whether the kids are up yet.

He's the antithesis of the great dads I know, who are every bit as much a parent as the moms.

According to the ad writers, the things that would improve pop's life include the Amazin' Beer Chiller, a battery-operated contraption that chills 12- and 16-ounce cans of beer in two minutes using ice and water.

He'd also be better off with a pool cue bearing the NFL logo.

Pool and football. Talk about your manly man.

If you believe the stuff in news releases, dads spend most of their time drinking, playing and relaxing, not pushing swings, supervising bath time or doling out snacks.

Hammocks.com, for example, offers all sorts of swinging places for dad to hang. The model they call the Biggy Daddy Special features a rope hammock with pillow, wood stand and accessories — all for a nickel under $500.

Dad can relax outdoors after he tires of sitting inside in his Inada Shiatsu Massage Chair. But then, who would tire of a model that lets him vegetate in style, with synchronized music and massage, for the low, low price of $3,500?

While he's relaxing indoors or out, dad could fire up what one pitchman called "something stylish and smokin'."

And when you're buying him cigars, remember, they come in many colors, but the mark of a good cigar is uniform color.

Or so the pitchman said.

Dads who prefer smoking up the yard to smoking a stogie might prefer a grill — charcoal, gas or infrared.

I could go on with suggestions: personalized car mats, a fishing boat, binoculars. Or tools. Although I equate buying dad a screwdriver with buying mom a toaster.

My dad never wanted gifts. "Why'd you waste your money on that?" he'd growl, shaking his head.

He was a child of the Depression. As long as you had a clean shirt, there was no need to buy another.

Sadly, I won't hear him growl this Father's Day. No one expected last year's special day for dads would be his last. People seldom do.

So maybe you shouldn't wait. Don't count on having those 24 days.

Forget the commercialized day and the overpriced insulting gifts. Just follow the lead of that 4-year-old and tell dad right now if he's the greatest.

Because if he is, you're as lucky as that laughing little girl.

Printed in the United States
94052LV00003B/255/A

9 781434 309853

CUBA

CUBA

Victoria Sherrow

Twenty-First Century Books
Brookfield, Connecticut

Published by Twenty-First Century Books
A Division of The Millbrook Press, Inc.
2 Old New Milford Road
Brookfield, Connecticut 06804
www.millbrookpress.com

Library of Congress Cataloging-in-Publication Data
Sherrow, Victoria.
Cuba / by Victoria Sherrow.
p. cm.
Includes bibliographical references (p.) and index.
ISBN 0-7613-1404-0 (lib. bdg.)
1. Cuba—History—Juvenile literature. I. Title.
F1758.5 .S57 2001
972.91—dc21 2001018110

Photographs courtesy of AP/Wide World Photos: pp. 8, 31, 32, 48,
64, 72, 90, 106; The Granger Collection, New York: p. 12; ©
Bettmann/Corbis: p. 22; © Bill Lyons/Liaison Agency: p. 122

CONTENTS

CUBA

Fidel Castro approaches the Che Guevara monument on July 29, 2000, on the anniversary of the 1959 Revolution.

"LIFE IS VERY DIFFICULT"

The name "Cuba" evokes images of tropical beaches, first-rate cigars, and large sugar plantations. It is the largest nation in the Caribbean, yet it occupies an area of only about 42,857 square miles (111,000 square kilometers), similar to the state of Pennsylvania. Visitors to the "Jewel of the Caribbean," as it was once called, praise the sunny climate and lush scenery, as well as the creativity and spirit of the Cuban people. Cuban music and dances are popular throughout the world and have inspired energetic new art forms.

Cuba is also one of the most controversial countries in the world, with a unique political and economic system. It is the only Communist nation in the Western Hemisphere and one of the few in the world. Cuba is located only 92 miles (148 kilometers) from the world's most powerful democracy, the United States, and relations between the two governments have often been hostile. Nations around the world have said that the Cuban government denies its citizens human rights.

Political images of Cuba center on Fidel Castro, Cuba's "supreme leader" since 1959. No other modern country has been ruled for so long by the same person. Castro dominates Cuban life and makes many public appearances, wearing the military uniform of the 1959 Revolution. A powerful speaker, he has kept himself and his country in the news and has involved the Cuban military in foreign conflicts. Cuba has been the focus of international attention through the years.

Cuba consists of more than 1,600 islands, islets, and cays (keys), the two largest being the island of Cuba and the Island of Youth. The country's location and physical attributes strongly influenced its development during the Age of Discovery, continuing to the present day. Centuries ago, conquerors from other countries coveted this beautiful and fertile land, which became known as the "key to the New World." At times, Cuba was controlled by Spain, Britain, and the United States. Foreigners exploited the country's resources and workforce and became wealthy while many Cubans lived in poverty.

During the late 1950s, revolutionaries led by Fidel Castro overturned the government and created a new regime. Cuba was now free of foreign control. Many Cubans felt a sense of hope, along with renewed national pride. The revolutionary government provided many social benefits to the people, particularly the rural poor. It also imposed strong limits on political and economic freedom, academic freedom, and personal expression. Soon, the Soviet Union (USSR) became Cuba's main political ally and trading partner and strongly influenced Cuban life.

Since 1959, Cuba has gone through many changes and endured hard times, particularly in the 1990s. Between 1959 and 1989, Cuba received extensive financial help from the USSR. The USSR system of a central Communist government collapsed in 1989, and the various nations in the Soviet bloc broke away. Cuba lost its favored-nation trading status with those countries. At the same time, the price of sugar (the mainstay of Cuba's economy) fell as the world's sugar supply exceeded the demand.

The year 1990 marked the onset of what Fidel Castro calls the "Special Period in Times of Peace," a time of serious economic problems. Since then, food and other basic goods have been carefully rationed and are hard to obtain. People line up to buy bread, shoes, clothing, paper products, and other things, if and when they are available. "Life is very difficult," a

Cuban man told a *Newsweek* journalist in April 2000. "There is not enough milk, there are not enough clothes, there's not enough rice."[1]

Castro acknowledged that Cuba faced big challenges, including "how to ensure that no child goes without milk, that the sick do not lack the medical care they need, that there are minimum levels of food, electricity, water, domestic fuel, transportation and many other products and services required by the population."[2]

The government pledged to preserve its healthcare and education systems, which it regards as two major achievements of the Cuban Revolution. However, a lack of funds hindered social programs. Hospitals could not stock soap, surgical supplies, and other things; schools suffered shortages of books and paper goods.

In response, Cuban officials changed the nation's economic policies to allow some activities once condemned as "capitalistic." At the same time, the government reaffirmed its commitment to social equity—equality for all and a society with no class divisions. Some Cubans, however, have more access than others to material goods because they can obtain dollars, a currency that has a higher value than Cuban pesos. Foreign tourists enjoy scarce foods and amenities that average Cubans cannot obtain for themselves or their families.

This book will describe Cuba's fascinating history and long struggle for independence. It will explore the country's economy and political life since the 1959 Revolution and show how people live today. What does the future hold for the government that Castro has controlled for so long? Will Cuba change more of its economic policies and form of government to adapt to a changing world? How do Cubans themselves see their future?

The port and city of Havana in an engraving from 1720

CHAPTER ONE

FROM COLONY TO REVOLUTION

Glimpsing the coast for the first time in October 1492, explorer Christopher Columbus called Cuba "the loveliest land ever beheld by human eyes."[1] The islands are rimmed with beautiful sandy beaches and enjoy a warm climate, with temperatures ranging between about 70 and 86 degrees Fahrenheit (21 and 30 degrees Celsius). Rainfall and underground sources provide adequate water. About one-fourth of Cuba is mountainous, much of it covered with forests. Flat plains lie between the mountain ranges. Millions of years ago, geologic events created a soil made up of limestone, clay, and shale, a superb blend for growing tobacco and sugarcane. A colorful variety of plants, animals, and birds make their homes in Cuba.

Europeans who embarked for these unknown lands across the Atlantic sought new trade routes to the Far East so they could avoid passing through the Ottoman Empire. They also sought wealth and new territory. The Roman Catholic Church, a powerful political force in Spain, planned to send missionaries to spread their religious beliefs and values abroad.

NATIVE PEOPLES

For thousands of years, native peoples lived on the islands now called Cuba. Pre-Ceramic tribesmen, the Arawak-Siboneys (Ciboneys) and Guahanacabibes, were nomadic hunters and gatherers who lived in caves along the coast. The Tainos, who inhabited the islands of Cuba and Hispaniola, arrived around the beginning of the twelfth century. Sailing from South America, they settled mostly in eastern Cuba and lived in organized villages. They cultivated crops, such as maize, beans, squash, peanuts, and tobacco, and hunted and fished for their food. They also enjoyed a game called *batos* that resembles today's baseball.

The Arawaks, the largest group, had high cheekbones, straight black hair, and deep copper-toned complexions. By the fifteenth century, the Arawaks were living in settlements located near water where they grew manioc (yucca), yams, potatoes, corn, and beans and fished and hunted birds for food. They wove clothing from cotton they grew and crafted many objects from clay, including containers for baking a breadlike food from the ground cassava plant. Although the Arawaks outnumbered other native groups, they were less aggressive, and others sometimes attacked their settlements.

SPANISH CONQUEST
Christopher Columbus spotted Cuba during his first voyage to North America in 1492. While he was exploring the Bahamas, he heard natives talking about a large island they called "Colba," but Columbus wrote down the name as "Cuba" in his log entry dated October 23. As he left the Bahamas, Columbus believed he would soon encounter China or Japan.

On October 29, Columbus reached Cuban shores. The native people on nearby islands had said that Colba was a land of rich merchants who traded in spices and gold. Of course, the Spaniards found something quite different—a land dotted with palm trees, mountains, and villages, populated by fishermen and farmers who lived in round huts. The map of the world that Columbus had brought with him now required major changes. He wondered why things looked so different than he had expected.

The scouts sent by Columbus to explore the island reported that the people were friendly. The Spaniards

THREATS FROM THE WEATHER

Cuba enjoys a beautiful setting and stable climate (usually hot and sunny), with adequate rainfall, but it has suffered from property damage and loss of human life during hurricanes. Storms have hurt sugar crops and other agriculture, although in most years the harvest is safely brought in. The city of Havana, situated only a few feet above sea level, may also experience flooding during severe storms, as winds drive seawater ashore. During some storms, water has flooded the streets of Havana, especially the Malecon, a scenic 4-mile (6-kilometer)-long six-lane seaside road between Havana and the Atlantic Ocean. Storms also pose risks to the historic buildings in Havana and Santiago de Cuba.

About 1,200 people died and many acres of crops were lost when Hurricane Flora struck Cuba in 1963. Hurricane Lili, one of the worst storms in Cuban history, destroyed buildings and left thousands of people homeless in 1996. Lili brought fierce rains and winds of 90 miles (145 kilometers) per hour that toppled palm trees and damaged plantain and ground root crops, as well as destroying 16,500 tons of citrus. The International Red Cross (IRC) said that about 200,000 people were evacuated from their homes. The IRC provided emergency aid, including food, soap, and blankets, and it monitored the safety of drinking water.

Emergency aid was also needed after Hurricane Georges struck Cuba in 1998. The hurricane left five Cubans dead and caused destructive floods. Banana crops in San Antonio del Valle were damaged. The mayor of that town, Migdalia Leon, said: "The primary problem remains food." In response to this emergency, the World Food Program sent large quantities of rice, beans, and canned fish to Cuba. Unfortunately, this hurricane came on the heels of a devastating drought that destroyed 42 percent of the crops in five Cuban provinces.

found no gold but noticed something else that would prove quite valuable. Columbus wrote these words in his log on November 6: "On the way inland, my two men found . . . men and women, carrying firebrands in their hands and herbs to smoke, which they are in the habit of doing."[2] It was the first time that Europeans had observed the use of tobacco.

A new Spanish expedition reached Cuba in 1510. The next year, Diego Velásquez de Cuellar, a distinguished soldier, arrived with three or four ships and about three hundred explorers, including Hernán Cortés. Velásquez organized the first Spanish settlement at Baracoa. By then, Cuban natives had heard about the way the Spaniards mistreated the native people of Hispaniola, a part of Cuba that they had already settled. Taino warriors led by Chief Hatuey attempted to drive out the Spanish, to no avail. By 1513 the well-armed Spaniards had crushed the resistance and killed Hatuey. Guanahatebey Indians escaped by fleeing to the Sierra de los Organos on República de Chile. Caves and underground streams can be found in these large limestone formations, which are covered with vegetation.

Cuba became a Spanish colony. Within a few years, the Spaniards had organized several settlements and killed thousands of native people, forcing the rest into slavery. Many native Cubans even committed suicide to avoid Spanish control; others died from diseases introduced by the Europeans. The Spanish crown rewarded Velásquez and his men with land grants and slave laborers. The crown also issued permits, called *repartimiento,* which allowed the invaders to use Indian laborers for mining, in agriculture, on cattle farms, in public works, or as personal servants.

Abuses of the Indians were widespread, and some Spaniards asked the crown to stop this mistreatment. One of the most vocal protesters was Fray (Father) Bartolemé de Las Casas, a young Spanish priest who became known as the "Protector of the Indians." In response, the Spanish crown passed the New Laws, which aimed to help the Indians, in 1542–1543, but they were largely ignored. Plagued by disease and abuse, the native people in Cuba were reduced to a few thousand by the mid-1500s. Their culture was nearly destroyed.

A KEY PORT

Cuba soon became a way station where ships could prepare for expeditions to the mainland or stock up before returning to Spain. For instance, Hernán Cortés assembled his troops and equipment in Cuba as he prepared for his conquest of Mexico. The city of Havana—La Habana—was founded in 1514, and soon became the colony's political and cultural center and the largest port in the Caribbean.

New industries developed in response to the sea trade. Large herds of cattle were raised in Cuba to produce dried meat for seagoing crews. Yucca was made into cassava flour, which could also be carried on ships to feed passengers and crew.

During the 1530s, increasing numbers of foreigners came to the Americas seeking gold in Mexico and Peru. Ships loaded with bullion stopped in Havana en route to Spain. When gold supplies dwindled, the explorers began digging for copper and other metals. They found rich supplies of nickel in Cuba. Nickel adds strength when it is mixed with steel and other metals; a nickel coating helps to prevent rust. For the next two centuries, pirates from England, France, Holland, and other European countries would roam the Caribbean attacking treasure-laden ships. Some pirates invaded mainland Cuba.

THRIVING PLANTATIONS

The fertile soil of Cuba was well-suited to the cultivation of both sugar and tobacco, which became a major export. In the mid-1500s, Bartolemé de Las Casas wrote that the native people smoked "tubes [cigars] that they call by the name of *tobacos*."[3] The natives claimed that smoking relieved fatigue. De Las Casas further noted that some Spaniards had become "addicted to the use of them and on being reproached with it as a bad habit, replied that they could not bring themselves to give it up."[4] This crop would bring great economic benefits to Spain as tobacco use spread

Natural Wonders

Cuba is home to some unique animal species, including the smallest hummingbird in the world, called the "bee hummingbird" (*Mellisuga helenae*). It not only is the smallest bird but also the smallest warm-blooded animal in the world. The hummingbird measures about 2.25 inches (57 millimeters) long and weighs a mere 0.05 ounce (1.5 grams). Several Cuban postage stamps feature this colorful creature.

In 1996 scientists discovered a new type of frog in a remote mountain area near the eastern tip of Cuba. This frog could fit on a U.S. nickel coin and is the smallest terrestrial vertebrate in the Northern Hemisphere. A Cuban zoologist, Alberto R. Estrada, found it during an expedition in 1993 to Monte Iberia. Estrada and his long-time collaborator, Blair Hedges, a professor of biology at Pennsylvania State University, wrote about this animal, *eleuthero-dactylus iberia*, in a scientific journal in 1996.

Will this tiny frog survive? Cubans sometimes kill larger frogs for food, but for such a small species, the natural enemies are snakes and scorpions. However, the loss of tropical forests throughout much of the West Indies has deprived certain animals of their habitats. When Columbus arrived in Cuba, about 90 percent of the land was forest. By 1959 about 7 million trees had been cut down and none were replaced.

The Castro government began planting new trees. In 1987 the Cuban population took part in a massive program to plant more trees, and they put some 3 billion seedlings into the ground. In an article in the state-run newspaper *Granma International* on October 18, 1995, the government quoted José Martí, who said: "A region without trees is poor. A city without trees is sickly, land without trees is parched and bears wretched fruit."

During recent years, more Cuban timber has been cut down for firewood to deal with the energy shortage, but the government has restated its commitment to continue planting trees, including fruit trees.

throughout the world. Many Europeans who cultivated the crop and traded in tobacco products grew wealthy. The Spanish government oversaw the production and trade of this increasingly profitable industry, the mainstay of the Cuban economy.

The end of wars among France, Britain, and Spain resulted in treaties that outlawed piracy in the Caribbean. However, the way was opened for British ships to bring African slaves to the region. Slaves performed much of the labor on tobacco and sugar plantations. They brought their varied cultures, including Yoruba, Mandingas, Congos, Carabalies, and Bantu. Later, after the slave trade was outlawed, Chinese people were brought to Cuba to work as laborers under slavelike conditions.

The tobacco and sugar industries dominated the economy and the landholding patterns in Cuba. Instead of developing a variety of crops and livestock that would make people self-sufficient, large plantations were built to raise cane and tobacco and make rum for export. Plantation owners sought sources of cheap labor, which fueled the slave trade in Cuba.

CLASS DIVISIONS

Sharp class divisions developed along color and economic lines. Wealthy landowners dominated Cuban politics and retained special privileges for themselves. Spanish-born whites, called *peninsulares,* had more money and power than Cuban-born whites (*criollos,* or creoles), and *criollos* were divided into landowners and workers. Blacks were divided into slaves and free people. The 1774 census showed a population of 172,620 people, including 96,440 whites, 31,847 free blacks, and 44,333 black slaves.

Creoles resented the colonial government for giving Spanish-born whites preferential treatment in appointing civil and religious positions, even though Creole plantation owners contributed so much to the economy through tobacco, sugar, and cattle raising. Catholic religious organizations, including the Jesuits, an order of Catholic priests, exercised much power over politics and the education system and owned large plantations. Threatened by their power and influence, the Spanish crown passed laws in 1767 expelling the Jesuits (temporarily) from all Spanish colonies.

YEARS OF CHANGE

Despite tight Spanish control, the British were able to take over Cuba in 1762 during a swift military invasion. They occupied Havana from August 1762 through February 1763, then "returned" Cuba to Spain in exchange for Florida. During that brief time, the British increased both the slave trade and Cuban trade with other nations.

The French Revolution brought still more changes, as unrest in France inspired Haitian natives to rebel against the French who occupied Haiti, an island near Cuba. During the Haitian Revolution of 1796, many white plantation owners were killed and cane fields were burned, which destroyed that island's sugar industry. About 30,000 French refugees fled to Cuba along with some of their *mulatto* (mixed-race) workers. They brought new techniques for raising sugarcane and running plantations. Cuba became the foremost exporter of sugar to Europe, and sugar became the mainstay of the economy. Tobacco remained profitable, and coffee production was rising. The Spanish crown permitted slaves to be brought into Cuba without any taxes, which provided more cheap labor.

By the early 1800s, Cuba was prosperous, but wealth was concentrated in the hands of a few. Because so much land was used for sugar, tobacco, and coffee production, Cuba traded with the United States for other foodstuffs and materials it needed.

REBELLION

Cuban colonialists increasingly resented Spanish rule. They complained about high taxation from Spain, the lack of freedom of press and speech and assembly, and that native Cubans were not chosen for leadership positions. Spain had promised reforms, but they came slowly. Some leaders tried to change the political system. Governor Louis de Las Casas and a wealthy planter and statesman named Francisco de Arango y Parreno encouraged economic reforms and changes in the educational system that would enable more children to attend school. However, many influential Cubans promoted the continuation of slavery. Some people wanted Cuba to become part of Spain or the United States; others called for Cuban independence, but many members of the elite class did not support this movement.

During the early 1800s, Cuban nationalists staged several unsuccessful revolts. In 1868 rebel Cuban forces began an uprising that became the Ten Years' War. Plantation owner Carlos Manuel de Céspedes, who deeply resented the heavy taxes levied by Spain, organized the first group of rebels in Yara. Céspedes freed his slaves and demanded that Spain cease to control Cuba. Thousands of other rebels joined revolutionary groups throughout Cuba. Soldiers sent from Spain and their Cuban supporters, whom Spain supplied with rifles purchased from the United States, opposed them. About 50,000 Cubans and 208,000 Spaniards died during this war. When it ended, the Spanish government pledged to enact real reforms. After they failed to materialize, rebels continued to organize new revolts, but these groups were small and poorly equipped.

The dispute over slavery intensified. By 1841 there were at least 436,000 black and *mulatto* slaves in Cuba—more than 40 percent of its population. In 1868 the first of many slave rebellions broke out. As a result of these uprisings and the abolition of slavery around the world, slavery was abolished in Cuba in 1886. The fight for a free Cuba intensified in the final years of the nineteenth century.

The revolutionary José Martí, known in Cuba as the "Father of the Nation," was killed in the fight for independence against Spain.

CHAPTER TWO

AMERICAN INTERVENTION

The United States had long observed Cuba with interest and had even looked for ways to acquire or buy the island. In 1799, President John Quincy Adams referred to Cuba as "an apple that had to fall by gravity into the hands of the United States."[1] His successor, Thomas Jefferson, also thought that Cuba would make a fine addition to the United States.

American businesses invested in Cuban enterprises and made big profits. By the 1870s the American Sugar Refining Company controlled much of the sugar industry. The company operated nineteen refineries, which processed between 70 and 90 percent of the sugar Cuba shipped to the United States. In Europe the beet-sugar industry dominated European markets, which made Cuba even more dependent on trade with the United States. American investors were also involved in Cuban cattle raising, agriculture, iron-ore exploration, and other activities.

Tourism also increased, especially in Havana. As Americans and Europeans flocked to Havana, American businesses invested in hotels, casinos, and nightclubs. Gambling was a profitable segment of the tourist industry, and prostitution was common in tourist areas.

José Martí, born in Havana in 1853, led a concerted effort to liberate Cuba. Martí, a practical idealist who was also a poet, was the son of a Spanish artillery sergeant. He became interested in politics as a teenager and later graduated from law school. Martí became known for his revolutionary political writings, which inspired many Cubans but angered the Spanish government. He was briefly imprisoned in 1879, then exiled to Spain. Martí went to the United States in 1880 and began organizing Cuban exiles to fight for independence. From Santo Domingo on the nearby island of Hispaniola, he worked with other important revolutionary leaders, including Máximo Gómez, to unite Cubans of all races to fight Spain.

In April 1895, Martí, who had been named leader of the Armies of Liberation, wrote an article that appeared in the *New York Herald*. He said: "Cuba wishes to be free in order that here Man may fully realize his destiny, that everyone may work here. . . . The Cubans ask no more of the world than the recognition of and respect for their sacrifices."[2] But Martí himself would never live to see that dream realized. On May 19, 1895, he was killed at Dos Rios in his very first battle against the Spanish royalist army. He is often called the "Father of the Nation." His burial site in Havana became a shrine, and monuments and tributes to Martí can be seen all over Cuba today.

Cuban patriots revered Martí as their hero and inspiration, reciting his exhortation, *Cuba Libre!*— "Free Cuba." In September 1895, patriots set up their own government and declared Cuba a Republic in Arms. However, Spain refused to recognize Cuban independence. Revolutionaries urged other Cubans to stop producing crops or anything else that would benefit Spain. By 1898 a majority of Cubans supported rebellion.

Some Americans supported Cuban independence, and these feelings swelled after an American ship, the

"LA HABANA"

La Habana (Havana), the capital of Cuba, is situated on the northern coast. The original city, founded in 1515, was on the southern coast. But when Spain began exploring Mexico, the city was moved in order to serve as a port. La Habana was burned and plundered several times. During the late 1500s the Spanish built fortresses to guard the city from pirates and foreign invaders. A grand palace was built there to house the Spanish governors who ruled the colony on and off until 1902. One old fort, built in 1577, is the oldest building in present-day Havana. San Carlos de la Cabao is the largest fortress in the Americas.

La Habana was named the capital of Cuba in 1589, and it remains Cuba's main port and cultural center. The walls that the Spanish had built around "Old Havana" were demolished during the late 1800s to make way for suburban development. Villas, mansions, and public buildings went up. The city was named a UNESCO World Heritage site in 1982. Old buildings are being stabilized and restored. Palaces and colonial forts, such as the old cathedral and the Palace of the Captains General in the Old Havana section, are tourist attractions. Some of the grand buildings in Havana have been turned into cultural centers, where plays and concerts are performed. Other large former homes were converted to apartment houses. These include splendid neoclassical-style homes with lovely columns, arched porticos, wrought-iron trim, and tiled floors.

Maine, exploded and sank in Havana harbor on February 15, 1898. The cause of the explosion remains unclear and may have been due to a faulty boiler, but Americans blamed Spain. In April the United States joined Cubans in their war against Spain, which was called the Spanish-American War. That spring, the U.S. Congress adopted a resolution that said: "Cuba is, and by right ought to be, free and independent."[3] American troops achieved several land victories in Cuba early in the summer and disabled the Spanish fleet.

Spain surrendered on July 17, 1898, and gave up Cuba, as well as Puerto Rico, the Philippines, and the

West Indies. The United States now controlled these territories and assumed the role of victor against Spain. Cuban nationalists resented that their troops were excluded from negotiations to settle the war and from the victory celebrations. It was the U.S. flag that flew over Havana, not the Cuban flag. The U.S. government insisted that the new Cuban constitution contain provisions called the Platt Amendment, which gave the United States "the right of intervention for the preservation of Cuban independence and the maintenance of stable government." The amendment limited Cuba's ability to make treaties with other countries and allowed the United States to buy or lease land in Cuba for naval bases. When a permanent U.S. naval base was set up at Guantanamo Bay in 1903, many Cubans called it an unlawful seizure of territory. In 1934, under the urging of President Franklin D. Roosevelt, the U.S. Congress agreed to revoke the Platt Amendment, but retained rights to Guantanamo with its naval base.

A TROUBLED GOVERNMENT

Having cast off four centuries of Spanish rule, Cuba was briefly governed by the United States, then became independent. American troops withdrew in May 1902, and Tomas Estrada Palma became Cuba's first elected Cuban-born president. However, the United States continued to interfere in Cuban affairs and elections, as well as the economy. Americans had invested about $100 million in Cuba by the early 1900s. Many Cubans resented American influence.

The years that followed were fraught with political instability. Although the United States "officially" gave up control, it continued to support certain Cuban candidates for elected office and finance their campaigns. Money from American and European investment in Cuba enabled President Jose Miguel Gomez (1908–1912) to fund some social services and infrastructure and build new rural schools. But reforms came so slowly that poor black Cubans sparked an uprising in 1912. Various political factions made charges of fraud during both the 1917 and 1921 elections.

Changing conditions in the world sugar markets hurt the economy. During World War I (1914–1918) and the prosperous years that followed, sugar prices rose. But they fell dramatically after 1920 when the world's economy changed. Some countries imposed new sugar tariffs, which caused more problems for Cuba. A $50 million loan from the United States provided relief but left Cuba with a large foreign debt. As Cuban businesses failed, U.S. banks foreclosed on them.

American investments in Cuba soared to more than $1 billion during the early 1920s; by 1929, Americans owned $1.5 billion worth of property there. They controlled half of Cuba's sugar industry and invested heavily in other segments of the economy, including public utilities. During the 1920s, U.S. markets bought half their sugar from Cuba, which also supplied 45 percent of the world's sugar. Sugar exports made it possible to construct new hospitals, schools, and municipal and cultural buildings. But 1929 brought a severe economic depression in the United States that led to widespread poverty and unemployment, as well as rising political tensions between America and Cuba.

Cuban leaders failed to achieve real reform or satisfy different political factions. Liberal and Conservative candidates vied for power, and public protests occurred regularly. Reformers continued to complain about social injustices, especially racism and high rates of poverty, notably in rural areas. Politicians usually left office wealthy.

Americans contributed heavily to the campaign of General Gerardo Machado y Morales Gerardo, who was elected president in 1924, and aided other candidates whose policies favored their interests. Machado had promised reforms but ruled like a dictator. His government was criticized for corruption and terrible abuses, including the torture and murder of political opponents. In 1933 workers held a general strike, and the military revolted. Some noncommissioned officers took charge of Camp Colombia in Havana and arrested their superior officers. Fulgencio Batista y Zaldívar, an army sergeant, led the revolt. Batista, who came from a poor family of sugarcane cutters of mixed racial heritage, joined groups of university students who wanted to overthrow Machado. They succeeded and then formed their own government, headed by Ramon Grau San Martin, the revolutionary provisional president. Batista was awarded the rank of colonel and named chief commander of the Cuban military.

INCREASING UNREST

Cuban unrest continued, as new leaders took over, pledging to improve living conditions. Batista, who had resigned from the military, was elected president in 1940. Both the Communist party and Revolutionary Union party supported him, and these groups merged to form the Communist Revolutionary Union (Union Revolucionario Communista, or URC), a name that was later changed to Popular Socialist party (Partido Socialista Popular, or PSP).

A new constitution, passed in 1940, included universal suffrage and more benefits for Cuban workers, notably an eight-hour day, minimum wage, pensions, and social-insurance benefits.

During World War II (1939–1945), Cuba joined the Allies shortly after the United States entered the war in December 1941. Grau won the presidency back in 1944, a year before the war ended, and served for four years. Carlos Prio Socarras was then elected president.

During the late 1940s government corruption continued, and the Cuban people protested against dishonest officials. A few courageous leaders tried to reform different branches of government. Some foreign businesses and investors left Cuba because of new laws that gave more privileges to workers.

In 1952, Batista regained power by force with a military coup (takeover). He was subsequently "elected" president, but no other candidate was on the ballot. The Batista presidency was condemned for corruption and harsh, ineffective leadership and political repression. Dissidents were severely punished; some were tortured and killed. American gangsters were allowed to run the lucrative gambling industry so long as they gave part of their profits to the government. Cuba depended on American imports, and American firms controlled many aspects of the economy. Large numbers of American tourists visited Cuba.

On the other hand, Cuba had a free press and an extensive mass media that included 58 daily newspapers, 6 television networks, 270 radio stations, and more than 100 privately owned magazines. Despite the high rates of poverty, Cuba had the third-highest standard of living in Latin America. More schools were being built, and Cubans were better educated than most Latin Americans.

A presidential election was scheduled for November 3, 1958, and Batista was not up for reelection. Many Cubans looked forward to democratic elections and a new leader. Like other Cubans, members of the middle class did not support Batista's corrupt government. According to author and Cuban emigré Agustin Blazquez, the average Cuban "was pressing for a political, not an economic change."[4] Most Cubans hoped that the new government would improve social conditions and develop a more democratic government.

Cuban revolutionaries led by Fidel Castro, his brother Raul, and Argentinean revolutionary Che Guevara had more dramatic and profound changes in mind for the country.

CASTRO: THE "SUPREME LEADER"

Fidel Castro was born to a middle-class, landowning family in 1926. His father was a Spanish immigrant from Galicia, and his mother was a servant who bore Fidel before she and his father were married. As a result, young Fidel endured scorn and insults from children who knew about his "illegitimacy." (Nonetheless, Castro later had children with women he did not marry, in addition to a son, Fidelito, born during his marriage to his first wife. As an adult, his daughter Alina Revuelta defected from Cuba and often publicly criticized Castro and his regime.)

Castro enjoyed a private Catholic education and studied law at the University of Havana. He was a superior student who excelled in several sports and was also a well-known student leader. Father Llorente, a Catholic priest who taught Castro at a Jesuit boarding school, Collegio de Belen, in Havana in 1942, recalled the sixteen-year-old Fidel. He shared his memories with author Marcia Friedman who wrote, in *Cuba, A Country Study*:

I saw in him that he was a very special boy. . . . He was idealistic and very ambitious to become the best in the school at whatever it was. For instance, he came from a school in Santiago where they only played soccer. In Havana they played more sports, basketball, baseball, track as in the American schools. So he became immediately very interested in becoming a member of every team. He was very competitive, but in that moment, in a good way, not in a bad way.

Later, he would apply his enormous energy to governing Cuba. Spanish journalist Juan Luis Cebrian, who interviewed Castro extensively, observed his control over many aspects of the government. As quoted by journalist Jacobo Timerman in *Cuba, A Journey*, Cebrian said:

Nothing happens if he personally doesn't conceive it, and this can range from organizing a conference of nonallied nations to a film festival. . . . Castro molds his own image as leader with exquisite care.

In the space of seconds he can be terrible, human, cruel, amusing, transcendent. He wants to know everything, to talk about everything, to give an opinion of everything.

Castro makes personal appearances all over Cuba regularly, and most Cubans have the opportunity to see him in person at least once a year. He seems to enjoy meeting people and talking with them. Lee Lockwood, an American journalist who spent a great deal of time in Cuba during and after the Revolution, said in his book *Castro's Cuba, Cuba's Fidel*: ". . . the real source of his strength is his ability to communicate directly with the people and to dominate them with his personality." Lockwood concludes that the Cuban people support Castro do so because of "a combination of hero-worship, faith in his personal honesty, and appreciation of the practical accomplishments of his Revolution."

A march in 1960.
Fidel Castro is at left.

CHAPTER THREE

A REVOLUTIONARY SOCIETY

On July 26, 1953, Fidel Castro led a group of revolutionaries in an attack on the Moncada army barracks in Santiago de Cuba. It was the hundredth anniversary of the birth of Castro's hero, José Martí. The revolutionaries hoped to overthrow Batista's government troops, but the uprising failed, and Castro and his brother Raul and the other rebels were arrested.

At the trial, Castro denounced government corruption and the massive poverty and other social problems in Cuba. In his impassioned speech calling for Cuban independence, he quoted the words of St. Thomas Aquinas, John Locke, Jean-Jacques Rousseau, and the United States Constitution. Castro's speech contained words that have become famous: "History will absolve me."[1]

The government later granted amnesty to the rebels after the opposition party pleaded their cause and agreed to surrender some of their seats in the Cuban senate to Batista supporters. Besides, Batista concluded that the rebels could no longer threaten him, so he agreed to let the Castro brothers leave Cuba. They went to Mexico, where they continued to plan a revolt with an Argentine-born physician, Ernesto (Che) Guevara, who shared their beliefs. A small group of Cubans who supported the rebellion continued to work inside Cuba and prepared for Castro's eventual return.

In December 1956, on an old yacht called the *Granma*, Fidel and Raul Castro returned to Cuba with Che Guevara and eighty other revolutionaries. They waged their early battles against Batista's government troops in the Sierra Maestra, a remote mountain region in eastern Cuba. The guerrillas lived in hiding there as they planned and carried out various attacks. Castro expressed concern about the poverty in this region and promised to help rural Cubans someday.

The revolutionaries, consisting mostly of people under the age of thirty, waged a bold and determined campaign. They urged Cuban students to join the rebellion and also asked the military not to interfere with their activities. At one time, they were reduced to fewer than twenty fighters. On March 13, 1957, rebels attacked the Presidential Palace in Havana and tried to assassinate Batista and seize control of the public radio system. The attack on the palace failed, and Batista's government brought in a large number of troops to patrol the streets and guard the palace. However, that May, rebels were able to storm an army garrison and obtain many weapons, which they carried back to their hideouts.

In September 1957 the rebels began setting fire to sugarcane fields throughout Cuba, including the Castro family plantation in Oriente. They carried out this extreme action to prevent the Batista government and foreigners from profiting from Cuban sugar. Cubans were hurt and killed in the process. Guerrilla groups began winning battles throughout southern Cuba. They urged Cuban workers to strike in protest against the government.

In the end, it took three years for the rebels to oust the Batista government. At midnight on New Year's Eve, Batista fled, taking an estimated $300 million. The ex-dictator eventually settled in Spain. Other government officials also fled or were arrested.

On January 2, 1960, Che Guevara and Camilio Cienfuegos led their rebel troops triumphantly into

Havana. Castro made a victory speech before the nation on January 8.

The Batista regime had deposited millions of dollars in foreign banks. Castro claimed that the national treasury contained $500 million when Batista took office, but only $70 million remained after he left. Castro said that his government would use this money for various social programs.

Castro emerged as the leader of the new government, while his brother Raul became a top official who would serve in key government positions, as minister of defense, second secretary of the Communist party, and commander of the Revolutionary Armed Forces (RAF). Che Guevara served as minister of the interior, and he also became involved in revolutionary activities in other Latin American countries.

Once Castro took charge, he set out to instill his political ideals in the population. In a speech at a meeting of the Organization of Latin American Solidarity, he said: "Whoever stops to wait for ideas to triumph among the majority of the masses before initiating revolutionary action will never be a revolutionary."[2]

At that time, many Cubans regarded Castro as a reformer who would purge government corruption and alleviate social problems. Castro moved to eliminate graft, gambling, and prostitution. He said that government officials would not use their positions for personal gain or to exploit the people. He and his staff continued to wear their guerrilla uniforms and pledged to live simply, without material luxuries. Many foreigners hailed him as a "hero" and invited him to visit their countries. The United States officially recognized the new government.

American officials, among others, warned Castro that some members of his new government were Communists. They assumed that Castro would want to prevent these people from shaping the new government. Castro denied that he planned to create a Communist regime. He had never given specific details about the kind of government he envisioned. In May 1959 he had remarked: "Every people has the right to its own ideology. The Cuban Revolution is as Cuban as our music."[3] After the Revolution, many Cubans were disappointed when Castro did not hold free elections or reinstate the Constitution of 1940.

Public executions were also held and televised. More than five hundred officials from the Batista government were tried in "people's courts," then executed by firing squads. Castro called these people "war criminals." When some members of the U.S. Congress called the executions a "bloodbath" that should be stopped, Castro replied: "If the Americans don't like what's happening in Cuba, they can land the Marines and then there will be 200,000 *gringos* [slang term for people from the United States] dead."[4]

Castro hoped to receive financial aid from abroad, but American officials who met with the Cuban leader, including Vice President Richard Nixon, said he did not openly request such aid. He called his April 1959 visit to the United States a "goodwill" trip. It is likely Castro did not want to make any deals with the United States that would allow American officials to influence Cuban affairs in exchange for money. However, Castro confided to friends that he thought the United States would offer aid without being asked. This did not happen.

The Cold War between the world's two great "superpowers"—the United States and the Soviet Union—was at its height. Soviet officials thought that Cuba's location made it a strategic asset. They offered economic assistance, and Castro accepted. Soviet oil began arriving in Cuba in May 1960.

A COMMUNIST AGENDA

In 1961, Castro acknowledged that he planned to develop a new Cuba based on Lenin's view of communism with a strong centralized government that would control the economy and other major areas of

COLD WAR CRISIS

When Castro publicly acknowledged in May 1961 that Cuba was to be a Communist nation, the United States government imposed a full trade embargo and attempted to isolate Cuba by pressuring other countries to halt diplomatic relations with the island nation. The Organization of American States (OAS) expelled Cuba as a member and imposed economic sanctions.

Castro formed strong ties to the former Soviet Union (USSR), then under the leadership of Premier Nikita Khrushchev. Cuban leaders contended that the United States was a threat to their national security. In April 1962, the Soviets sent medium-range missiles to Cuba.

After U.S. intelligence aircraft spotted the missiles on October 15, 1962, President John F. Kennedy knew that he had to respond to these enemy weapons located only ninety miles off the Florida coast. For several days, President Kennedy and a specially appointed crisis committee secretly discussed alternative plans, including an air strike on the missiles or a ground-based invasion of Cuba. Some advisers recommended a blockade of Cuban waters, which would give the Soviets time to think about what to do, and the president chose that option.

According to an account in *The Kennedy Tapes: Inside the White House During the Cuban Missile Crisis*, Kennedy told congressional leaders: "Whatever we do is filled with hazards. If we stop one Russian ship, it means war. If we invade Cuba, it means war. There's no telling." In an address to the nation on October 22, Kennedy informed Americans about the presence of offensive nuclear missiles in Cuba. That same day, the president demanded that Khrushchev promptly remove the missiles.

A fearful world watched and waited anxiously to see how these two superpowers would resolve the conflict, which was the most dangerous confrontation of the Cold War. Many people around the world believed that World War III was about to begin. Government officials in various countries made emergency plans in case of a nuclear attack.

On October 26, Khrushchev sent Kennedy a message offering to remove the missiles. In exchange, the USSR demanded that the U.S. government promise it would never invade Cuba and that it would remove U.S. missiles from Turkey. After some negotiation, the matter was settled, averting a nuclear disaster.

life. Communist theory states that countries go through stages before they reach "true communism," with socialism as a phase in that process. In socialism, the idea is that everyone contributes to society, according to their ability, and that people receive according to their work. Communism is based on the idea of distributing goods and services "to each on the basis of need." In line with this, Castro said he wanted a society where there was no longer "a 'dollar sign' in the minds and hearts of our men and women."[5] He said Cubans should regard their obligation to their fellow humans as their most basic responsibility.

The government banned the independent press and placed all media under its control. People were forbidden to assemble for political purposes or to debate political issues freely. The government also took charge of the University of Havana and various professional associations, some of which had criticized the new government. Castro appointed judges in the judicial system, which he used to punish and eliminate his enemies.

To shape people's attitudes and values and gain support, the Castro government used the education system and the media. A vast network of radio and television equipment was already in place. The government promoted socialistic, nationalistic, and anti-American attitudes, depicting the United States as an enemy that threatened Cuban independence and exploited its own people.

Various organizations were also set up to promote Communist programs and ideals. They included trade unions, the Federation of Cuban Women, the National Association of Small Farmers, and Committees for the Defense of the Revolution (CDRs). The new government actively discouraged religious practices and taught schoolchildren that religion was unnecessary. It also abolished Christmas, Three Kings Day, and various religious festivals. Public holidays celebrating important days in the history of the new government were added, including January 1, Liberation Day, which commemorates the day in 1959 on which the revolutionaries declared victory, and May 1, International Labor Day, celebrating workers around the world. July 26 observes National Revolution Day, when Castro's group attacked the Moncada barracks in 1953. October 10 is the anniversary of the onset of the First War of Independence in 1868.

The government also set out to control the sources of economic production. Within a year, banks, industry, and energy production were nationalized and placed under the control of the Juceplan—Central Planning Board. Castro said that because the people were now the government, the people themselves owned all these things. Rationing was introduced to ensure that people had minimum amounts of food, clothing, and certain other goods, but the government said rationing would be "temporary."

In 1972, Cuba joined COMECON, the trade organization of the Soviet bloc, as it existed at the time. As in the Soviet Union, the Cuban Communist party controlled the executive as well as the judicial branch of government and local and national assemblies. All other parties were outlawed in Cuba. (The current constitution, adopted in 1976, formally says that Cuba is governed by one political party—the Partido Communista de Cuba—Communist party of Cuba.

In 1960 the new government confiscated property held by foreign corporations. American companies had controlled much of Cuba's banking business, import business, oil refineries, nickel mining, and sugar industry, and the U.S. government estimated the losses at $2 billion. The Cuban government refused to compensate these companies. Many Cubans expressed pride that their leaders had stood up to their powerful northern neighbor.

NEW SOCIAL PROGRAMS

The new government faced many problems. About 600,000 able-bodied Cubans lacked jobs. Nearly 37.5 percent of the people were illiterate, and some 70 percent of the children in rural areas had no schooling. Health statistics showed high rates of disease and widespread malnutrition.

Housing was another concern. More than half of the 6 million Cubans lived in poor housing, slum apartments, shacks, or huts, many with no toilets and running water, and about half had no electricity. Utilities, which had once been controlled by U.S. companies, were expensive. Rents had become so high that city housing often cost one-third of a family's income, making housing costs among the highest in the world. Rural farmers also paid high rents for the land they were using. About 1.5 percent of Cuba's landowners held more than 40 percent of the land area. The government enacted an Agrarian Reform Law and set the maximum permissible land holding at 966 acres (391 hectares), which meant that nearly 2,000 acres (810 hectares) of Castro's own family's land was seized. (Later, a new law would turn over tracts larger than 165 acres [67 hectares] to the state.)

The government took over homes and other property left by Cubans who fled the country. People who remained were allowed to keep one place of residence. If they owned more than one residence—for example, a city apartment and beach house—they must choose one. The Castro government reduced rents by about 50 percent. (Later, they were set at no more than 10 percent of a person's salary.) Electricity rates were also lowered. The government set out to destroy slum tenements and to make sure that no Cuban was homeless. Thousands of new housing units were built in rural and urban areas, and some new towns were organized in rural areas.

The government also addressed health problems. Tuberculosis plagued about 100,000 Cubans. Infant mortality rates were higher than the average around the world, and life expectancies were below the average. Hospitals lacked enough beds, equipment, and personnel to serve the population. Castro implemented dramatic reforms, including universal, free health care, and began setting up clinics in rural areas that had no facilities. The government declared that everyone would have access to a physician.

Cuban leaders announced a campaign against illiteracy, and Cuban citizens were urged to take part in that effort. Urban youths made up the majority of those Cubans who moved to the countryside and taught people to read and write. Castro declared: ". . . Cuba will be the first country of America which, after a few months, will be able to say it does not have one single illiterate."[6] Within twenty months, the government created 10,000 new schools—double the number of rural schools built during the previous fifty years.

Other reforms aimed to improve agricultural production and reduce rural poverty. The government praised the value of work and said all Cubans must respect manual labor. Castro called work "not a punishment but a necessity in the life of man. . . . it is necessary to create a devotion to work, to see work as it is and not as a punishment. In the past, work was an instrument of exploitation of man. Today, it is an instrument for the redemption of man, for the elevation of man, for the progress of man."[7] To demonstrate their commitment, Castro and other government officials worked in the fields during harvest times.

CUBAN EXILES

A number of Cubans disagreed with Castro, and Catholic Church officials were among those who spoke out against the new regime. Some Cubans believed Castro would not stay in power very long, so they waited quietly. People who openly criticized the Revolution or Castro faced persecution.

Other Cubans actively tried to unseat his government. In some cases, they received assistance from the U.S. Central Intelligence Agency (CIA). In 1961 farmers in Escobray province began a rebellion that would last for six years.

Many Cubans left. In previous decades, some Cubans had emigrated, usually to the United States. In 1910 about 44,000 Cubans lived in the United States; in 1959 they numbered around 124,000. In the wake of the Revolution, more than 200,000 people left Cuba. They included staunch anti-Communists and political opponents of Castro who feared for their lives. Most emigrants belonged to the higher economic classes, including professionals, skilled workers, and property-owning Cubans. As a result, Cuba lost many talented people, which resulted in a serious shortage of doctors, industrial experts, and other professionals.

Some exiles formed a close-knit community in Miami, Florida; others moved to various parts of Florida and New York City, Illinois, California, and New Jersey. Cubans who left were not allowed to take their possessions or money with them. They worked hard to rebuild their lives and contribute to their new communities.

Some exiles planned to overthrow the new regime. With help from the CIA, 1,400 Cuban emigrés from the United States launched the Bay of Pigs invasion in 1961. They landed on the beaches of the Bahia de Cochinos to begin the invasion but were stranded after Cuban air force planes struck their supply ships. Within three days, the invasion was over. Two hundred men had died, and the rest surrendered.

The Cuban government harshly criticized exiles as traitors, and the press referred to them as *gusanos*—worms. Those who tried to overthrow the government or to assassinate Castro were called terrorists. Castro aroused more patriotism and support by rallying Cubans against the United States.

OPERATION PETER PAN

A number of parents made the painful decision to send their children alone to the United States. Some parents were taking part in counter-revolutionary activities and feared for the safety of their families. Parents also thought that the government might send their children off to special training facilities in the Cuban mountains or the Soviet Union, or they worried that the children would not be able to grow up in their Catholic religion. Others were upset by changes in Cuban schools and disliked Castro's comments about an "Army of Education."

The Cuban Children's Program, which was founded by Father Bryan O. Walsh, a priest at the Catholic Welfare Bureau in Miami, organized "Operation Pedro Pan" (Peter Pan). Walsh agreed to accept a few hundred children in America, but the numbers grew. Between November 1960 and October 1962, about 14,000 Cuban girls and boys between the ages of 6 and 17 were sent to the United States—the largest political exodus of children ever recorded in the Western Hemisphere. Some of the Cubans who helped to plan the airlift, obtain visas for the children, and put them on airplanes were caught and put in jail.

One former child refugee, political scientist and author Maria de los Angeles Torres, later said: "We left very early in the morning. We were to tell no one that we were leaving because there was always a fear that the Cuban government wouldn't let us go."[8]

Once they reached the United States, the children lived with relatives or friends or in homes or camps set up by Catholic groups. Their parents then asked the Cuban and U.S. governments to let them join their children in the United States. About 5,000 children were reunited with one or both parents within the first six months; others waited longer to see their parents, and thousands of others were never reunited. More than 150,000 relatives of the "Peter Pan" children eventually came to the United States. About 50,000 additional young people received travel visas to leave Cuba, but the United States terminated flights out of Cuba in October 1962 for political reasons. This also prevented parents from joining their children already

FORCED LABOR IN EASTERN EUROPE

Between 1978 and 1991 the Cuban government sent about 80,000 young men and women to Eastern European countries as cheap labor. Their pay was sent directly to the Cuban government, but they were told that 60 percent of it would be deposited in their Cuban bank accounts. They were also told they would receive clothing, comfortable living quarters, and language lessons.

Carlos Morel was sent with other young Cubans to Czechoslovakia in 1986. Morel, a thirty-one-year-old graphic designer and draftsman, wanted to leave Cuba and had been told that the plane to Czechoslovakia would be stopping in Montreal, Canada, where he planned to defect and then join his grandmother in Miami, Florida. However, the plane flew nonstop to Europe with no layover. Morel was not able to reach Miami until four years later on his return trip to Cuba, when the plane did stop in Montreal. Morel later told his story to Damarys Ocaña of the *Miami Herald*. In "The Secret Servitude," which appeared on January 9, 2000, Morel described the meager food, crowded housing, and hard work that he and his fellow Cubans endured. He claimed that some Cuban workers resorted to taking corn or fruit from nearby farms to supplement their meager meals of rice and onions. Morel said: "My first reaction was to try to leave, but you would hear the rumors, 'so-and-so got caught at the border.' So after that, it was a waiting game, waiting for my contract to expire so I could defect during a layover."

Workers were shocked to learn that clothing, housing, food, and other expenses were deducted from their pay each month. They were also required to donate money to various Communist causes, including the Cuban military. Instead of receiving on-the-job technical training, they did hard manual labor in shoe factories, breweries, textile mills, and construction sites. Some women claimed that they were sexually harassed. Another worker who was sent to Czechoslovakia, Eneida Hernandez, told Ocaña that she and other workers went on strike to protest poor food and abuse. They were sent back to Cuba, where, she reports, government-sponsored mobs harassed her: "They yelled at me and called me all kinds of names: traitor, whore, *gusana* [worm]. They threw eggs and rocks at my house." Hernandez said that the government informed her that the wages the workers had earned in Czechoslovakia had not been kept for them. When she asked to leave Cuba, officials told her she would first have to repay the government for the round-trip cost of her flight to Czechoslovakia.

in the United States. Flights resumed in December 1965.

Many children lived in overcrowded camps until they could be placed with families in the States. While some received loving care in foster homes and orphanages, others were abused. Some were emotionally traumatized when their families could not join them. They also faced language and cultural barriers, as well as homesickness and other problems. Nonetheless, many became professionals in the fields of education, health care, government, journalism, and religious organizations.

Author Yvonne Conde was ten years old when she left Cuba for Miami. She later researched Operation Pedro Pan and found that the Catholic Church was the major force behind it, the U.S. Welfare Department provided funding, and the U.S. State Department gave a church official the power to issue visa waivers. CIA documents cast doubt on the CIA's claim that it was not involved in this operation. Cubans who remained in the country after their children fled to the United States told Conde that the Cuban government kept track of their children and used that information against them during police interrogations. For their part, the Cuban government has accused the United States of spreading frightening rumors that caused parents to send their children away.

MAINTAINING SUPPORT

During those tumultuous years, the revolutionary government worked hard to maintain support and quash dissent. Castro made many public appearances and speeches and used newspapers, radio, and television to communicate with the people, something he has continued to this day.

To enforce laws, the government uses police as well as civilians in the Committees for the Defense of the Revolution (CDRs). The number of CDRs grew through the years, exceeding 100,000 in the 1990s. Cubans are expected to take turns patrolling neighborhoods to prevent crime and report any illegal acts, such as prostitution, black-market trading, or antigovernment activities. Castro told Cubans that "their Revolution" is at stake, and they must guard it carefully.

In 1991 the government created "Rapid Response Brigades," made up of security personnel and civilians, to identify dissenters. Some Cubans have accused brigade members of maliciousness and brutality, asserting that brigade members beat up people in the street. Critics claim that the brigades are another means used by the government to terrorize potential dissenters and punish those who speak or act against it.

MIXED RESULTS

The revolutionary government launched an ambitious social agenda that included subsidized health care, education, day care for preschool children, and housing. Many other services, provided by the government, were cheap. For example, utilities cost very little. In 2000 these figures were, on average, 15 pesos a month for electricity and 3 pesos a month for water (22 pesos = $1.00).

During the 1960s optimism about the future, coupled with noticeable improvements in people's lives, bolstered support for the government. However, the state's economic policies have been far less successful. Castro had hoped to boost sugar production to 10 million tons by 1970, but it never reached those levels. Rationing continued, and there were ongoing shortages of consumer goods.

Loans from foreign countries and aid from the Soviet Union helped to subsidize Cuban social programs. The amount of Soviet aid has been estimated at about 25 percent of the gross national product and included military supplies and technology, as well as about 13 million tons of oil each year. The USSR also bought sugar and nickel at higher prices than the going rate.

Although nobody outside Cuba is certain, experts think that the country borrowed between $8.5 and

$35 billion during the 1960s and 1970s. When interest rates rose during the early 1980s, many countries, including Cuba, faced debt crises. Cuba could not pay for all the goods it imported. Critics said the government had tried to do too much too soon and that Cuba remained too poor to finance such extensive social programs.

More Cubans expressed dissatisfaction in the 1980s when living standards did not improve as expected. They had done what the government asked, but the rewards were not always there. Thousands of Cubans sought to leave the country. The Peruvian embassy received 11,000 requests for political asylum in 1980 alone, and the United States said it would accept Cubans who wanted to emigrate. The government allowed these exiles to leave via the port at Mariel. Castro used this opportunity to send criminals, mentally ill people, and political prisoners out of Cuba in boats, rafts, and other devices that were put to sea. During the "Mariel Boatlift," as it was called, about 125,000 Cubans headed for Miami.

LOSS OF SOVIET SUPPORT

Castro had often said that wealthier Communist countries would aid poorer Communist countries. However, in the late 1980s, dramatic political changes occurred in the Soviet Union and its bloc countries in Eastern Europe. As the Soviet bloc dissolved, it no longer gave economic support to Cuba. Leaders of Latin American countries that relied on Soviet support were stunned. Some, including Castro, did not permit much news about Soviet political events to be published or broadcast.

Loss of Soviet markets and higher oil prices in the early 1990s hurt Cuba. It lost 70 percent of its markets almost overnight in 1989, as well as its source of technology, oil, and other materials needed for industry and production. This had devastating effects on Cuban agriculture, industry, and daily living. The Special Period had begun.

The intersection of Consulado and Neptuno streets in Old Havana, January 1959.

CHAPTER FOUR

A CHANGING ECONOMY

The loss of Soviet support caused major economic problems in Cuba. The Cuban government does not reveal all of its trade information, but information from Cuba's trading partners and international trade organizations showed that, between 1989 and 1993, there was a 35 percent drop in gross domestic product. The economy declined severely in 1996. Analysts estimate that it grew a mere 2.5 percent in 1997 and about 3 percent in 1999.

In response, Cuban leaders reduced the bureaucracy, tightened rationing, and permitted a limited market economy. United States dollars had been banned in Cuba, but Castro allowed them again in 1993. All tourists were required to use U.S. dollars, although the government said it hoped to switch to Eurodollars in 2000. Castro said: "As true Marxist-Leninists we have to take this course of action, with all the courage and realism demanded by the circumstances. However, this does not imply, as some people seem to think, a return to capitalism, and much less a crazy and unchecked rush in that direction."[1]

Economic conditions worsened after the U.S. government erected new trade barriers. In 1992, Congress passed a law that bans U.S. companies and subsidiaries from trading with Cuba. Canada and various European nations said they would continue to trade with Cuba, and the United Nations passed a resolution calling for an end to the U.S. embargo. Pope John Paul II, the head of the Roman Catholic Church, and various international human-rights organizations also criticized the embargo.

By 1996, Cuban-American relations seemed to be thawing slightly. But in February of that year, the Cuban military shot down two light aircraft flown by Cuban-American pilots from the Miami-based group "Brothers to the Rescue." Cuba said that the planes were in Cuban airspace; U.S. officials said they were in international airspace. The International Civil Aviation Organization (ICAO) conducted an investigation and found that the planes were in international airspace. They also said that the U.S. pilots had not received adequate warnings before the Cubans opened fire.

Congress called for new sanctions against Cuba, and President Bill Clinton signed the Helms-Burton Act (called the "Cuban Democracy Act"). It allows legal action to be taken against a company or individual that benefits from properties the Cuban government expropriated after the 1959 Revolution. Governments around the world condemned this act. Critics said the United States had no right to penalize foreign companies and employees for doing business with Cuba. Human-rights organizations said the embargoes made importing goods more difficult and costly and caused problems for the Cuban people.

Castro has blamed Cuba's economic problems and shortages on the embargo and Helms-Burton Act. Political observers say that this helps the Cuban government to direct people's hostility at the United States, rather than at their own leaders. Critics of Castro's explanation say that the United States is not responsible for shortages in Cuba. For instance, Jacobo Timerman wrote:

> *Though I'm convinced that it would favor specific U.S. interests to establish normal relations*

with Cuba and not to interfere in its internal affairs, I couldn't believe that a country able to trade with almost the entire world with the sole exception, among the great powers, of the United States, is incapable of organizing its economy and enabling its fertile soil, which receives generous rainfall, to produce food.[2]

A weak sugarcane harvest in 1997, coupled with lower international prices for sugar and nickel, exacerbated Cuba's economic problems. The government could not repay loans it had obtained from European banks to buy equipment and fertilizer to boost the sugar crops.

Since 1992, Cuba has lacked money for imported goods, and people have endured shortages in many basic items, as well as things usually taken for granted. Even Cubans who have extra money often cannot buy things they want. Unemployment became a problem, especially among young people, during the late 1990s. To improve the economy, the Cuba government looked for new industries and resources, and it sought to boost agriculture, tourism, the fishing industry, and oil exploration. Cubans have also been forced to "tighten their belts" in numerous ways.

A STRONG WORK ETHIC

Cubans are expected to work and contribute to the economy. The majority work in one of these areas: agriculture and cattle ranching, the government, the military, or in various industries (including nickel and cement). In the past, most people worked in agriculture either full-time or during the harvest. Today, about 20 percent of the workforce engage in agriculture. About 30 percent work in the government or government services, while some 22 percent are employed by industry. Others work in commerce, transportation, or communications. There are relatively high numbers of scientists and technologists, about 2.7 per 1,000 residents, compared with 3.6 in the United States.

The government plays a strong role in determining career paths. People are steered into jobs and professions that reflect their particular abilities and mesh with the country's needs, as determined by the government. Outstanding scholars are urged to pursue careers in engineering, medicine, and other professions. The Cuban government has also discriminated against people who did not show loyalty to the Communist party. People have lost opportunities for higher education or certain jobs because they did not join the party.

People with full-time jobs often hold another job, including a home-based small business. More Cubans became self-employed after the government eased restrictions and allowed a limited number of people to apply for licenses to run small-scale businesses. These earnings are then taxed. People who work as physicians, government officials, teachers, store clerks, or for a radio station or newspaper office, for example, may also run a small restaurant or make crafts. People sell produce, baked goods, baskets, pottery, jewelry, or used goods to fellow Cubans and tourists. They also provide services, such as manicuring, hairstyling, shining shoes, or repairing watches or appliances. Some people sell snacks or take-out food, such as candy or pizza, on the street. In 1998 the government estimated that one out of twenty Cubans was self-employed.

The economic crisis has made it difficult for many families to make ends meet even when both men and women work at one or more jobs. As of 2000, the average monthly salary was about $8–$10 a month for workers, ranging to about $30 a month for professional people. (22 pesos = $1.00) Government pensions were 110 pesos a month, on average.

Absenteeism occurred more often in the 1990s as salaries for certain jobs declined. To motivate workers, the government offered extra pay to employees who performed additional jobs after finishing their regular assignments. For instance, after cleaning an assigned area of the hospital, a person could earn more money by cleaning another area. Good workers have been rewarded with access to hard-to-obtain items, such as meat, soaps, and paper products.

However, Cubans who work in the tourist industry, such as taxi drivers, waiters, bartenders, chambermaids, and others who collect tips, earn more, sometimes upward of $10 a day. Prostitution also surged during the late 1990s, and those who engaged in this activity could earn hundreds of dollars a week. Some professionals have even left their jobs to pursue other opportunities. Schools experienced shortages of English teachers as they left to work in the tourist industry. Although teachers are highly respected, some took less prestigious jobs at hotels or other places serving tourists.

As a result, the Special Period created two economic groups in Cuba: those with dollars and those without. People with dollars, whether they come from friends and family abroad or from tips, prostitution, or the black market, have access to more goods and services. In the government-run "dollar stores," dollars can buy scarce consumer goods, such as jeans, imported foods, toys, CDs, and electronic devices. Castro has complained about the impact of dollars on Cuban society. He described it once as a disease process, saying: "We're surrounded by viruses, the bacteria of alienation and egoism that the capitalist system creates."[3]

AGRICULTURE: BASIC TO THE ECONOMY

Cuba's agricultural policies focus on increasing exports and growing more food for the population. Sugar, tobacco, and citrus fruits (chiefly oranges and grapefruits) are the main exports. Most of the largest sugar plantations are located in central Cuba, as are

ADVANCES IN BIOTECHNOLOGY

Cuba has become known for its scientific know-how and is the home of a prestigious biotechnology institute, the Center for Genetic Engineering and Biotechnology. Located outside Havana, the center has been working on vaccines to fight AIDS and dengue fever and has been developing medicines to dissolve blood clots. It is also working on ways to genetically change animals, fish, and plants to help them resist disease and grow faster.

The center produces and exports medicines and medical supplies to China, India, Eastern Europe, and other parts of Latin America. The Cuban government is seeking foreign partners to help with marketing and distribution. Dr. Manuel Limonta, the director general, told journalist John J. Putman: "We can offer lower costs in development and production."

the main citrus-fruit plantations. Other popular crops include rice, sweet potatoes, bananas, and coffee.

Although harvests declined after 1994, sugar remains the mainstay of the economy, because the climate and soil are so well-suited to this crop. It is also more profitable than many alternatives. During the 1990s, Cuba began exporting more sugar to the Middle East and Iran and Egypt. Along with Russia and China, these countries are Cuba's biggest sugar customers. Some analysts think that Cuba may barter sugar for Iranian oil.

Increasing production is a major goal. The government acknowledged the need for better equipment and more fertilizer. Farmers lack enough laborsaving machines and sometimes enough fuel to run the machinery that is available. Workers sow seeds by hand and use plows drawn by oxen. In the rice fields, workers, primarily women, sort, rake, and dry the crop manually.

The government has actively encouraged people to raise food for their own use, and it promotes organic farming, using biological pest control and biopesticides. Small farming plots have been created in urban areas so that groups of people can work the land and grow beans, corn, tomatoes, and other vegetables. The government also runs programs to educate people about growing food and nutrition.

Cuba has sent agricultural advisers to other countries to study farming methods. Luis Sanchez Almanza toured Australia for this purpose. He said: "The aim [of Cuban programs] is also to empower people to take control, be active producers of foodstuffs and important agents in helping to solve a national problem."[4]

To deal with the milk shortage and reduce the cost of importing milk, the government has increased soy production. Soy is a good source of protein, and soy milk can be substituted for cow's milk.

In October 1993 the government gave state farms more autonomy. Many farms were changed to cooperatives, and farmers in the cooperatives were given more independence than ever before. They made group decisions about what to plant and how to pay workers. During the late 1990s the government announced that farmers could sell whatever they produced above their quota (the crops they must raise for the government to distribute to the people). Cuban farmers sell "surplus" fruits and vegetables directly to citizens, and some say this new policy helps the economy and motivates them to raise more crops.

EXPANDING TOURISM

Tourism has been steadily growing, although not as fast as the government had hoped. Years ago, Castro called tourism "decadent," but he now welcomes tourists, who bring in needed hard currency. The government ensures that tourist facilities receive the foods and other things they need for visitors, who come mostly from Canada, Latin America, and Europe.

In 1996 tourism became Cuba's top source of hard currency, the first time this had happened since 1959. Tourism brings nearly $2 billion to Cuba each year. The number of hotel rooms reached 27,000 in 1996, which was more than the combined total for Puerto Rico and the Bahamas, two popular Caribbean vacation spots, at that time. In 1998, Cuban officials said there were 1.4 million visitors, and they expected that number to reach 2 million in 2001.

To meet increased demand, more infrastructure is needed, including thousands more hotel rooms. Importing enough food and other materials for tourists is an ongoing challenge. Foreign investors see chances for growth. Canadians played a large role in developing the international airport in Cuba, which is vital for developing tourism. More luxury cruise ships also plan to stop in Cuba, so docking facilities are being expanded.

Americans who wish to travel legally to Cuba (for educational, religious, or humanitarian reasons) must obtain a permit from the U.S. government. Journalists, government officials, and Americans with families in Cuba are among those who receive permits; others attend international conferences or exhibitions or participate in sports or cultural events.

As of 2000, U.S. laws stated that American tourists may spend no more than $100 a day in Cuba and may bring back up to $100 in Cuban goods. Fines of up to $50,000 may be imposed on people who are caught violating these rules.

Nonetheless, thousands of Americans visit Cuba without permission. They travel by way of other countries, usually Mexico or the Bahamas. Cuban officials do not stamp U.S. passports, knowing this would cause problems for the tourists. Only a few of these illegal tourists have been prosecuted. One visitor who sails to Cuba to fish said: "A lot of Americans come here basically because it's a beautiful country."[5] Visitors praise the friendly, hospitable atmosphere and warm-hearted Cuban people. They say that Cubans do not discriminate against people because of their nationality. One visitor and author noted: "If you display a sincere interest in the country, you will undoubtedly make friends with the locals."[6]

Private restaurants often cater to tourists. Home-based restaurants called *paladares* ("palates") can be found in both cities and rural areas, in people's homes or yards. One *paladar* owner in Bauta, outside Havana, operates a pizza business and sells each pizza for 10 cents. He told journalist Charles Strouse: "I have two jobs, but I love making pizza. The people like it. They wait in lines. It is better than what the state serves."[7]

In addition to beautiful beaches and a lively nightlife, Cuba has superb fishing areas, such as the Cienaga de Zapata on the south coast and the Playa Giron on the coast of the Bay of Pigs. Bass and bonefish are plentiful. Americans are among the anglers and fishing-tour operators who enjoy such excursions. One New York lawyer who has been fishing in Cuba said, "Wonderful fishing. First-rate...I'm talking rod and reel. Bonefish. More bonefish than you can imagine. Two thousand dollars for a week of fishing. Best money I ever spent." The famous author Ernest Hemingway, a sports fisherman, spent much time in Cuba and his former home there is now a tourist attraction.

Travel writer Frank Bruni said that tourism causes some dilemmas for Cuban leaders:

> *Tourism brings Cuba money that is desperately needed . . . but it has other, less desired effects. There is, for example, an immediately evident black market of enterprising Cubans who offer to arrange for foreign tourists to stay in private houses where they can entertain Cuban guests, an option unavailable at most hotels, which post sentries at the elevators to make sure such inter-*

actions do not take place. There is also a network of paladares, or makeshift restaurants in private apartments, and the smallest and most authentic of these are run illegally. . . . They are found only with the assistance of the self-styled "tour guides" who roam Havana's sun-baked side-walks, whispering cautiously to tourists.[8]

During his visit in July 1999, Bruni said that when these "tour guides" talked to him, they were stopped and questioned by police, "who seemed to be just about on every corner."[9]

Journalist Brian Campbell, who visited Cuba in 1997, said:

Prostitution has openly returned, as have con-men and middlemen who sell stolen cigars in whispered conversations with foreigners. These people are intensely disliked by Cuban workers. I spoke to one man, a doctor, who explained why. He and his wife, a psychologist, earn 650 pesos a month (about $30) but have no access to dollars. A prostitute could make the equivalent of their monthly earnings in one day. A bartender or waiter working in a tourist hotel could also earn dollars regularly. It creates an inequality which the socialist system has sought to avoid.[10]

A Growing Fishing Industry

Although the warm waters around Cuba do not contain the abundance of fish often found in colder regions, Cuba has been building its fishing industry, with help from the United Nations Food and Agriculture Organization (FAO) and the United Nations Development Program (UNDP). During the 1990s, Cuba also sought foreign business partners to help optimize its resources and increase freshwater and saltwater species. Cubans are working with advisers from Asia, Canada, and Europe to develop programs to increase production of saltwater fish on fish farms. Cuban leaders want foreign investors to provide advanced technology. They also began repairing and remodeling their fishing fleet, which operates in international waters.

Between 1997 and 2000, production increased by thousands of tons. The production and export of processed fish products also increased, and government economic planners sought to strengthen this part of the economy.

Shellfish, including shrimp and spiny lobsters, are common in the waters around Cuba. As of 1999, Cuba's top seafood export was lobster—10,000 tons were exported in 1998. The whole lobster catch went to the international market, tourism, and the government stores that sell items only for dollars. The main foreign markets for Cuban lobsters were Japan, France, Spain, Italy, and Canada. The Cuban Fishing Industry Ministry has been developing new shrimp farms in a region where the climate favors year-round production.

Cubans also fish for their own consumption or for sale to others. They pay a small fee of about one peso a month to belong to local fishing clubs. This permits them to fish in local waters and to keep up to 33 pounds (15 kilograms) of fish a day. Any amount of fish over that must be turned over to the state to be distributed.

OIL PRODUCTION
The government has launched new oil exploration efforts. Until 1991, Cuba imported about 13 million tons of crude oil annually from the Soviet Union. When that oil was no longer available at discount prices, Cuba could not afford to import enough oil to meet its needs. Cuba had imported 13 million tons of oil from the Soviets in 1989; in 1992 it could only acquire 6 million tons. The shortages affected both industries and households and led to frequent power

outages. It meant that Cuba could import just 30 percent of the materials it needed for sugar production, so the harvest was the worst in thirty years. As a result, food and other consumer goods were scarce— only about two-thirds of what had been available in 1989.

During the 1980s, Russia sent seismic vessels to Cuban waters to explore the region for petroleum deposits. The data collected showed that there might be rich deposits of oil offshore. In the early 1990s, Cuba signed agreements with oil companies from Europe and Canada. Foreign investment made it possible to extract Cuban oil, and production doubled between 1990 and 1999 to about 30,000 barrels a day.

After repaying its foreign oil-company investors, Cuba was able to supply about 20 percent of its own energy needs with domestic oil in 1997; the next year that figure climbed to 28 percent; in 1999 it reached 50 percent. This domestic fuel cost only about one-third to one-half as much as imported fuel.

However, the government believed that much richer deposits were untapped. In 1999, Guillermo Hernandez, head of Cupet, Cuba's state oil company, said: "The geological conditions along with other factors indicate there might be good oil fields— important oil fields—even giant oil fields in Cuba's exclusive economic sound in the Gulf of Mexico."[11] A geologist, Hernandez graduated from the University of Miami and the French Institute of Oil Exploration. For years he had believed that oil could be found in the Gulf, but the Cuban government lacked the technology and money to explore. By the end of the 1990s, new kinds of oil rigs could drill 6,500 feet (1,980 meters) underwater, which made it possible to collect oil and gas from deepwater wells. Experts predict that even more-advanced rigs would be capable of drilling 11,500 feet (3,505 meters) deep.

Still, the Cuban government could not afford the costs involved in drilling for this oil, which were esti-

OUTSTANDING CIGARS

Cuba produces some of the world's finest cigars, including the brands Montecristo, Romeo y Julieta, Partagas, Bolivar, Cohiba, and Upmann. Cigar exports rose from 72 million in 1996 to 126 million in 1998. The government once owned the tobacco-growing industry, but as of 1999, private farmers working on small pieces of land were growing 90 percent of all Cuban tobacco.

Much of this prime tobacco is grown in the fertile soil of the western province of Piñar del Rio. The seeds are planted in seedbeds in October or November; later, the seedlings are hand-planted in the fields. During the ninety-day growing season, farmers carefully weed the fields and watch out for pests. After the leaves are picked, sorted, and dried for up to forty-five days, they are sent to a processing plant.

For factory workers, hand-rolling the cigars is a painstaking, monotonous process. Skilled workers are expected to produce about a hundred cigars a day. To make their jobs more pleasant, factories hire people to read to the workers during the day, or they play music from the radio over a speaker system. This custom has existed for many years.

mated at $23 million per offshore well. Cupet approached major oil companies around the world offering the chance to drill in various offshore sites, most of them off the northern shore. Cuba would share in the proceeds. Only major oil companies can afford such a risky venture. Nine of the top twenty oil companies in the world are based in the United States, and U.S. laws banned them from working with Cuba. To lure investors, Cupet offered foreign companies better terms than those found in standard contracts. The government also hired a European service company to update the geophysical surveys in the Gulf of Mexico. A French company, Total Fina, spent about $40 million during a four-year period but did not find any oil. It then halted its exploration activities in Cuba.

The costs of importing oil have increased, and prices in 1999 were 90 percent higher than in 1998, causing serious energy shortages in Cuba. The government eagerly sought ways to supply its domestic energy needs so that it would have more money for housing, transportation, and other things. It hopes to develop nuclear energy and is also considering the use of peat reserves, which are mainly located in Matanzas province.

DOLLARS FROM ABROAD

As of 1997, about 1.5 million Cubans lived outside the country, about 1.2 million of them in the United States. During the 1960s and 1970s the Cuban government discouraged citizens from communicating with Cubans who had defected to other countries. People who maintained those connections were criticized, and some were accused of the crime called "ideological deviation." Ties to relatives living abroad have become stronger since 1978. The Cuban government has revised these policies, too, in response to the economic crisis.

Cuban exiles, mostly Cuban-Americans, send large sums of money (called *remisas*) to relatives and friends in Cuba. These remittances come in small amounts, but they add up to between $500 and $900 a year per exile, according to some estimates.[12] Through its sources of information, the CIA estimated the amount at $1 billion.[13] Between 1995 and 1999 the number of Cubans with access to hard currency grew from 40 percent to 62 percent. Relatives also send clothing, medicines, and other goods.

Pedro Monreal, with the Center of Studies on the International Economy in Havana, wrote that foreign remittances are Cuba's main source of foreign exchange, and that, in 1998, they were equal to about 35 percent of Cuba's imports.[14] Analysts think that this assistance enables large numbers of Cubans to avoid living in poverty. One retiree in Havana said: "If

CHAPTER FIVE

POLITICS AND HUMAN RIGHTS

The Cuban government is strongly centralized and remains firmly committed to socialism. Through the years, Cubans have experienced some changes in government policy. Yet critics condemn the government for repressing dissent and penalizing people who protest peacefully or propose changes in the laws. Critics maintain that the government deprives its citizens of basic freedoms and human rights and takes harsh measures against those who disagree with its leaders or challenge its policies.

CENTRAL AND LOCAL GOVERNMENT

A strong central government based in Havana controls Cuban affairs. The chief lawmaking body is the National Assembly, with 589 members, who are chosen by citizens to fill five-year terms. The assembly holds two sessions each year. When it is not in session, the Council of State assumes the assembly's duties. The 31 members of that council are chosen by the National Assembly from among its own members. They enforce laws, direct government agencies, and formulate foreign policy.

Cuba's 14 provinces are divided into about 170 municipalities, and each province has an assembly that conducts local government. Members are elected by popular vote, and they handle local affairs, including schools, economic enterprises, health-care services, transportation, and sports and recreation facilities. The Isle of Youth is Cuba's largest offshore island. It does not belong to a province and is under central government control.

Political candidates must be approved by the Communist party to appear on the ballot. Citizens over the age of sixteen are eligible to vote, and turnout for various local and national elections is generally high. Cubans are readers, and visitors are impressed with their knowledge of national affairs and local politics. People who have spent time in Cuba note that Castro speaks directly to the people often about politics, social issues, current events, and other topics. As a result, he is a major source of information and ideas. Jacobo Timerman wrote: "Any topic elicited a reference to some speech of his [Castro's]."[1]

The Cuban legal system includes the People's Supreme Court, which consists of a president, vice president, and five divisions (called chambers), each with its own members. Chambers include a president, at least two other professional judges, and numerous lay judges (citizens who hold regular jobs while also serving on the court). The chambers are categorized as civil and administrative; criminal, state security, military, and labor. The National Assembly elects the justices. Lower courts include 14 provincial courts (one for each province) and about 170 municipal courts, distributed throughout the country.

In July 1992, Castro enacted constitutional amendments, some of which affected municipal and provincial government. The reforms also changed the system of the local "people's power" assemblies, and allowed direct election of deputies to the National Assembly and to provincial assemblies. It recognized some private property.

The new constitutional reforms of 1992 stated that the Cuban government was "secular" (rather than "atheist") but was religiously tolerant. It banned discrimination against religious believers, who previously had not been allowed to join the Communist party.

Repressing Dissent

People have strongly criticized the Castro regime for repressing various forms of political protest and for its harsh treatment of political dissidents. Laws restrict freedom of speech, assembly, and the press, and people who break these laws may be arrested and punished. They also forbid people from leaving the country without permission from the government. People who do so can be arrested and imprisoned for "illegal exit."

Cuban officials have broad authority to repress any kind of dissent. For example, the penal code forbids Cubans from speaking with a foreign journalist without permission from the government. It is illegal to imitate or joke about Castro in the press, radio, television, or onstage. Officials can use the law against "dangerousness" to prosecute many different kinds of nonviolent protest. According to Human Rights Watch, an international human-rights organization, criminal offenses include "meeting to discuss the economy or elections, writing letters to the government, reporting on political or economic developments, speaking to international reporters, or advocating the release of political prisoners."[2]

In 1997, Hector Palacio Ruiz was sentenced to eighteen months in jail for referring to Fidel Castro as "crazy." He was convicted of violating the section of the Cuban penal code that discusses a crime called "disrespect," which involves threatening, defaming, or insulting a public official. Palacio, the head of a dissident group called the Democratic Solidarity party, had criticized the government and called for reforms during an interview with a German television network.[3]

Political Prisoners

The Cuban government has frequently denied the existence of political prisoners—people sent to prison because of their political beliefs and activities—on the island. However, during the late 1990s, international human-rights groups estimated the number of such prisoners at between 390 and 500 people. Nearly all of them were convicted of nonviolent activities. Charges against them included "disrespect for authority" and "disseminating enemy propaganda."

Some Cuban dissidents and political prisoners have become well known to people around the world. One of them is Elizardo Sanchez Santacruz. Sanchez was imprisoned for eleven years for speaking out against the Castro regime. He presently is the head of the Cuban Committee for Human Rights and National Reconciliation.

According to this organization, political prisoners often suffer even more than other kinds of prisoners. They may spend long periods of time, ranging from months to over a year, in pretrial detention, often in isolation cells. Sometimes they are placed in solitary confinement right after they are convicted, and these cells may lack any kind of bedding, light, or ventilation. Human Rights Watch says that the treatment of political prisoners violates the Convention Against Torture and Other Cruel, Inhuman or Degrading Treatment or Punishment, which Cuba ratified in 1995.

International human-rights organizations say that conditions in Cuban prisons are very poor. In a 1999 report, Human Rights Watch said conditions were "substandard and unhealthy" and that prisoners live in overcrowded facilities and "face physical and sexual abuse."[4] They suffer from malnourishment and do not have access to adequate medical treatment.

CRITICISM FROM HUMAN-RIGHTS ADVOCATES

People from around the world, including international human-rights organizations, have asked the Cuban government to free political prisoners.

Some Cubans have also spoken out against the treatment of political prisoners, complaining that people should not be put in jail for speaking out against the government. This means that they also may become targets and be penalized for their remarks. Young Cubans are active in the struggle for human rights. Cuban Youth for Democracy seek changes in the education system that will permit more freedom of expression.

In 1998 the United Nations considered a resolution that would condemn Cuba for its human-rights abuses. The resolution failed to pass by a margin of three votes. Eighteen countries abstained from voting. Cuban Hector Palacio was among those who had hoped the measure would pass. Palacio claimed that he had been detained eighty-six times and imprisoned fourteen months because of his political activities. He said: "Cuban dissidents live in a permanent state of fear for their own safety and the safety of their families."[5]

In 1999 and 2000 the United Nations did pass a measure condemning the way the Cuban government treats political dissidents. The international human-rights group, Human Rights Watch, issued critical reports on Cuba in both years, the latest in a series of such reports from that group.

At times, Cuban officials have responded to pressure from other nations or individuals. The Reverend Jesse Jackson, a well-known African-American leader, obtained the release of twenty-six prisoners in 1984. In 1995 a few people were freed when the First Lady of France, Danielle Mitterrand, visited Cuba. About two hundred political prisoners were released when Pope John Paul II visited Cuba in 1998. Castro said this was a goodwill gesture in honor of the Roman Catholic leader.

An Ongoing Struggle

Dissidents continue to risk imprisonment for speaking freely in Cuba. During the summer of 1999, a group of six dissidents, including five men and one woman, began a forty-day fast, asking Castro's government to release political prisoners and permit more freedom of expression in Cuba. During their fast they said they would pray for respect for human rights and a general amnesty toward Cuban political prisoners. One member of the group, Marcos Torres, declared that the group hoped to "challenge the political structure" of the country.[6]

The Life and Freedom Fast continued until July 16 for the Fasters of 34 Tamarindo Street, as they called themselves. Supporters stopped by the house regularly, and the dissidents spoke to foreign visitors. Previously, the government had taken measures to stop such protests and had arrested protesters, but foreign reporters noted that the government was letting this one proceed. At one point, however, someone cut the electrical wires leading into the apartment where the protesters were staying, and some of their supporters were detained and questioned. Dr. Oscar Elias Biscet, one of the Fasters, said that a man who supported the group was later denied the use of an exit visa he had obtained to leave Cuba.

Biscet himself had been imprisoned numerous times. In 1994 the government had accused Biscet, an Afro-Cuban physician, of "dangerousness" because he criticized the regime and supported nonviolent protest, as exemplified by Mahatma Gandhi and Martin Luther King Jr., to gain religious freedom and other civil rights for his fellow Cubans. In 1998 he was expelled from the Cuban National Health System and was banned from practicing medicine in Cuba. His wife, a nurse, also was not able to obtain employment as a result of his activism.

During 1998 and 1999 Biscet was arrested several times and was sometimes confined with dangerous criminals. In November 1999 he was sentenced to three years in prison on charges of "public disorder" and "dishonoring patriotic symbols." He had hung a Cuban flag upside down during a news conference. Biscet was placed in solitary confinement for forty-two days. His wife, who visited him, said that he had lost 20 pounds (9 kilograms) and suffered a severe mouth infection that resulted in the loss of several teeth. Biscet is currently an Amnesty International Prisoner of Conscience, and other human-rights organizations have called for his release.

Human-rights issues may affect the tourist industry. Dr. Pamela Falk of Queens College, New York, said that some Canadians, Europeans, and others who have helped to build up tourism have expressed anger when human-rights activists are imprisoned.[7] If large groups of people decide not to visit Cuba unless the government changes certain policies, tourism could suffer.

FAMILIES KEPT APART

Critics of Castro and his regime also complain about the way they keep families apart. One example is the family of Cuban physicist Luis Grave de Peralta. He was fired from his university post after resigning from the Communist party in 1992 in protest of the way the Cuban press was attacking the movement toward democracy in the Soviet Union. After he wrote a long manuscript documenting contradictions and false statements in Castro's speeches and writings, he was arrested. The government charged him with the crime of "rebellion through peaceful means" and sentenced him to thirteen years in prison.[8]

Amnesty International declared Peralta a Prisoner of Conscience, and foreign human-rights advocates intervened with Castro to release him from prison. After Peralta was released in 1996, he was required to emigrate from Cuba and was told that his wife and two sons could follow later. The children had U.S. visas and Cuban exit permits. However, the Cuban government would not let his wife leave with the children. The government also dismissed her from her job as a teacher because of her husband's dissent. As of the year 2000, the family remained in Cuba, and the government would not change its position.

Many others have fought for family members who are still in Cuba to be allowed to join them in other countries. Castro's own daughter, Alina Revuelta Fernandez, struggled to get her daughter out of Cuba after she fled from the country. Fernandez, a writer, has been extremely critical of her father's government.

Stick-ball in Havana.

CHAPTER SIX

LIVING IN CUBA

The people of Cuba are a true "rainbow" that includes Caucasians, Africans, and Asians, as well as those of mixed heritage. There were about 11.5 million Cubans in 2000, about 40 percent white and 10 percent black. The remaining 50 percent are *mulatto*—of mixed white and black heritage. A small minority are Chinese, descendants of workers who came to Cuba during the last half of the 1800s, while another very small number are Jews. Through the years, different racial and ethnic groups have intermarried, a practice the government approves.

All Cubans are eligible for certain social services no matter where they live. Since the Revolution, people in rural areas have had access to education and health care they did not have before. Cubans have many things in common, but their lifestyles differ depending on where they live and what kinds of jobs they perform. About 70 percent of all Cubans live in cities—more than 2 million in Havana, as of 1999. Other large cities include Santiago de Cuba, Camagüey, and Santa Clara. Urban Cubans usually live in apartments but spend much of their time away from home, at work, at school, at cultural and athletic activities, or outdoors. City life tends to be fast-paced.

Rural life often revolves around the seasonal activities of raising crops. For example, in a town like Viñales farmers grow beans, rice, manioc (yucca), and tobacco, and they cultivate lime trees and bananas.

The landscape features pine trees instead of tall buildings, and many residences have porches.

DIFFERENT KINDS OF HOUSING

Cubans live in different kinds of housing, depending on their location, job, and family history. *Bohios*—traditional wooden dwellings with thatched roofs from the royal palm—are still built and used in rural areas, as they were centuries ago. In rural areas—for example, parts of Republica de Chile in the western province of Piñar del Rio—people might live in concrete apartment buildings, as well as single-family dwellings, including *bohios*. Many rural homes are built of cement and stucco and painted in vivid pastels. For centuries, working-class people have often lived in single-story homes with tiled roofs. During colonial times, the wealthy built large mansions.

In the years following the Revolution, the government set rents at about 10 percent of the main wage earner's salary. Installment plans enable people to purchase their homes after a given number of years. Restrictions against conveying property have been imposed, then lifted, on and off, through the years. In 1986 people were once again prohibited from selling private dwellings. This led to some awkward situations, such as divorced people living together even when they did not want to, because they had no other housing options. Cubans have traded properties with permission from the government.

After 1959 most of the mansions were turned into museums or government buildings, while others are used for multifamily housing. Older buildings feature pillars and wide portals in the avenues and squares. Wide windows and balconies give buildings an "open" feeling, while other elements screen the light. Many colonial buildings also feature stained-glass windows. The government also built and operates modern, low-cost apartment buildings. Some buildings are done in the plain, Soviet style; others have interesting modern designs or a traditional tropical look.

In recent years, many buildings have become more crowded and run-down. Jacobo Timerman described the housing he saw in the late 1980s:

> Dwellings have been divided and subdivided. Mattresses are scattered on the floors, in courtyards and corridors, and are aired during the day. . . . The rooms are divided by sheets hung wall-to-wall on ropes. If someone has political access to the officials who allot material, it's possible to obtain bricks, plasterboard, glass, wood . . . with which the subdivisions are improved. The hardest articles to obtain are still paint and glass.[1]

Fewer housing units were built after materials became increasingly scarce in the 1990s. Some new construction was of poor quality and did not hold up well. Pipes broke, and people needed permission to replace them. It was also difficult to replace windows and other building parts. Architects and people in the building trades found themselves without enough work. Conditions worsened during the 1990s. However, since Havana was named a World Heritage site, numerous historic buildings in Old Havana have been restored.

A serious housing shortage developed during the 1990s, and large families, which are common in Cuba, often occupy an apartment or home with a few small rooms. A family of six people who live in an apartment with two bedrooms and a living room, bathroom, and small kitchen are considered well-off. Two or more generations frequently live together out of necessity. People with high political positions have better access to housing, among other privileges, another reason that competition for positions in Cuba is keen.

Nearly every Cuban home has electricity and running water, but these utilities have often been unavailable since the Special Period began in 1990. Kitchen appliances run mostly on gas, which also is sometimes in short supply. During those times, people may cook with kerosene burners or use charcoal. People store water and keep batteries and candles on hand for power outages. During the Special Period, water was only available at certain times of the day in many areas.

After the Revolution, practical needs took priority over architectural creativity. About two-thirds of the architects in Cuba left after 1959. Others went to work for the state, which launched new social building projects, including art schools and agricultural cooperatives. State firms gave architects, who earn about $15 a month, strict guidelines. They lacked access to international design ideas and materials. Changes were occurring in 1999, as architects created striking restaurants and hotels. They discussed their desires to develop innovative, contemporary structures. The magazine *Arquitectura Cuba* resumed publication. Graphic artists contributed to buildings, adding murals and other design elements.

GETTING FROM PLACE TO PLACE

Most Cubans use public transportation. Any car, much less one with air-conditioning or special features, is a luxury. The government decides who can purchase cars. They cost thousands of dollars, and few people can afford one even if they had permission. Fuel shortages and the lack of repair parts keep many car owners from using the vehicles they do have.

Most of the cars on Cuban streets are American cars from the 1940s and 1950s, Ladas purchased from the former Soviet Union, or small models made in South America. People who have cars take good care of them and find spare parts anywhere they can. Some paint their cars to match their homes, using the same paint. They even improvise or make their own parts to keep their cars running.

Transportation became a major problem during the Special Period. Getting to and from work and other places is an ongoing challenge because of gas shortages and the lack of repair parts. Many people ride bicycles except for long-distance travel. Buses and trucks that carry passengers are often packed with people. One type of truck, a *camello*, offers cheap fares and can hold up to 250 passengers.

There is often no public transportation in rural areas, so people walk or use bicycles, often old ones, or rely on horse-drawn wagons or other animals. Passing motorists may offer someone a ride. Author James Suckling described country roads in Cuba during a trip in 1999:

> *Although large asphalt roads traverse Cuba's interior, there's very little traffic. You're more likely to see rusty bicycles and haggard horses than automobiles and trucks. Local villagers wait along the road for an occasional bus or for a car to stop and give them a lift.*[2]

COMMUNICATIONS SYSTEMS

Communications services in Cuba are sparse and sometimes unavailable because of equipment shortages and power outages. According to the United Nations agency the World Bank, as of March 2000, there were about 35 phone lines per 1,000 residents, compared with 661 in the United States.[3] There was 1 Internet host per 10,000 people, compared with 1 per 509 persons in the United States. Cubans who want to hear news that is not controlled by the government get information from abroad through phone calls and letters, or from Florida radio stations.

Households usually have a television set, often an old one. There are approximately 241 TV sets per 1,000 Cubans, compared with 2,115 per 1,000 people in the United States. It is difficult to get repair parts. The government operates two TV channels and broadcasts

A Distinguished Visitor

Religious Cubans were heartened by the visit of Pope John Paul II in January 1998—his first visit to the islands. For five days the Pope made public appearances and met with Castro and other officials, and he said open-air Masses in five cities. The events were reported around the world in the print media, radio, and television. News channel CNN, which has correspondents in Cuba, reported that the Pope said he had come "as a pilgrim of love, of truth, and of hope. . . ."

During his visit, the Pope did speak about certain moral and political issues. He condemned the U.S. embargo of Cuba, saying that such embargoes "are always deplorable because they hurt the most needy." Addressing a crowd of about 50,000 young Cubans, he decried the fact that Cuba is the only Latin American country with legal abortion on demand. In the late 1990s the number of abortions was equal to the number of births each year. The Pope asked the government to permit Catholic schools and let parents "choose for their children . . . the ethical and civic content and the religious inspiration which will enable them to receive an integral education." Speaking about human rights, John Paul II asked the Cuban government to free people "imprisoned for reasons of conscience, for ideas which though dissident are nonetheless peaceful," according to a report by Larry Rohter in *The New York Times* on February 13, 1998.

As he left Cuba, the Pope said: "May Cuba . . . open itself up to the world, and may the world open itself up to Cuba." After the visit, Cuban church officials said they were communicating better with the government and that the "climate" of church-state relationships improved. More Cubans were practicing and discussing religion openly. Priests said more adults were being baptized and more children were enrolled in Catechism and Sunday school classes. The number of people attending Bible study groups also rose.

the programs on these channels, including cartoons and children's shows, news, sports competitions, movies and soap operas.

Educating a Nation
The government provides free education, including lunch and, for younger schoolchildren, some milk.

Free, universal education is often cited as a major achievement of the Cuban Revolution. The government claimed that no schools have closed down since the Special Period began, but economic problems have hindered the education system. Between 1995 and 2000, the Cuban government spent about $2.5 billion each year on education, which was twice the amount spent in 1994. However, computers are in short supply, and many students share textbooks.

During Spanish colonial days, only upper-class children in urban areas had much access to education. In 1899 only 16 percent of all those eligible to attend school were enrolled. When the United States occupied Cuba, plans were made to expand educational opportunities throughout the country. By 1902 about 40 percent of the school-age population were enrolled in school. They included young people from various provinces. Those rates rose to about 60 percent in 1931, with lower enrollments and high dropout rates in rural areas.

The literacy rate and the percentage of the school-age population enrolled in school remained about the same through the 1950s. Cuba did have higher literacy rates and more schools per capita than other Latin American countries.

Castro declared 1961 the Year of Education. The government set out to enroll all eligible children in school and to improve adult literacy rates. About 300,000 youths and adults went to rural areas to teach others. Within less than twenty years, literacy rates exceeded 90 percent and are now thought to be around 95.2 percent. More than a thousand libraries were also built throughout Cuba during that time.

The school curriculum was modeled on the Soviet style, which emphasized memorization and a lecture format without much student-teacher interaction. Educational materials stress Cuban history and culture, along with patriotism and revolutionary ideals. The stories used to teach reading praise Fidel Castro, Che Guevara, and the Revolution. Schoolchildren recite revolutionary sayings, such as *"Seremos como el Che"*—"We will be like Che Guevara."

School is compulsory for Cuban children from age five to fifteen. Children begin attending free nursery schools at six months and remain there until age five or six. After that, they attend primary school. Two free uniforms are provided to students in primary and secondary schools each year. Most children go to and from school on foot or bicycle.

Primary students attend classes from about 8 A.M. to 4:20 P.M., with a two-hour break at noon. They study basic language skills and composition in Spanish, arithmetic, physical education, art, and ideological orientation, which involves training in the morals and behaviors expected of them in Cuban society. Beginning in the last year of primary school, students study English. Primary-school students also study basic agriculture and learn how to grow crops. When they finish primary school, they may continue to study or join the Youth Movement, which combines study with service and vocational training.

Secondary-school students attend classes on weekdays and Saturday mornings year-round except for July and August, with a short break at the New Year. If their mothers are working outside the home, they can eat lunch at school. Classes include Spanish, mathematics, science (biology, chemistry, physics), geography, history, and technical/agricultural production. The rest of their schedule depends on whether they are studying a vocation or training to be teachers.

Eligible students then go to preuniversity studies at the age of fifteen or sixteen. These last about three years. Students with special talents attend schools that specialize in those areas. Young people who show athletic ability or dancing talents may be selected to attend a special boarding school that provides training facilities and other things they need. Exceptionally bright students may be invited to attend the Vladimir Ilyich Lenin Vocational Institute.

Young people are expected to contribute to the economy, and agricultural studies and experience are part of their curriculum. At age eleven, children begin working in agriculture in the fields about 35 to 40 hours each school term. They may be sent to pick coffee beans or cut sugarcane, for example, while living in a farm labor camp. To develop a sense of community, schools stress group games, and students help to care for school buildings and grounds.

Cuba's four universities are located in La Habana, Las Villas, Camagüey, and Oriente. To be admitted to a university, a student must complete secondary school, pass the entrance examination, take part in an interview, and show what officials consider the proper attitude and behavior. Critics complain that the government removes teachers who disagree with government policies and admits only students who support the Castro regime. Students do not have freedom to speak out against government policies. Like other education, college is free but is only available to selected students.

Changes in the world and global economy led to changes in Cuban schools, too. One educator said: "The problem today is to maintain socialist principles when we have to use not only socialist but capitalist means."[4] Now, in addition to their basic texts about Marx, Engels, Lenin, and Che Guevara, Cuban students have what one educator called "a more creative education" in which they talk more and learn about "the problems of today."[5]

English is now a compulsory second language. Teachers of English study for five years and take part in a program that includes grammar, linguistics, English literature, and area studies of countries where English is spoken. English classes begin in the last year of primary school and continue into secondary school. Adults may also take English classes. English skills are regarded as a way for Cubans to have more access to the international community and communicate with tourists.

Food rationing became more restrictive during the Special Period. Cubans can obtain certain basics each month: fixed amounts of rice, beans, sugar, eggs, coffee, and cooking oil; small amounts of meat (usually pork or chicken); and vegetables and fruit. Each person is allowed one portion of bread each day, and children under age seven are given milk each day. People record their purchases in a ration book (*libreta*) provided by the government.

Government food rations are supposed to provide about 30 percent of a person's daily needs, but they are small compared with what people eat in countries where food is plentiful. As of 2000, monthly rations included one dozen eggs, 6 pounds (2.8 kilograms) of rice, 1 pound (0.45 kilogram) of beans, 1 pound of coffee, and 5 pounds (2.3 kilograms) of sugar (which supplies only calories, not vitamins, minerals, or other nutrients). Beef or chicken was provided only twice a month. Milk was usually unavailable, except to children under age seven and pregnant and lactating women. Black marketeers continued to trade in produce and meats. They are punished severely when they are caught. Someone who sells beef illegally might be sentenced to fifteen years in prison.

Rural Cubans can augment their food rations by growing their own fruits and vegetables and raising chickens for eggs and meat. Some people also grow their own coffee beans. Bread and milk are delivered to villages, sometimes in horse-drawn carts or in trucks. Rural Cubans travel to centrally located villages to buy other kinds of foods and goods.

Cuban foods are often highly spiced, and rice and beans appear at most meals, along with bananas, root vegetables, avocados, and pork, when it is available. *Congri* is a popular dish containing rice and black beans, while kidney beans are combined with rice to make *arroz moro*. Coffee, beer, and rum are popular beverages. Most Cubans prefer strong black coffee, with sugar. Coffee-loving Cubans have bemoaned the coffee shortages during the Special Period.

Meals for special occasions such as Christmas Eve, New Year's Eve, or weddings usually feature a pig, which is roasted on an outdoor fire. Cubans enjoy iced beer, crisp pork rinds, white rice, black beans, yucca served with a garnish of onion, lemon, and parsley, corn fritters, fried bananas, and tomato salad on these occasions. Desserts may include guava marmalade, sweetened grapefruit peel, and yucca crullers with anise-flavored syrup. Rum is sometimes served with coffee and dessert.

The government owns and operates stores that stock certain scarce foods and other goods. Soap, matches, toilet paper, other paper products, pens, and cosmetics have been especially hard to obtain. People line up when stores receive shipments, and they might wait for hours, even a day or more. Some people hire others to hold their places in line while they go to work or run errands. In government-run "dollar" stores, people with U.S. dollars can buy canned hams, sweets, butter, and other scarce food items. However, most Cubans are paid in pesos, not dollars. Cubans who receive dollars from abroad shop in these stores; in turn, the government uses these dollars to buy imported goods from countries that do not accept Cuban pesos as payment.

UNIVERSAL HEALTH CARE

Free health care for all Cubans is one of the revolutionary government's proudest achievements. Health statistics have improved since 1959. Life expectancy—74 for men and 77 for women—is similar to that in developed countries. Infant mortality rates are about 12 per 1,000 births, about the same as in the United States and lower than in other Latin American countries. In 2000 there were 5.3 Cuban doctors for every 1,000 residents, compared with 2.6 in the United States.[6]

The Cuban system emphasizes patient education, prevention of illness, and community medicine. Citizens are expected to get an annual medical checkup and take personal responsibility to keep themselves healthy. Children receive immunizations against contagious diseases. Doctors are located on city blocks to serve the families in the neighborhood, which could number 120 or more. Outside the major cities, a doctor and nurse are usually available in local medical clinics. People with serious conditions go to hospitals located in different regions. Although every Cuban is assured a minimum standard of health care, high-ranking government officials and people who can pay with dollars have access to the most advanced medical treatments.

Since 1990 economic problems have plagued Cuba's health-care system. The government has been unable to obtain certain supplies and medicines. As a result, people have become more resourceful. Cubans have been growing traditional herbal plants to treat illnesses; health-care workers have used alternative treatments, such as acupuncture and homeopathy; and hospital personnel have improvised equipment.

Energy shortages also affect health-care facilities. Doctors carry flashlights in their lab coats because the lights are likely to go off several times each week. Patients bring their own soap, towels, sheets, and other items to the hospital.

Some visitors come to Cuba to receive more sophisticated medical care than what is available in their own countries. The International Center for Neurological Restoration in Havana is known for its excellent physical therapy facilities. Victims of the Chernobyl nuclear plant disaster in the Ukraine region of the former Soviet Union have been treated for leukemia and other medical problems in Cuba.

Cuban leaders were criticized for their treatment of AIDS patients after they introduced a mandatory testing program for the HIV virus and quarantined people who tested positive. The patients were sent to compounds run by the state, where they were housed, fed, and given medical care. These people were separated from their families and communities. Those with active symptoms were hospitalized, again at state expense. The government declared that these measures were needed "for the common good."[7] In their view, restricting these individuals helped society as a whole. As of 2000, the AIDS rate in Cuba was less than one case per 100,000, very low for the region. However, critics say this result was achieved at the expense of individual rights.

SPIRITUAL CUSTOMS

Spanish conquerors brought their Roman Catholic religion to Cuba and founded missions and churches. Catholicism became the main religion among Cubans of Spanish heritage. Cubans from Africa and Asia brought other traditions, as did Jews, and various Protestant groups also developed. During the years of Spanish rule, slaves were forbidden to practice their own religions, but they continued to do so, even while pretending to accept Catholicism. This led to the development of new religions that blended the symbols and practices of African religions with Catholicism.

The best-known and most widespread Afro-Cuban religion is Santeria, based on the traditions of the Yoruba tribe in Nigeria. Santeria is widely practiced in Santiago de Cuba. Practitioners, called *santera*, perform ceremonies for people who come seeking help for problems, such as poor health. They may be told to offer food sacrifices to the gods or take special baths. Another Cuban religious tradition is called Spiritism. Followers of this religion may call on different protectors for help. Another Afro-religious tradition is Palo Monte, rooted in central African Bantu beliefs. Some white Cubans also practice these religions.

Symbols of these religions can be seen on the walls of public buildings. Cuban men may wear beaded necklaces in the color that represents a certain deity.

For instance, red and white are the favorite colors of the god Changó. People also sometimes place fruits and other religious offerings in paper bags at the base of royal palm trees. Small dolls, as symbols of dead ancestors, can be seen on shelves, tables, or cabinets inside people's homes.

After the Revolution, the Castro government stifled religious practices and penalized religious practitioners. Many of the exiles who fled from the island left because they feared they would not be able to practice their religion freely. The government claimed it was taking a "neutral" stance and would not support religion in Cuba. Essentially, the government banned practitioners from attending universities and pursuing certain careers.

People still celebrate festivals with religious significance. For example, the carnival festival in Santiago de Cuba is held in honor of the feast day of their patron saint, James the Apostle. Teams of dancers, musicians, marchers, and floats compete for prizes during the week of celebrations.

Religious groups engage in social work and support government policies that provide health care, for example. Caritas, the social service agency of the Cuban Catholic Church, receives international donations, which it uses to aid both Catholics and other Cubans in need. The church has regularly been in conflict with the government because it advocates the release of political prisoners and has asked for more civil liberties. Most Protestant groups belong to the Cuban Council of Churches. Since 1992 they have undertaken numerous projects with groups from other countries to carry out self-help projects.

By the 1990s about half of all Cubans had been baptized, and an estimated 70 percent identified themselves as Catholic.[8] The Protestant and Santeria groups also increased in number during that decade. Between 1992 and 1996, the number of Protestant congregations nearly doubled, growing from 900 to

COMMUNITY PATROLS

Many rules govern everyday behavior in Cuba. People are expected to take part in civic activities, such as blood-collection drives and patriotic assemblies. Every fourth Sunday each month is "Defense Sunday," and Cubans help with the Committee for the Defense of the Revolution, or CDR, projects, such as building nuclear fallout shelters. Community meetings are held for different reasons—for example, to discuss the meaning of President Castro's latest speech.

People may not legally buy or sell homes or apartments, although there are ways to swap them. They must obtain change-of-residence permits to move (for example, if a married couple decides to live with relatives). The permits are temporary, and permanent arrangements must be made with the housing authorities, who measure homes to make sure the space contains at least 12 square yards (10 square meters) per person. Local Board of Health representatives check homes regularly for cleanliness, so that diseases will not spread.

Each city block is governed by the local branch of the CDR. The leaders see that people fulfill certain community tasks, such as recycling, patrolling the streets, and conducting public-health campaigns (for example, childhood vaccinations). They make sure that everyone living on the block has permission to be there. One CDR leader told journalist John Putman that they watch closely for antisocials—"those who don't work or study, who hustle or rob, who do nothing for anyone, not even themselves"—and report them to the police.

1,700.[9] However, only a fraction of these people formally practiced their religion regularly. According to religious experts, about 400,000 to 500,000 regularly attend weekly religious services. Among Protestants, Evangelical faiths increased the most. These groups tend to meet in people's homes or apartments rather than in a church building.

The government's antireligion stance has changed somewhat over the years. In 1986 the government began to eliminate formal discrimination against religion. In December 1997, Castro declared that Christmas would be celebrated as a national holiday for the first time in more than thirty years to honor the visit of Pope John Paul II, whom the government had invited to come to Cuba. The Archbishop of Havana, Jaime Cardinal Ortega, urged Cubans to focus on the spiritual aspects of the holiday, not "commercialization."[10]

Nonetheless, Cuban religious leaders have complained that the government still refuses their requests for more freedom. It was difficult to gain permission for religious processions, which are strictly regulated, and the government often will not admit foreign priests and nuns. Religious groups also lack access to the state-controlled media for religious broadcasts. Catholic schools for children are forbidden, and the church is not allowed to print and distribute church bulletins or other literature. Government officials complained that counterrevolutionary groups might try to use the churches to gain an advantage. In September 1998, Orlando Marquez, a spokesperson for Jaime Cardinal Ortega, said: "It is obvious that there is still a lack of understanding by the authorities of the role that the church should have in society. There are still limitations that are unnecessary."[11]

SOCIAL EQUITY?

The Cuban constitution and Communist agenda call for a "classless" society, with racial and gender equality. People debate whether these goals have been achieved. For example, government leaders and bureaucrats have special privileges, more access to jobs, and more material advantages than average Cubans.

The revolutionary government has provided more opportunities for people who were once poor or unemployed, including Afro-Cubans, women, and rural Cubans. Many enjoy better living standards as a result of universal education and health care. There are far more minorities in skilled, professional, and managerial jobs, including the Cuban military, than was true before the Revolution.

Cuban law states that men and women should share equally in household tasks and child-rearing. However, surveys show that most Cuban women still do more than half of the household and child-related work along with their outside jobs. The government does provide day care, which helps more women to work outside the home and also enables the government to play a larger role in child-rearing. Women say they now have equal opportunities for education. Few women hold high government positions, although female government officials and professionals are more abundant in Cuba than before the Revolution. Some Cuban women complain about a "macho" mentality among men who believe they deserve special privileges, including the right to have sexual affairs outside their marriage.

Social services tend to favor children and the elderly. "There are two privileged classes in Cuba, the young and the old," said Rosa Perez, a resident of Havana.[12] Cuban Children's Day is celebrated on the third Sunday in July.

PRIDE IN THEIR CULTURE

Observers say that, despite their problems, Cubans take pride in many aspects of their culture and society. Racism has declined significantly since 1959, and violence is rare. The education and health-care systems serve everyone.

Many Cubans are also glad that materialism is not stressed in their culture. A retired teacher named Margarita Sosa said: "I don't think material things can buy happiness. My children were not children with many toys, but they were happy. They had what they needed: a parent who was here to answer their questions and to talk."[13]

During the Pan Am Games, Cuban Ana Quirot Moret wins the 400-meter run in Pan Am record time, on August 6, 1991, in Havana.

CHAPTER SEVEN

ARTS AND RECREATION

A blend of African, European, and Caribbean elements in Cuba has created a unique, fascinating culture and creative arts. As tourism to the island has increased and Cuban performers tour the world, more people are experiencing Cuban art, music, dance, and theater. Music, in particular, has a rich history, and the visual arts, including filmmaking, have become increasingly important.

Right after the Revolution, Castro's government discouraged certain forms of popular music in favor of classical music from the Soviet Union, but that changed in later decades. Some groups have been banned for creating music that the government deemed inappropriate. To ease economic problems, the Cuban government has permitted more musicians to sign recording contracts with U.S. companies. Their earnings go primarily to the government.

The Cuban government supports art, music, and literature and has promoted African-American culture, all through the Ministry of Culture, established in 1976. Havana remains the nation's cultural center, with its museums, movie theaters, live theaters, and concert stages. The famous National Ballet of Cuba is there, and the Havana International Ballet festival is held each November. However, the government proudly points out that cultural events are held around the country so that everyone has access to the arts. Cuba boasts more than two hundred art museums.

SON AND SALSA: A MUSIC-LOVING NATION

Music is an integral part of Cuban life, both as a form of entertainment and a leisure activity. People like to sing, dance, or play music informally, as well as listen to professional musicians. The guitar is basic to Cuban music and reflects the Spanish influence; the double bass, trumpets, maracas, and different types of drums are the other basic instruments. Street bands perform on conga drums, clay pipes, guitars, and bass.

Popular Cuban rhythms include the cha-cha, conga, bolero, rumba, *son*, guaracha, mambo, and salsa. Afro-Cuban culture combined with Spanish flamenco rhythms generated several important musical forms and influenced jazz, too. The habanera rhythm evolved from the *danza criolla* and *contradanza* and influenced the tango and other South American rhythms. *Son* came from the eastern provinces, in the mid-1800s, while the bolero emerged in the 1880s when composer Pepe Sanchez wrote "Tristezas." Alberto Villalon and Sindo Garay are two of the best-known early bolero composers. The rumba also developed in the late 1800s, in poor African-Cuban communities.

Son blends brass horns, piano, and bongo drums. a combination of African and Spanish music that developed in rural areas. During the early 1900s it became popular in cities, where it was played by larger bands with modern instruments. A *son* group usually includes a small three-cord guitar called a *tres*, standard guitars, various hand drums, and other percussion instruments. Brass instruments are added for jazz pieces.

In 1950, Enrique Jorrin composed what is regarded as the first cha-cha, "La Enganadora," and Perez Prado brought out the mambo in 1952. During the 1970s the Los Van Van orchestra, founded by Elio

Reven, became popular for dancing. This group mixed jazz with unique combinations of trombones and violins for a sound that was dubbed *songo*. Salsa followed several years later, combining sounds from Cuba, Puerto Rico, and the Dominican Republic. Cuban salsa boomed in popularity during the late 1980s and early 1990s. A form of salsa called *charanga* includes the flute and violin, with a bass, piano, conga drum, and vocals.

Certain Cuban performers have influenced jazz over the decades. Chano Pozo, a Cuban percussionist, was part of the great "bebop" band led by Dizzy Gillespie, starting in the late 1940s. Afro-Cuban drummers added a unique sound to a Stan Kenton recording called "The Peanut Vendor." Machito and Chano Pozo are prominent figures in modern jazz.

People around the world became familiar with Cuban-born musician and actor Desi Arnaz, costar of the popular television show "I Love Lucy," which he made with his wife Lucille Ball during the 1950s. The show remains popular year after year and is shown in reruns around the world in many languages. The Cuban-American pop singer Gloria Estefan has become famous worldwide. Albita (Albita Rodriguez) sang at the inauguration of President Bill Clinton in 1997. She and her band, composed of three women and herself, defected while performing during the spring of 1993 in Mexico. They crossed the border to El Paso, Texas. With help from the Cuban exile community in Miami, they resumed their careers. Albita's music includes folkloric and Cuban "country music." Her first album was produced in Cuba during the late 1980s and became the best-selling export album in Cuba at that time.

Chuchu Valdes, a jazz piano legend, is known for his innovative blends of Afro-Cuban jazz and salsa. With his fifteen-piece band Irakere, Valdes won a Grammy Award in 1979 and performed at Carnegie Hall. The artist was barred from playing in the

United States for pay in the years that followed, but returned in 1995 on an "academic exchange" visa and played informally at different clubs in New York City. Valdes could have left Cuba but remained because of his strong connection to his musical and cultural roots. He has extensively toured Europe, appears at international festivals, and has run Cuba's annual jazz festival.

Some Cuban singers are known for political protest ballads or folk songs. The music of Silvio Rodriguez and Pablo Milanes, who founded a musical movement called *la nueva trova*, is popular throughout Latin America and Spain. Their songs describe the lives and problems of average Cubans. Rodriguez began his career in the late 1960s and quickly became one of Cuba's most popular songwriters. He is known for his virtuoso guitar playing, rich compositions, and expressive singing. His album "Mujeres" (1978) is often cited as his masterpiece. Singer/composer Carlos Varela, who first appeared onstage in 1989 at age twenty-six, has written songs in which he questions the Revolution. Unlike some other critics, he has been permitted to live in Cuba.

Strained relations between Cuba and the United States have kept musicians from the two countries from collaborating as much as they would like. In 1995, American trumpet player Manny Duran said: "We have a lot to learn from [Cuban musicians]—and they have a lot to learn from us."[1] In recent years, the Cuban government has issued more travel visas for performing artists. They include Vocal Sampling, a Cuban *a cappella* group that performed in San Francisco and New York in November 1995.

In 1997, American musicians and spectators attended the Havana Jazz Festival. David Sanchez, an American saxophonist who performed there, said of Cuban music: "It's the smartest pop music I've ever heard, and, while it is for a dancing audience, it is really complicated and profound."[2]

Cuban folk musicians received broader attention in 1999 when they were featured in the popular film *The Buena Vista Social Club*. A recording of the same name sold millions of copies and won a Grammy Award. The group played to large audiences during a tour of Europe and the United States.

OUTSTANDING DANCERS

Cuba is famous for an array of dance forms—traditional, popular, and classical. The National Folklore Group performs around the world, as well as in Cuba itself. The Trinidad Folkloric Ballet is known for its Afro-Cuban dance and music. Dancers at the famous outdoor nightclub the Tropicana give electrifying performances. Besides watching such performances, tourists can take part in "dance trips" where they learn popular Latin dance steps during their Cuban vacation.

Foreign critics have noted the wealth of talent in Cuba. Writing for *The New York Times* in 1979, Clive Barnes said: "One is simply amazed at the quality of the dancing. Why should a small country like this have produced so many excellent dancers?"[3]

Classical ballet has a proud history. The chief founder and an acclaimed soloist of the Ballet Nacional de Cuba is Alicia Alonso, one of world's great dancers. After studying and working in New York City, she returned to Cuba in 1946 and developed her own ballet company. The company received government support after the Revolution and became known as the National Ballet of Cuba. Its offices and studios are located in an early twentieth-century convent in one of Havana's elegant old neighborhoods.

The national company performs standard classics, folklore pieces, and modern compositions. It performs at the Teatro Garcia Lorca in Havana, as well as all over the island itself, and on tours outside Cuba. As a result, Cubans are educated about ballet and can see performances by leading dancers. Potential ballet students come from all over Cuba and are chosen from auditions, where experts identify candidates. Training is free.

Cuban ballerinas are known for their beautiful classical movements and form, and male dancers display technical brilliance. Ballerinas Mirta Pla and Aurora Bosch, and later, Josefina Mendez and Viengsay Valdes, have been stars of the company. Top male dancers are Jose Manuel Carreno and Carlos Acosta. Acosta, who has danced primarily in the United States and London, was born in Havana in 1973, the youngest of eleven children.

Acosta began studying ballet at age nine. He told one journalist: "I always loved dancing, but not ballet. I used to break-dance all the time. I was quite famous in my old neighborhood in Havana."[4]

At age sixteen, Acosta won the prestigious Gold Medal at the Prix de Lausanne (Switzerland) international competition. One British critic called Acosta "a firecracker of a dancer who spins nonstop, flies through the air, has phenomenal splits and yet never loses the elegance and refinement of his classical training."[5]

In 1993 he signed with the Houston Ballet Company and has appeared in cities all over the world, performing leading roles in *Don Quixote*, *Romeo and Juliet*, and *Orfeo*, among others. Acosta gives financial support to his family in Cuba, whom he visits regularly. Observers claim that the government permits Acosta and certain other dancers to perform in other countries in order to prevent them from defecting.

Asked why she founded a ballet company in Cuba, Alicia Alonso said: " . . . I thought it was very important to bring culture to the people. The arts are essential to human beings, and dance is an art that expresses everything. Cuba deserved a company, it deserved a school. . . . Today we have one of the best companies in the world, and one of the best schools in the world, and a tremendous amount of talent."[6]

LITERATURE

Spanish literature in Cuba dates from colonial days, when people of Spanish descent became known for their poetry. The revolutionary hero José Martí became popular for his poetry at the turn of the twentieth century.

Most educated Cubans were reading Spanish and North American literature before 1959. Since then, the Castro government has urged Cubans to explore their own literary heritage, as well as materials with socialist themes. Writers receive salaries from the government (which also determines what will be published). The highly literate population buys large numbers of the books that are in print. Poetry and mysteries are especially popular. Important contemporary Cuban writers include Alejo Carpentier (1906–1980), Jose Lezama Lima (1910–1976), and Miguel Barnet, who in 1968 wrote the best-seller *The Autobiography of a Runaway Slave*.

Several Cuban exiles have also become famous writers. Playwright Eduardo Machado, a Cuban-American, wrote *Floating Islands*, a series of plays that follow four generations of a Cuban family from the late 1920s through the Revolution and into their years of exile in California. Machado left Cuba for the United States in 1961 when he was eight years old. His family kept their memories of Cuba alive by talking about them often.

Poet Heberto Padilla moved to the United States in 1980. Padilla, who is homosexual, said the Cuban government had imprisoned him for "crimes" against conventional morality. After he spoke out against the way the government treated certain exiled writers, including Cabrera Infante, Padilla was sentenced to several months of forced labor and treated for "psychological maladjustment." An international group of prominent authors urged the Cuban government to release Padilla and let him leave Cuba. He was sent to Florida with a few items of clothing.

Writer Zoe Valdes left Cuba in 1995. Valdes said that the government banned her books, which had to be smuggled out of the country and published abroad. She criticized the Castro regime, saying: "They're afraid of intellectuals and they're very repressive."[7] Valdes said that writers who displeased the government might be tortured or imprisoned. She also claimed that government officials had forced poet Maria Elena Cruz Varela to stand in a road and chew up her poems, then sent her to prison for two years.

Author Gustavo Perez Firmat, who moved to North Carolina, said, "I feel alienated from the current regime but not from the island's culture and history."[8]

A Growing Film Industry

Cubans love movies, and American films are often shown there, although the quality may be poor because the newer films are usually "pirated" versions, taped in U.S. theaters. Renting American films is expensive, so few are brought legally to Cuba.

Cuban filmmakers have gained increasing recognition since the first film in Cuba was made in 1897. A 1986 Cuban film that was shown abroad is a satiric social commentary titled *She Sold Candies*. It tells the story of a female metallurgical engineer who cannot find work, so she decides to make and sell candies instead. One of the most highly acclaimed feature films, released in 1995, is the dark comedy *Guantanamera*, directed by Tomas Gutierrez Alea. Alea is one of Cuba's best directors, with more than eighty films to his credit. The film, which was criticized by the Cuban government, explored the problems experienced by a Cuban family trying to make arrangements for a relative's funeral. *Guantanamera* won second prize in the fiction category at the XVII International Festival of New Latin American Cinema in 1996.

Another 1995 film, *Fresas y Chocolate* (*Strawberries and Chocolate*), won the Silver Bear award at the Berlin

Film Festival. Very popular in Cuba, the film, centers on the relationship between two young men, one a devoted socialist and the other a homosexual, around the time of the Mariel boatlift in 1980. The film was praised for its excellent performances, directing, and screenplay.

The International Festival of New Latin American Cinema is held in Havana each December. Hundreds of competing films, along with other noncompeting films, take part. During the festival, about 1,500 people from around the world watch films in Havana while movie fans see films throughout the country. The awards ceremony is held in the Karl Marx Theater.

BOLD STUDIO ART

During the early colonial days, religious art dominated Cuban fine arts, while classical landscape painting became popular in the 1800s. The San Alejandro Academy was founded in 1818. Cuban artists engaged in the modern movement of the early 1900s. In 1927 the first major exhibit of modern Cuban art was held, featuring paintings by Victor Manuel, Carlos Enriquez, and others. Ten years later, the first Modern Arts Salon was introduced.

Modern Cuban art often features bold graphics and vivid colors. Rene Portocarrero (1912–1985) was one of the foremost Cuban avant-garde artists and was particularly known for his murals. Another world-famous Cuban modern artist, Wilfredo Lam, studied in Europe and painted in the studio of Pablo Picasso. In 1943, after his return to Cuba, Lam painted *La Jungla* (*The Jungle*), a famous work that now hangs in the Museum of Modern Art (MOMA) in New York City.

The Cuban government took an active role in sponsoring fine arts after the Revolution. In 1962 it created the National School of Fine Arts, and added the Fine Arts College of the High Institute of Arts in 1976.

In the 1990s recognized artists included Manuel Mendive, a Santero priest whose modern-style works are influenced by Afro-Cuban religious images, sculptor Kcho, and Tania Bruguera, an installation artist.

AWARD-WINNING ATHLETES

Numerous sports are popular in Cuba, and the government sponsors sports programs in schools and communities. Sports are also a major activity for the Pioneros—the José Martí Pioneers—Cuba's most important youth organization, with more than 2 million members.

Cuban athletes have done well in international competitions, such as the Olympics. At the 1996 Summer Olympic Games, held in Atlanta, Georgia, Cuban athletes earned 7 gold medals along with a number of silver and bronze medals. They earned 29 medals at the 2000 Olympics, including 11 gold, 11 silver, and 7 bronze. Cubans have also done well in the Pan American Games and served as the host country in 1991. That year marked the first time a Latin American country earned more medals than the United States, as Cubans won 140 gold medals.

Cubans love baseball, and the Cuban national team won the Olympic gold medals in 1992 and 1996. Each year, teams from all over Cuba compete in a national series. They are divided into two leagues: Occidentales and Orientales. Various teams compete in series games held in Havana and the provinces to determine who will compete in the finals. The top team from each of the two leagues plays in a seven-game series each year, and the winner is the national champion. Havana hosts the finals of the National Baseball Series, held from November to January. In recent years, top teams have come from Santa Clara, Havana, and Piñar del Rio.

Cuban players are known for their speed and determination. Some of the finest players of the 1990s were third baseman Omar Linares, pitchers Jose Ibar and Jose Contreras, and shortstop German Mesa. The Cuban team has visited other countries to play against leading teams. Two exhibition games between the Cuban team and Baltimore Orioles took place in 1999. This was the first time a U.S. professional team had played in Cuba in forty years. Cubans were eager to attend the game on March 29, and seats were given out "by invitation only." Fidel Castro was among the 50,000 spectators. Jose Contreras pitched for the Cuban team. The exciting contest went to eleven innings and ended in a victory for Baltimore. In May, the two teams played again, this time in Baltimore, and the Cubans won, 12–6. Cuba reached the finals at the 2000 Olympics in Sydney, Australia, and won the second-place silver medal after the U.S. team defeated them.

During the 1990s, more than fifteen Cuban baseball players defected to play for U.S. teams. In 1995, Livan Hernandez, a talented twenty-year-old pitcher, left the Cuban national team and was signed by the Florida Marlins. Hernandez became a national sports figure when he was chosen as a starting pitcher in Game 1 of the 1997 World Series against the Cleveland Indians. To get to the Series, the Marlins had defeated the Atlanta Braves for the National League title. Hernandez was chosen most valuable player (MVP) for his brilliant performance in the series. Although Livan Hernandez is officially considered a "traitor" by the Cuban government, his countrymen have followed his career with enthusiasm. One man told a *New York Times* correspondent: "Livan has demonstrated the high quality of Cuban baseball, that our players can compete and succeed spectacularly at the highest level. So how can we not be proud of him?"[9]

In 1996, Livan's half-brother Orlando Hernandez, another top pitcher, was banished from the Cuban team, even though he told government officials he had not known that Livan planned to defect. In order to resume his career, Orlando left Cuba in December 1997, in a boat that carried his wife and three others, along with some water, brown sugar, cans of Spam, and gas for the 35-mile (56-kilometer) trip. After twelve hours, they reached an uninhabited shore in the Bahamas but nearly ran out of food before a U.S. Coast Guard helicopter picked them up three days later. They obtained humanitarian visas through Costa Rica, which prevented them from being sent back to Cuba. Orlando Hernandez later signed a four-year contract for $6.6 million with the New York Yankees, where he is known to fans as "El Duque."

Baseball clearly runs in the family. Livan and Orlando's father was a great Cuban pitcher whose style influenced his sons. Orlando, who began playing ball at age seven, recalls a happy childhood in Cuba: "I didn't have the best material things in the world, but in my heart my life was the best in the world."[10]

Boxing is the second most popular sport in Cuba, and Cuban boxers have won international competitions. Amateur boxer Teofilo Stevenson won three Olympic gold medals (1972, 1976, and 1980). He is equally well known for his sportsmanship and was honored with the UNESCO Pierre de Coubertin Fair Play prize in 1989. At ceremonies in Atlanta celebrating the centenary of the Olympics, Stevenson was the one Latin American among the twenty-five athletes who were specially honored. He retired from boxing in 1986 and has served both in the Cuban parliament and as vice president of the Cuban Boxing Federation. Felix Savon won the gold medal for the 201-pound (91-kilogram) class heavyweight boxing in the 1996 Summer Olympics.

Volleyball is another popular sport, and Cuban players excel. Since the 1970s the Cuban women's team has been ranked among the top six teams in the world. They won the world championship in 1978, 1994, and 1998 and earned gold medals at the Summer

"Es Estanderte"–The Caribbean Storm

One of the most remarkable Cuban athletes is track star Ana Fidelia Quirot, who joined the national athletics team in 1983. During that decade, she won both national and international awards, including the World Cup in the 400-meter and 800-meter races. In 1989 she won the world title in both those races as well as the 400-meter relay. The regional press selected her as the Latin American Woman Athlete of the Year, and *Track and Field News* named her its Athlete of the Year.

In 1993, Quirot suffered terrible burns over more than 50 percent of her body as the result of a kitchen accident. Courageously, she not only recovered but began training again. She returned to competition two years after her accident and won the silver medal in the Central American Games. She won the women's 800-meter race in the 1995 World Championships and went on to win the Olympic silver medal at the Atlanta Games the next year.

Quirot, who was awarded Cuba's Medal of Dignity, is popular for her amazing discipline and optimism. She now serves in the Cuban parliament.

Olympics in Barcelona (1992), Atlanta (1996), and Sydney (2000). In the 1990s the team also won two World Cups. Mireya Luis and Regla Bell played key roles in their team's success. Cubans have nicknamed this team "The Spectacular Brunette Women of the Caribbean."

The men's volleyball team has likewise been ranked among the best in the world. They won gold medals in the 1989 World Cup and 1998 World Championship. They came in sixth in the world at the Atlanta Olympic Games.

In track and field, Cuba won its first Olympic medal in 1964 when sprinter Enrique Figuerola won a second-place silver in the 100-meter race. Maria Caridad Colon became the first Latin American woman to win an Olympic gold medal in the javelin competition when she placed first at the 1980 games.

THE CUBAN "GISELLE"

Alicia Alonso was born in Havana in 1921 and began studying ballet at age ten at the Musical Pro-Art Society Ballet School, which was founded by wealthy arts patrons. After moving to the United States in 1936 with her new husband, Fernando Alonso, she studied at the American Ballet School. In 1938, Alonso made her professional debut, and the next year, she joined the American Ballet Caravan (now the Ballet Theater of New York). Despite serious vision problems that began when she was nineteen, Alonso became known around the world for her interpretation of romantic and classical roles, particularly "Giselle" and "The Sleeping Beauty." Critics praised her poise, footwork, grace, passion, and dramatic skills and said she was the greatest Giselle of the twentieth century. Alonso worked with the most talented choreographers and ballet directors in the world, including George Balanchine, Michel Fokine, Jerome Robbins, and Agnes de Mille, and top choreographers designed ballets just for her.

In 1948 she returned to her homeland and, with her husband, founded the Alicia Alonso Ballet (later renamed National Ballet of Cuba). Between 1955 and 1959, Alicia Alonso was invited to appear with the Montecarlo Russian Ballet, and she was the first ballet star from the Western Hemisphere invited to perform in the then-Soviet Union, where she danced at the Bolshoi and Kirov theaters. She toured in Europe, Asia, Latin America, and Australia. Alonso continued to spend part of her time with the American Ballet Theater until 1959, when the Cuban government began to sponsor her company. While serving as director of the state ballet, she also became a noted choreographer. After she and Fernando were divorced in the mid-1970s, he started a new company in Camagüey. Alonso later married dance writer Pedro Simon. She continued to perform into her seventies.

In a 1998 interview with Jordan Levin of the *Los Angeles Times*, Alonso said: "Cubans are very expressive. They have a wonderful ear for music, a tremendous sense of rhythm and plasticity. That is in the expression of the company, in the way we look at dancing itself."

Javier Sotomayor is one of Cuba's best-known track-and-field stars. He won his first world high-jump title in Budapest, Hungary, in 1986, when he jumped 2.44 meters, breaking the world record of 2.42

meters. In 1989 he jumped 2.45 meters. Sotomayor later broke his own record by jumping 2.53 meters, then went on to win the gold medal at the 1992 Olympics. As of 2000, Sotomayor still held the world record for the high jump: 2.6 meters, which he had set in 1993. This beloved athlete has made numerous goodwill tours and was admitted to the Cuban parliament in 1998. He has been praised for refusing to sign lucrative contracts to promote commercial sporting goods.

FUN AND GAMES

Cubans also enjoy impromptu sports and games. People get together spontaneously on the street and form teams to play a ball game called *"cuatro esquinas"*—four corners. Children fly imaginative homemade kites on windy days, and also enjoy games of marbles or hide-and-seek. They find places to hang a basket to start a basketball game or improvise soccer goalposts made of stones or place a net across an old table for Ping-Pong. Cards and chess are also popular.

If they don't feel like going out, Cubans find ways to enjoy themselves, just sitting and talking with friends and family, often outdoors. One favorite leisure activity is dominoes, played in couples or larger groups. People of all ages can be seen playing cards or dominoes.

Elian Gonzalez and his father, Juan Miguel Gonzalez, return to Cuba on June 28, 2000.

CHAPTER EIGHT

INTERNATIONAL RELATIONS

Despite its small size, Cuba has often been involved in international affairs and military conflicts. Cuban relations with the two world "superpowers" of the twentieth century, the United States and the former Soviet Union, have affected world events, as well as life inside Cuba.

Although Fidel Castro is said to be quite interested in foreign affairs, especially those involving the United States, the average Cuban has limited access to spoken ideas and printed materials from outside Cuba. According to Jacobo Timerman, Cubans live under "an impenetrable glass dome" that affects "their lives, their energies, their innermost human nature."[1] He believes that Castro sees himself as playing a significant role in world affairs.[2]

In the late 1980s, as the Soviet political philosophy and form of government changed, the Cuban government censored written materials from that country. Two popular Spanish-language Soviet magazines, *Sputnik* and *Novedades de Moscu,* could no longer be distributed in Cuba. The government-run newspaper *Granma* explained that these magazines now showed "a fascination with the North American way of life. . . ." and "subversion of values. . . ."[3]

Since 1989, Cuba has strengthened its relations with other countries, including Canada and various

Middle Eastern and European nations. The government reached out diplomatically to other Latin American nations and to Canada and Europe to increase foreign trade and investment. It encouraged joint projects with nongovernmental organizations (NGOs), so that more people from other countries could develop relationships with Cubans outside the realm of politics. In 1995, Fidel Castro signed a new foreign-investment law. It allowed 100 percent foreign ownership of some businesses in Cuba and promised foreign companies protection against expropriation of assets. These measures were especially important to Cuba's economic survival because of the trade embargo the United States has maintained since 1962. Cuban exiles and other critics of the Castro regime continue to support the embargo and to complain about the Cuban government.

SPREADING REVOLUTIONARY IDEAS

Since 1959 the Cuban government has tried to gain international support. The Fair Play for Cuba Committee printed and distributed materials that described the goals and ideals of the Revolution and contained some of Castro's speeches. In 1966 the government began printing *Granma*, a weekly review of news in Cuba, available in English. Although the publication was hard to obtain in the United States, it later became available on the World Wide Web.

The Cuban government tried to promote communism in the rest of Latin America. With help and supplies from the Soviet Union, it built a strong army that took part in conflicts on several continents, sometimes working with Soviet troops.

A CHANGING MILITARY INVOLVEMENT

After the Revolution the Cuban government developed a well-trained, well-equipped military, which was subsidized by the Soviet Union. Raul Castro, who was named general of the army in 1976, played a key role in this process. The military was told to be prepared at all times to defend Cuba from a U.S. invasion. The whole Cuban population was organized into militias and defense brigades, part of what the government calls the "whole people's army."

Cuban troops were involved in numerous foreign conflicts. Che Guevara led troops into the Congo and Bolivia during the 1960s. In 1965, Cuban troops fought in Zaire. An estimated 20,000 Cubans went to Angola (1985–1986) to help the Marxist government defeat a guerrilla movement from South Africa. More than 15,000 fought in Somalia on the Ethiopian side of that country's war in the 1970s. Cuba sent advisers and health-care workers to aid Nicaragua after the Sandinistas ousted the Somoza dictatorship in 1979. Other Cuban military advisers went to Algeria, Syria, Zanzibar (now part of Tanzania), and the Congo; they aided the left-wing Manley government in Jamaica and the Marxist government in Grenada.

In the late 1980s the Soviet Union stopped sending military planes, equipment, and supplies, and the Cuban military cut back its foreign operations. In recent years, most military personnel have been assigned to work within Cuba on various projects to improve the infrastructure and economy.

Compared with other Caribbean nations, Cuba's military is large. More than 100,000 men and women are on active duty, with about 135,000 more in the reserves. Men between the ages of sixteen and fifty must serve at least two years on active duty.

TENSE U.S.-CUBAN RELATIONS

The United States has had no formal diplomatic relations with Cuba since 1961, although there is a U.S. Interests section in Havana and a Cuban Interests section in Washington, D.C. The two nations have strong political disagreements and different values. A U.S.

State Department publication described some basic differences between the way people in Cuba and people in the United States look at the world:

> . . . the United States and socialist Cuba are extreme opposites in their beliefs as to what constitutes social and political rights for its citizens. Americans have been taught from childhood that we all have the right to dissent, to vote for change, and to organize politically. We do not consider social benefits as rights; we feel instead that such things as medical care, jobs, housing and higher education are benefits to be earned through work. Cubans, conversely, see medical care, guaranteed employment, housing, and education as basic rights, but have been taught that control over society is required to provide these rights.[4]

The Cuban government criticizes American culture as overly competitive and materialistic and too concerned with the individual. They also point out that the United States has far more crime and violence than Cuba and that nobody in Cuba is homeless.

Observers say that Fidel Castro blames Cuba's economic problems on the United States and also promotes the idea that the United States might attack Cuba at any time. During his visit to Cuba in the late 1980s, Jacobo Timerman noted:

> Every day one reads in the newspaper, hears on radio and television, has it proclaimed in all the schools, that Cuba is prepared to repel a United States invasion, and never is there any mention of the Kennedy-Khrushchev agreement, thus far respected by the two powers, guaranteeing Cuba's territorial integrity.[5]

Journalist Mirta Ojita wrote in 1998 that Cuban children continue to carry out air-raid drills and "dive under their desks in schools all over the island" in case of a U.S. attack and pledge that they will defend the Cuban flag against "los Americanos."[6]

At times, relations between Cuba and the United States have moved toward normalization. When Jimmy Carter was president (1977–1981), Cuban exiles were allowed to travel to Cuba. Beginning in 1994, U.S. citizens have been permitted to own a noncontrolling, minority interest in a foreign company that conducts business in Cuba. However, the revenue from these operations must not be the foreign company's major source of revenue. Some companies, including Days Inn and Choice Hotels International, own a share of foreign companies that have built hotels in Cuba.

During the early 1990s, it seemed as if the United States might lift its long-standing embargo against Cuba. A number of U.S. corporations sent people to Cuba to look over potential investments. Some Canadian and European companies thought that U.S. companies might soon offer to buy out their business interests in Cuba. However, after the Cubans shot down two Brothers to the Rescue planes in 1995, the U.S. government responded by enacting the Helms-Burton Bill, which added new economic sanctions against Cuba. The process of normalization was stalled once again.

As of 2000 the embargo was still in effect, and U.S. laws required that Americans have special permits to travel to Cuba or transfer funds and most material goods to that country. Some items, such as food and other things that meet basic human needs, were exempted. American economic sanctions against Cuba have drawn much criticism. The American Association for World Health says that the embargo has harmed the health and nutrition of the Cuban people by making it harder for Cuba to import foods and medicines. Other critics include the United Nations and Human Rights International. Pope John Paul II has called the embargo "unjust and ethically unacceptable."[7]

The embargo sparks heated debates. Strongly anti-Castro groups of Cuban exiles in the United States continue to lobby Congress to maintain these economic sanctions. Some embargo supporters demand that Castro meet three conditions before the trade sanctions are lifted: release political prisoners, legalize political activities, and hold free elections. Jesse Helms, a Republican senator from North Carolina, strongly believed the embargo should continue:

> *Flooding Cuba now with U.S. investment and American tourists will do nothing to bring democracy to Cuba. To the contrary, it will give new life to Castro's crumbling regime. . . . Foreign investors cannot do business with private Cuban citizens—they can go into business only with Castro. . . . They must pay Castro in hard currency for the workers. Castro then pays the workers in worthless Cuban pesos, while keeping the rest.[8]*

Opponents of economic sanctions argue that ending the embargo not only will help the Cuban people but will also help to bring political change. Christopher Dodd, a Democratic senator from Connecticut, called the embargo "ineffective and counterproductive."[9] The embargo also "prevents Cuban and American diplomats and military leaders from establishing meaningful channels of communication in order to prevent serious misunderstandings."[10] Dodd wrote:

> *Defenders of the Cuban embargo strategy assert that by isolating the regime economically we will*

force Fidel Castro to capitulate and hold demo-
cratic elections. Or alternatively, that the suf-
fering of the Cuban people will become so
unbearable that they will rise up and remove
their political leaders, by force if necessary. I saw
no tangible evidence during my visit to Cuba
that either scenario looms large on the horizon.[11]

Analysts point out that U.S. policy is inconsistent, because it permits trade with China, Vietnam, and other countries that do not tolerate political dissent and have state-run economies. Yet it continues its embargo against Cuba.

Many Americans are curious about this country, which is often in the news, because of its remarkable music and athletes. They say that Cubans and Americans should not be separated for political reasons. More cultural exchanges have been occurring. In 1999 pianist Byron Janis returned to perform in Havana for the first time since December 1958. Other Americans made appearances in 1999, including a group of seventy pop, country, and jazz musicians that included Jimmy Buffett and Burt Bacharach, as part of a group called Music Bridges. A Tony Award-winning musical, B*ring In da Noise, Bring In da Funk*, also arrived, and a segment of the MTV show *Road Rules* was filmed in Cuba. More Cuban music, dance, and theater groups have been performing throughout the United States, too.

Small changes occurred in 1999. The Clinton administration announced some small steps that relaxed restrictions on money transfers and travel. They permitted Americans to send foods and medicines more freely and to set up offices in Cuba. American officials also met with Cuban officials to discuss mutual antidrug efforts to keep drugs from moving from Cuba to Florida. Critics of the Cuban government said more people-to-people contact might even help the cause of Cuban dissidents and could weaken Castro's assertions that the United States is trying to destroy Cuba.

RELATIONS WITH CANADA AND EUROPE

Cuba has strengthened its economic and political ties with other nations. In 1993 numerous countries sent aid to Cuba when two disasters struck. The first, Hurricane Flora, was called the "Storm of the Century." The second was a widespread epidemic of optic neuritis. Spurred by its churches and non-governmental organizations, Canada sent humanitarian aid to Cuba. Oxfam Canada, the Jesuit Center, and the United Church of Canada were involved. During that time the Cuba-Canada Interagency Project (CIDA) took shape in order to promote collaboration. In 1994 bilateral trade between the two countries added up to millions of Canadian dollars. Cuban officials met with Canadians in June 1996 to sign the Charter of Principles that described the cultural links and collaboration between the two countries. That year Canada sent 2,000 tons of paper stock to the Cuban Ministry of Education to be used for textbooks.

Canadians, both in the government and among the general public, also protested the Helms-Burton Act of 1996. Nearly 2 million Canadians typically visit Florida each year and spend around $1.3 billion. They launched a boycott campaign, urging fellow Canadians to stop traveling to Florida in order to put pressure on the U.S. government.

During the 1990s, Castro made state visits to several European countries. In 1995, President François Mitterrand of France met with Castro at a private luncheon, receiving him as a foreign dignitary. During that visit, Mitterrand criticized the U.S. embargo, saying: "[Cuba] no longer represents any threat to world peace, nor any threat to the Americans."[12] He also said he hoped that Castro's visit would encourage "real liberty" in Cuba. Earlier in 1995 the president's wife, Danielle Mitterrand, had visited Cuba and made a hospital donation of $2.5 million on behalf of a human-rights group called the France Liberties Association.

ANTI-CASTRO EXILES

Many Cuban exiles living in the United States and elsewhere continue to condemn the Cuban government. Some Cuban-Americans pressure government officials to maintain economic sanctions against Cuba. While most politically active exiles protest peacefully, others have resorted to violence or tried to assassinate Fidel Castro. Cuban exiles who deplore these tactics say that terrorism is not the way to resolve things. They focus on expressing their own views in the media and supporting candidates who share their attitudes about Cuba. Some take part in quiet demonstrations, as the Cuban exiles in Paris did during Castro's visit in 1995. These exiles protested the fact that the French president had received Castro as a legitimate leader.

Militant Cuban exiles have tried to kill Castro and incite rebellion in Cuba. Some continue to train in paramilitary camps for the day when he dies and the country goes through another change. In December 1997, Andres Nazario-Sargen, a seventy-eight-year-old exile who fought with Castro but later called the Cuban leader "a Hitler-style totalitarian" said: "Gradual change is only in the minds of people who are used to democracy. . . ."[13] Nazario-Sargen looks forward to Cuba's liberation, after Castro's death.

Polls of Cuban exiles, taken in 1997, showed that younger Cuban-Americans (those under the age of sixty-five) held moderate views and favored dialogue with the Cuban government as a way to move the country toward a more democratic system. An organization called Cuban Change seeks normal relations between Cuba and the United States.

While most Cubans who leave the country go to the United States, others head for Costa Rica, Mexico, the Bahamas, Canada, or Europe. After years of conflicts over Cuban emigration, in September 1994 the U.S. and Cuban governments agreed that 20,000 Cubans would be legally permitted to emigrate each year.

Many Cubans want to leave, and about 500,000 Cubans apply for the 20,000 legal visas that the U.S. government grants each year. Thousands of others flee illegally, attempting to reach Florida in boats.

It is expensive to leave the country legally. Cubans must first obtain a U.S. visa and an exit permit from the Cuban government. The permit costs $600 a person. The cost for a permit to visit and then return is $150. Passports cost another $50. People must also have a medical checkup that costs $400. It costs another $20 to use the airport, in addition to the cost of the airplane ticket. Few Cubans can afford these expenses. Those who wish to leave legally often rely on help from relatives living abroad.

People may also seek political asylum if they reach U.S. shores illegally. They must reach land itself and can be stopped if they are apprehended in the waters between the two countries. Those who leave by boat must evade the Cuban Coast Guard and then deal with the weather and conditions on the sea. Despite grave risks, and the fact that Cubans have died in their quest to leave Cuba, people continue to leave illegally. On July 13, 1994, the Cuban Coast Guard spotted a tugboat carrying 73 people. They aimed heavy-duty water hoses at the people, killing 43, among them 23 children.

One of the most dramatic exits from Cuba took place in 1992. Orestes Lorenzo Perez, a pilot in the Cuban Air Force, had defected earlier that year by flying his MIG-23 plane to Florida. General Raul Castro informed Perez's wife that she and the children would never be allowed to leave Cuba. Lorenzo went on a hunger strike and asked the media to pressure the government to release his family, but to no avail.

He then devised a daring plan to fly back to Cuba and pick up his family in a light plane. On December 9, Perez flew a 1961 Cessna from the Florida Keys to Cuba. Friends had told his wife and children to wait for him on a highway near Matanzas. Perez flew very low to avoid being spotted, and he turned off his radar. He had timed every part of the trip carefully, knowing that he had just fifteen minutes to land and pick up his family then get far enough away to avoid being apprehended. Despite a fast and risky landing, the family made it into the plane, and Perez flew safely back to Florida, again flying low until he reached the 24th parallel. When the plane landed, it was coated with salt from flying so close to the ocean.

"FREE ELIAN!"

Late in 1999, an incident involving a young boy brought conflicts between Cuba and the United States into sharp focus. On Thanksgiving Day, five-year-old Elian Gonzalez was discovered off the coast of Florida floating on a life raft. He was one of three survivors of a group of twelve Cubans who had left for the United States on a small boat. Nine others, including his mother and her boyfriend, drowned.

In Miami, Elian went to stay with the family of an uncle, all Cuban exiles, while the U.S. Immigration and Naturalization Service (INS) reviewed his case. Back in his hometown of Cardenas, Elian's father, Juan Miguel Gonzalez, demanded that his son be returned to Cuba. The Cuban government also insisted that U.S. officials return the boy at once.

A heated debate ensued over Elian's fate. Cuban exiles held public demonstrations outside the home of the Miami relatives and demanded that Elian be permitted to stay in the United States. Spencer Eig, a member of the legal team hired by the Miami relatives, said: "We all feel very strongly that Elian's life

Plots Against Castro

In May 1998 a boat with four Cuban exiles aboard was stopped near Puerto Rico. Officers of the U.S. Coast Guard found weapons, including sniper rifles, nightscopes, and rounds of ammunition. One of the exiles, Angel Alfonso Aleman, a resident of New Jersey, claimed: "I placed them there myself. They are weapons for the purpose of assassinating Fidel Castro." Alfonso had spent eighteen years in Cuban jails because of his anti-Castro activities. He said he had been a revolutionary in Cuba before 1959 but not a Fidelista.

In August, Alfonso and Jose Antonio Llama and Angel Hernandez Rojo and five others were accused of plotting to kill Castro during meetings in Venezuela and Guatemala. Alfonso said: "The main thing is to take Castro out, by any means necessary. . . . I am prepared to accept the consequences."

Another member of what has been called the "anti-Castro underworld" is Luis Posada Carriles, a Cuban exile who had spent his life trying to overthrow the government. Posada claimed that he organized bombings of Cuban hotels, restaurants, and nightclubs in 1997, aimed at overthrowing Castro. In his autobiography, *The Roads of a Warrior*, Posada described his activities through the years to topple Castro's regime. He said he received training during the early 1960s from the CIA.

The Cuban government identified Posada as a dangerous criminal and a terrorist. Posada said: "We didn't want to hurt anybody. We just wanted to make a big scandal so that the tourists don't come anymore. We don't want any more foreign investment." Posada, who claims to be a Venezuelan citizen, says he owns several passports that allow him to travel to different places and meet with people to plan his activities. Posada has been wounded during attempts on his own life.

will be destroyed if he's sent to the custody of Fidel Castro in Cuba."[14]

Cubans saw things differently, and many described his stay in the United States as a "kidnapping." Carmen Rivero, an eighteen-year-old Cuban college student, said: "He must return. His family is here. They've been trying to change his mind in

Miami with toys and gifts. He may not get that in Cuba but the most important thing is family love. . . . "[15] The Cuban government encouraged large demonstrations at which people waved Cuban flags, sang patriotic songs, made speeches, and carried signs saying "Free Elian!" More than 50,000 Cubans marched into Cardenas on January 7, 2000. One Cuban said: "It's true we have many economic problems. But we do our best for our children."[16]

American politicians chose sides. Some said that Elian should be permitted to remain to fulfill his mother's dream. Others said that the child belonged with his surviving parent, stepmother, and baby half-brother. They noted that Elian had spent a lot of time with his father, who had joint custody, and that a parent is normally expected to make decisions regarding a young child. Polls taken throughout the first half of 2000 showed that a majority of Americans believed that Elian should be returned to his father so long as he was a fit parent.

The INS said that their investigation showed the father and Cuban grandparents had a loving, close relationship with Elian and he should be sent back home. Attorney General Janet Reno supported the INS decision, as did the National Council of Churches, which sent representatives from Cuba to meet with Elian's family.

Journalists also joined the debate. Deborah Sharp, who spent a month traveling in Cuba and inter-viewing people, described scenes from Cuban life:

> . . . on this Havana playground, where parents line the fences to keep a watchful eye, the children appear happy and well-loved. Some here say eco-nomic difficulties have drawn traditionally close Cuban families even closer. And many parents here deeply resent the idea that a life of plenty in the USA would be preferable to a Cuban life of Elian.[17]

"HOARDING TOYS"

Critics of the Cuban government expressed dismay when Victor Rolando Arroyo was arrested in January 2000 by Cuban state security police for having more than 150 toys in his home. His home was being used as a distribution center for toys and gifts that were collected during an international campaign sponsored by Cuban civic organizations. They were being given to needy Cuban children on the holiday of the Three Wise Men. More than 100 had already been given to these children. Their families lacked hard currency needed to obtain these kinds of toys and clothing on their own. Arroyo was charged with the crime of "hoarding toys" and sentenced to six months in prison.

On March 21, a federal judge dismissed the lawsuit by relatives who sought to keep Elian in the United States. The Miami relatives asked an appeals court to grant him a political asylum hearing. Attorney General Janet Reno said: "It has been four months since Elian was separated from his father and lost his mother. It is time for this little boy, who has been through so much, to move on with his life at his father's side."[18] President Bill Clinton supported this idea.

The Cuban government then sent Elian's father to the United States with his wife and baby. Juan Miguel Gonzalez was quoted as saying that he wanted to take Elian back to Cuba. However, people debated whether he was speaking freely, and some said the Cuban government would not let him express his true feelings. The Miami relatives refused to turn Elian over to his father.

After concluding that there was no other way to reunite father and son, Attorney General Reno sent armed agents into the Miami home before dawn on April 22 to remove Elian and take him to his father. An appeals court later ruled that Elian was too young to apply on his own for political asylum, and he flew back to Cuba with his father.

These events outraged many Cuban-Americans and showed their deep bitterness toward the Castro regime. They revealed the kinds of conflicts that may occur among families with members in both Cuba and the United States. They also sparked much public debate about U.S.-Cuban relations.

As the twenty-first century began, tourism was Cuba's number-one industry.

CHAPTER NINE

CUBA IN TRANSITION

As the twenty-first century began, Cuba was working hard to resolve its economic problems while remaining faithful to the socialist revolution. Castro remained firmly committed to his agenda. He said: "The Revolution will not renounce its principles. And it will never be forced to its knees before the United States."[1] Throughout the country, signs encouraged people to remain loyal to the Revolution and to keep fighting for a better life for all. Some of these signs read: "No one should lose hope."[2]

The Cuban system has survived, despite the ban on trade between the United States in Cuba and the withdrawal of Soviet economic support after 1989. The government has changed some aspects of the Communist system to be more capitalistic.

The people of Cuba work to help themselves, cooperating with each other and sharing their expertise to tackle problems. Groups of Cubans have joined local farming projects to boost organic production by cooperatives. The Federation of Cuban Women sponsors self-employment programs for women through its collaboration with the United Nations Development Program (UNDP). With help from Oxfam-Canada, two Cuban organizations—the Martin Luther King Jr. Memorial Center and Felix Varela Center—have worked to improve housing. Local people's councils and community-based workshops help to organize and participate in these and other projects. The European Union (EU) and Canada have helped with projects to expand management-training skills for university students to prepare Cubans to function in a more decentralized economy and help local entrepreneurs compete more effectively with foreign businesspeople.

The people of Cuba have shown themselves to be energetic, resourceful, and flexible. They are well-educated and have good basic health care. Yet big economic challenges, including low wages, frequent power outages, and cutbacks in services, including cultural events, have been discouraging.

People born after 1959 now make up about 45 percent of the Cuban population. They have not known any other kind of government but the Castro regime. Many of these people and members of the older generations have strong feelings and ideas about how to solve Cuba's problems. Some say that it is possible to retain parts of the current system they appreciate, such as a strong education system, high literacy rates, free health care, low crime rates, and a clean environment, while still making political changes and increasing personal rights.

AN UNCERTAIN FUTURE

Around the world, people wonder what the future holds for Cuba. Generations of Cubans have worked hard for personal and national dignity and independence. They have hoped that the future would bring better times for themselves and their children. An aging dictator, a changing world order, and economic problems mean that Cuba must continue to adjust. How will the government change in the process? What social values will remain in place? What new kinds of personal freedoms may emerge? Will the changes be dramatic or relatively peaceful?

Although Cubans did not have much direct contact with other countries for decades and Castro himself said that the people lived in a protective "glass bowl," that has been changing, too. More contact with people from other places is bound to affect Cubans in different ways.

Do Cubans support their government? People who have visited in recent years or have studied the country say that the majority support the ideals of the Castro revolution. According to James Suckling: "Contrary to U.S. media reports, popular support for Fidel Castro and his revolution remain strong—it's just that many would like some of the amenities of life that their visitors have."[3]

Kenia Serrano, a twenty-one-year-old Cuban leader of the Union of Young Communists, expressed his opinions at a meeting at the University of Texas (Pan American) in Edinburg, outside of Houston, in 1995. Serrano said: "If by democracy, you mean homelessness, or you mean the democracy of racism, or where every four years parties organize a carnival and millions of dollars are spent, where candidates promise everything and nothing changes, then no, we don't want that kind of democracy."[4]

Other young people in Cuba feel differently. There are several independent youth movements working for political change in Cuba. They include Cuban Youth for Democracy, which seeks to restore academic freedom in schools and universities. This group objects to the firing of teachers who express views that differ from the government, for example. Spokesperson Heriberto Leyva said that these firings are "evidence of the continued political apartheid practiced by the current government in the education field and the complete subjugation of Cuban education to the totalitarian control of the Communist Party."[5]

Members of the same family may have different opinions and sometimes debate politics vigorously. Journalist Christopher Marquis recorded a conversation between a woman in her fifties and her thirty-three-year-old son who had lived in Miami for eighteen months. The woman expressed exasperation with the Castro government, saying: "Fidel runs this place like his own farm."[6] Her son countered by pointing out the disadvantages of capitalism, based on his experiences: "[In Miami] you work like a slave, and you think you're a king. It's a little room, and you call it a studio or an efficiency. You have a car that isn't yours; it's leased. Your house isn't yours; you rent it. There are so many debts."[7] He said he dreaded the "plague of consumerism" that might strike if the Cuban government changed dramatically. His mother persisted: "There, you can change the government after four years. . . . I'm dying for a chance to change things."[8]

Pablo Milanes, an international singing star, said: "We prefer to live in this kind of society. We have the possibility to do our art. It makes a lot of money but that is not fundamental for us. If we care about that, we would live in another country and be millionaires."[9]

Travel author Frank Bruni said that Cubans express varied opinions: "Some Cubans . . . told me bluntly that they could not wait for Castro to die. Others praised him as a brave leader who had created a triumphantly humane system."[10]

An American physician who spent a great deal of time in Cuba told journalist T. Z. Parsa: "Things are changing fast these days—you can see it all around. . . . The Cubans are an incredibly well-educated people— they're learning very quickly how to live with a free market. The transition won't be as hard as it was in Eastern Europe."[11]

Valdes Vivo, director of the Cuban Communist party's Nico Lopez school for advanced studies, predicted that Cuba would be more a part of the outside world. He said: "Cuba is no longer an island. There are no islands anymore. There is only one world."[12]

When journalist Jacobo Timerman visited Cuba in the late 1980s, he concluded that *waiting* was a dominant theme in Cuban life, both past and present.

Cubans waited centuries to break free of foreign rule. They waited decades for a strong leader who would improve social conditions and the economy and recharge the nation's pride. After the Revolution, they adjusted to other changes and worked hard, then waited for the rewards of their sacrifices. Timerman saw long lines outside stores and government offices and at bus stops. On a road near Havana, he encountered a woman carrying a television set. She had waited a long time for this luxury item, which her children had sent from Venezuela through a tourist. She had gone to Santiago to pick up the set, then waited for a bus to bring her back to Havana. When Timerman offered her a ride, she was waiting for a bus to take her and the TV home. He wrote: "Cubans are waiting for an outcome, a result, a finale. Those of us who go there are waiting, too, hoping to discern clearly what it is the others are waiting for. . . ."[13]

A decade later, photographer Marcia L. Friedman visited Cuba to capture images of the country and its people during the late 1990s. In her book *Cuba: The Special Period*, Friedman wrote: "[Cuba] has become a country where the outside world, though scrutinized, is allowed to come inside, but those inside can look out only through censure screens . . . wanting, hoping, and waiting. . . . I tried to capture a place and people frozen in time; a people with the ability, education, and desire to propel themselves and their country into a prosperous technologically advanced country it could be. And while they wait, the world watches."[14]

TIMELINE

1492	Christopher Columbus reaches Cuban coast and claims these islands for Spain
1511–1515	Spain conquers Cuba and builds numerous settlements
	Spanish crown approves free trade of slaves into Cuba
1791	Rebel slaves from Haiti flee to Cuba
1811–1812	Slaves rebel for freedom
1868–1878	Ten Years' War between Cuban rebels and Spanish colonial forces
1886	Slavery is abolished in Cuba
	Second war for independence, led by José Martí (killed in action in May), fails to oust Spanish rulers
	Spanish American War: Cuban patriots, supported by U.S., overthrow Spanish colonial government
1900–1901	U.S. enacts Platt Amendment and maintains control over Cuban affairs
1901	Cuban republic is established with Tomas Estrada Palma as its first president
1903	U.S. sets up naval base at Guantanamo Bay in Cuba
1924	Gerardo Machado elected president
1933	Machado is ousted by military coup; Cespedes takes over as president; Ramon Grau San Martin takes over late that year

	Fulgencio Batista leads uprising; Carlos Mendieta installed as president; U.S. cancels Platt Amendment
1938	Communist party is officially recognized as a legal organization
1940	Cuban constitution is adopted; Batista is elected president
	Fidel Castro leads unsuccessful attack on Cuban military
	Castro and his followers are allowed to leave Cuba under an amnesty agreement with Batista's government
	Castro returns to Cuba with his brother Raul, Che Guevara, and other revolutionaries
1957	Fidelistas begin series of successful attacks against the Batista government
1959	Rebels seize control of Cuban government in Havana, and Batista flees the island; U.S. recognizes the new government; Castro regime tries and executes members of Batista regime and enacts rural reforms
1961	Castro government allies itself with Soviet Union and expropriates foreign properties on Cuba; bans religious TV and radio broadcasts in Cuba
	U.S. imposes economic embargo on Cuba, exempting food and medicines
	U. S. government breaks diplomatic relations with Cuba; with U.S. support, Cuban nationalists launch unsuccessful coup attempt at Bay of Pigs
1962	Cuban Missile Crisis (October 22–28); Cuba is banned from Organization of American States (OAS); U.S. bans Cuban exports and announces it will cut off aid to countries that assist Cuba
	Cuban-owned assets in the United States are frozen
1965-1971	"Freedom Flights" by which 250,000 Cubans will emigrate to U.S.

1968	Cuban government begins rationing oil products and completes nationalization of private sector businesses in Cuba.
	Cuban economy sags when country fails to meet targets for sugar harvest; Cuba joins COMECON, the trading association of Soviet bloc nations.
1975	OAS begins discussions with Cuba to normalize relations
	New Cuban constitution declares Castro is president of the Council of Ministers, commander of the Cuban armed forces, and first secretary of the community party
	Cuba and U.S. sign agreements regarding maritime boundaries; each government installs an "interests section" in the other's capital city.
1978–1979	Cuba and United States move toward some normalization of relations.
	Thousands of Cubans seek political asylum at Peruvian embassy in Havana; about 125,000 Cubans leave for Miami during Mariel boatlift
1981	U.S. government forbids citizens to spend money in Cuba and thus prohibits travel to Cuba
1985	U.S.-sponsored "Radio Martí" begins broadcasting to Cuba
1989	U.S. allows limited travel to Cuba and permits expenditures of no more than $100 a day
1991	Soviet President Mikhail Gorbachev announces the withdrawal of all Soviet troops from Cuba; in the wake of the dissolution of the Soviet bloc, Soviet aid to Cuba ends
	"Special Period" of economic problems begins
	U.S. Congress passes "Cuban Democracy Act" sponsored by Senator Jesse Helms, which bans foreign subsidiaries of U.S. companies from trading with Cuba and bans travel by U.S. citizens to Cuba

Thousands of Cubans try to reach U.S. illegally by boat as economic conditions worsen

Cuban government enacts some reforms that permit limited ownership of privately owned businesses

Cuban government launches effort to identify and interrogate human-rights activists throughout Cuba

President Bill Clinton signs bill that penalizes foreign companies that transact business with Cuba and permits U.S. citizens to sue investors who use property the government seized from them after the Revolution. (This provision is suspended annually throughout the 1990s.)

1997 U.S. publishes report pledging assistance from U.S. and other countries if Cuba takes steps toward democratizing its government

1998 Pope John Paul II visits Cuba and urges more religious freedom for Cubans, the release of political prisoners, and the end of the U.S. embargo

1999–2000 Conflicts erupt among U.S. and Cuban governments and Cuban-American exiles over the case of Elian Gonzalez, a boy who was rescued from the sea where his mother and others drowned en route to Miami.

SOURCE NOTES

Introduction: "Life Is Very Difficult"

1. Quoted in Brook Larmer and John Leland, "Elian's Cuba," *Newsweek*, April 17, 2000, p. 32.
2. Quoted in Jim Genova, "Cuba Fights to Defend Socialism," *People's Weekly World*, August 26, 1995, at http://www.hartford-hwp.com/archives/43b/026.html

Chapter One: From Colony to Revolution

1. Quoted in Peter G. Bourne, *Fidel: A Biography of Fidel Castro* (New York: Dodd, Mead, 1986), p. 1.
2. Zvi Dor-Ner and William Scheller, *Columbus and the Age of Discovery* (New York: William Morrow, 1991), p. 170.
3. Dor-Ner and Scheller, p. 171.
4. Dor-Ner and Scheller, p. 171.

Chapter Two: American Intervention

1. Quoted in Bourne, *Fidel: A Biography of Fidel Castro*, p. 5.
2. Elizabeth de Lima-Dantas, "Historical Setting," in James D. Rudolph, ed., *Cuba: A Country Study* (Washington, D.C.: The American University Press, 1985), p. 19.
3. Quoted in Martin Kenner and James Petras, eds., *Fidel Castro Speaks* (New York: Grove Press, Inc., 1969), p. 5.
4. Agustin Blazquez, "Cuba: This Missing Page," Cuban American Democracy Project (CADP) 1999, at http://www.cadp-nyc.org/manuscripts/new%20manuscripts/cuba

CHAPTER THREE: A REVOLUTIONARY SOCIETY

1. Quoted in Bourne, *Fidel,* p. 101.
2. Quoted in Kenner and Petras, *Fidel Castro Speaks,* p. xiii.
3. Quoted in Lee Lockwood, *Castro's Cuba, Cuba's Fidel* (New York: Macmillan, 1967), pp. 280–281.
4. Tad Szulc, *Fidel: A Critical Portrait* (New York: Morrow, 1986), p. 179.
5. Quoted in Kenner and Petras, p. xiv.
6. Quoted in Kenner and Petras, p. 24.
7. Quoted in Kenner and Petras, p. 53.
8. Quoted in Patty Davis, "Cuban-Americans Struggle with Memories of Childhood Airlifts," at CNN: http://cnn.com/US/9801/12/pedro.pan/

CHAPTER FOUR: A CHANGING ECONOMY

1. Quoted in Jim Genova, "Cuba Fights to Defend Socialism," *People's Weekly World,* August 26, 1995, at http://www.hartford-hwp.com/archives/43b/026.html
2. Jacobo Timerman. *Cuba: A Journey.* (New York: Vintage Books, 1992), p. 60
3. Quoted in Larmer and Leland, "Elian's Cuba," *Newsweek,* p. 33.
4. "Cuba Greens Its Agriculture: An Interview with Luis Sanchez Almanza," *Green Left Weekly,* December 11, 1994, at http://www.hartford-hwp.com/archives/43b/003.html)
5. Quoted in Mireya Navarro, "Cuba Draws the Curious, Despite the Law," *The New York Times,* January 31, 1999, p. 90.
6. James Suckling, "Unforgettable Cuba," *Cigar Aficionado,* June 1999, p. 71.
7. Quoted in Charles Strouse, "Cuba Today Isn't Much Different Than the Soviet Union Just Before Its Collapse," *Miami Sun-Sentinel,* January 30, 1998, at http://www.sun-sentinel.com/news/daily/detail
8. Frank Bruni, "Island of Forbidden Fruits," *The New York Times,* August 8, 1999, pp. 15 and 17.
9. Bruni, p. 17.
10. Brian Campbell, "The Wonderful Spirit of the Cuban Revolution," in *An Phoblacht/Republican News,* October

9, 1997, at http://www.irlnet.com/aprn/current/October09/09cuba.html

11. Murray, Mary. "Cuba Opens Offshore Oil to Foreigners," MSNBC News, Nov. 29, 1999, at http://www.msnbc.com/news/321024.asp

12. "In Cuba, Hard Times Eased By Remittances From Abroad," *Caribbean Life* (Brooklyn/Staten Island Edition), February 29, 2000, p. 6, and *Newsweek* article, April 17, 2000.

13. "CIA: Cuba's Economy Sputters On," November 29, 1999, at http://www.msnbc.com/news/253684.asp

14. Quoted in "In Cuba, Hard Times Eased. . . . "

15. Quoted in John J. Putman, "Evolution in the Revolution," *National Geographic*, June 1999, p. 6.

16. "In Cuba, Hard Times Eased. . . . "

17. Quoted in Putman, p. 15.

Chapter Five: Politics and Human Rights

1. Timerman, p. 26.

2. Human Rights watch, "Cuba, 1999," at http://www.hrw.org/reports/1999/cuba/Cuba996-01.htm accessed on July 24, 1999.

3. Cubanet, "Cuban Dissident Jailed for Calling Castro Crazy," September 4, 1997, at http://www.fiu.edu/~fcf/jailed.crazy9597.html

4. Human Rights Watch: "Cuba, 1999," at http://www.hrw.org/reports/1999/cuba/Cuba996-01.htm accessed July 24, 1999.

5. "Cuban Dissidents Uneasy After UN Vote," Cable News Network (CNN), from correspondent Susan Candiotti, April 23, 1998, at http://www.cnn.ru/WORLD/americas/9804/23/cuba.human.rights/

6. Mary Murray, "Cuba Hunger Strikers Vow Defiance," NBC News, November 29, 1999, at www.msnbc.com/news/287088.asp)

7. Robert Windrem, "Cuba's Economy Sputters On," November 29, 1999, at www.msnbc.com/news/253684.asp

8. Charles Lane, "Castro's Family Values," *Washington Post*, January 30, 2000, p. B-7.

CHAPTER SIX: LIVING IN CUBA

1. Timerman, p. 90.
2. James Suckling, "Unforgettable Cuba," *Cigar Aficionado*, p. 68.
3. Cited in *USA Today*, March 22, 2000.
4. Putman, "Evolution in the Revolution," *National Geographic*, June 1999, p. 19.
5. Putman, p. 19.
6. Deborah Sharp, "Growing Up in Cuba," *USA Today*, March 22, 2000, p. 1A.
7. U.S. State Department. "Cuban Values and American Values."
8. Tim Golden, "After a Lift, Cuban Church Has a Letdown," *The New York Times*, September 13, 1998, p. 6.
9. Quoted in Golden, p. 6.
10. Quoted in "Dec. 25 Off Is Cuba's First in 30 Years," *The New York Times*, December 26, 1997.
11. Golden, p. 6.
12. Quoted in Brian Campbell, "The Wonderful Spirit of the Cuban Revolution," in *An Phoblacht/Republican News*, October 9, 1997, at http://www.irlnet.com /aprn/current/October09/09cuba.html
13. Quoted in Sharp, "Growing Up in Cuba," p. 2A.

CHAPTER SEVEN: ARTS AND RECREATION

1. Quoted in Tom Masland, "Cuban on the Keys," *Newsweek*, November 13, 1995, p. 84.
2. Quoted in Peter Watrous, "International Dissonance Aside, Harmony in Cuba," *The New York Times*, Dec. 24, 1997.
3. Quoted in "Revolutionary Moves"
4. Quoted in Sam Howe Verhovek, "Stardom Seasoned With a Yearning for Home and Kin," *The New York Times*, October 5, 1997, p. 6.
5. Quoted in Verhovek, p. 6.
6. Quoted in Jordan Levin, "Revolutionary Moves," *Los Angeles Times*, January 11, 1998, at http://www.cuba net.org/Cnews/y98/jan98/12e93.htm
7. Quoted in David Gates and others, "A Taste of Salsa," *Newsweek*, January 19, 1998, p. 44.
8. Quoted in David Gates, p. 44.

9. Quoted in Rohter, "Marlins Star Is a Hero Cuba Ignores," *The New York Times*, October 19, 1997.

10. Kenneth Shouler, "El Duque's Excellent Adventures," *Cigar Aficionado*, April 1999, p. 80.

CHAPTER EIGHT: INTERNATIONAL RELATIONS

1. Timerman, p. 31.
2. Timerman, pp. 47–49.
3. Quoted in Timerman, p. 115.
4. U.S. State Department, "Cuban Values and American Values," January 5, 2000, at http://www.cal.org/rsc/cubans/value.htm
5. Timerman, p. 114.
6. Mirta Ojito, "Divided Loyalties Tugging at Cuba's Children," *The New York Times*, February 18, 1998, A1.
7. Quoted in Ricardo Alarcon, *Cigar Aficionado*, April 1999, p. 90.
8. Jesse Helms, "Tighten the Screws," *Cigar Aficionado*, April 1999, p. 83.
9. Christopher Dodd, "End the Embargo," *Cigar Aficionado*, April 1999, p. 84.
10. Dodd, p. 84.
11. Dodd, p. 87.
12. Quoted in Craig R. Whitney, "Castro Given Big Welcome by Mitterrand," *The New York Times*, March 14, 1995, p. 5.
13. Mireya Navarro, "As Older Cuban Exiles Die, Young Pragmatists Emerge," *The New York Times*, December 6, 1997, p. A1.
14. Quoted in Deborah Sharp, "Dismay Follows Judge's Ruling in Miami," *USA Today*, March 2, 2000, p. 3A.
15. Quoted in Deborah Sharp, "Cubans See Elian's Case as a Kidnapping," *USA Today*, March 2, 2000, p. 5A.
16. Sharp, "Growing Up in Cuba," *USA Today*, March 22, 2000, p. 1A.
17. Sharp, "Growing Up in Cuba," p. A2.
18. Deborah Sharp, "Judge Refuses to Block Elian's Return," *USA Today*, March 22, 2000, p. 1A.

CHAPTER NINE: CUBA IN TRANSITION

1. Quoted in Genova, "Cuba Fights to Defend Socialism," *People's Weekly World*.

2. Quoted in Deborah Sharp, "Growing Up in Cuba," p. 2A.
3. Quoted in James Suckling, pp. 71-72.
4. Quoted in Margrethe Siem, "'Human Beings are the most important,'" says Cuban youth," *The Militant*, April 11, 1995 at www.hartford-hwp.com/archives/43b/016.html
5. Quoted in Cubanet, June 20, 1997 "Ideological Purges in Cuban Schools," at http://www.fiu.edu/~fcf /zpurgesschoolnorm697.html
6. Quoted in "Generations Divided Over the Future," *Miami Herald*, March 19, 2000, p. 2L.
7. Ibid.
8. Ibid.
9. Quoted in Mark Kurlansky, "Cuba, Si," *Mirabella*, January 1991, p. 153.
10. Quoted in Bruni, "Island of Forbidden Fruits," *The New York Times*, p. 17.
11. Quoted in Parsa, "Club Red," *New York Magazine*, p. 43.
12. Quoted in Putman, "Evolution in the Revolution," *National Geographic*, p. 19.
13. Jacobo Timerman, trans. by Toby Talbot. *Cuba, a Journey* (New York: Knopf, 1990), p. 15.
14. Marcia Friedman, *Cuba: The Special Period* (Samuel Books, 1997), Prologue.

BIBLIOGRAPHY

Bourne, Peter G. *Fidel, A Biography of Fidel Castro*. New York: Dodd, Mead, 1986.

Cisneros, Milagros. *Respectful Engagement: Cuban NGO Cooperation with Latin America, Europe, and Canada*. Philadelphia: American Friends Service Committee, 1996.

Conde, Yvonne M. *Operation Pedro Pan—The Untold Exodus of 14,000 Cuban Children*. New York: Routledge, 1999.

Dor-Ner, Zvi, and William Scheller, *Columbus and the Age of Discovery*. New York: William Morrow, 1991.

Friedman, Marcia. *Cuba: The Special Period*. Samuel Books, 1997.

Kenner, Martin, and James Petras, eds. *Fidel Castro Speaks*. New York: Grove Press, Inc., 1969.

Lockwood, Lee. *Castro's Cuba, Cuba's Fidel*. New York: Macmillan, 1967.

Manuel, Peter, ed. *Essays on Cuban Music: North American and Cuban Perspectives*. Lanham, MD: University Press of America, 1991.

Rudolph, James D., ed. *Cuba, a Country Study*. Washington, D.C.: The American University, 1985.

Ryan, Alan, ed. *The Reader's Companion Guide to Cuba*. San Francisco: Harcourt, Brace, Jovanovich, 1997.

Timerman, Jacobo. trans. by Toby Talbot. *Cuba, a Journey*. New York: Knopf, 1990.

Tremblay, Helene. trans. by Hilary and Paul Childs-Adams. *Families of the World: Family Life at the Close of the Twentieth Century*. Vol. 1: The Americas and the Caribbean. New York: Farrar, Straus, and Giroux, 1988.

Triay, Victor Andres. *Fleeing Castro: Operation Pedro Pan and the Cuban Children's Program.* Gainesville: University Press of Florida, 1998.

Ward, Fred. *Inside Cuba Today.* New York: Crown Publishers, 1978.

White, Mark J. ed. *The Kennedys and Cuba: The Declassified Documentary History.* Chicago: I. R. Dee, 1999.

ARTICLES

Anderton, Frances. "In Cuba, Seeds of a Design Renaissance," *The New York Times,* F1, F7.

Brantley, Ben. "Creator of Paradise Lost: Eduardo Machado," *The New York Times Magazine,* October 23, 1994, pp. 38–41.

Bruni, Frank. "Island of Forbidden Fruits," *The New York Times,* August 8, 1999, pp. 15, 17.

Campbell, Brian. "The Wonderful Spirit of the Cuban Revolution," in *An Phoblacht/Republican News,* October 9, 1997, at www.irlnet.com

"Castro Wants to Hear Details on Expected Easing of U.S. Sanctions," Cable News Network (CNN), March 20, 1998, at www.cnn.ru

"Cuban Dissidents Uneasy After UN Vote," Cable News Network (CNN), from correspondent Susan Candiotti, April 23, 1998, at www.cnn.ru

"Generations Divided Over the Future," *Miami Herald,* March 19, 2000, 2L.

Golden, Tim. "After a Lift, Cuban Church Has a Letdown," *The New York Times,* September 13, 1998, p. 6.

———. "Just Another Cuban Family Saga," *The New York Times Magazine,* April 23, 2000, p. 62ff.

Helms, Jesse. "Tighten the Screws," *Cigar Aficionado,* June 1999, pp. 80, 83ff.

"In Cuba, Hard Times Eased by Remittances From Abroad," *Caribbean Life* (Brooklyn/Staten Island Edition), February 29, 2000, p. 6.

Kurlansky, Mark. "Cuba, Si," *Mirabella,* January 1991, pp. 150–153.

Lane, Charles. "Castro's Family Values," January 30, 2000, *Washington Post,* B-7.

Larmer, Brook, and John Leland. "Elian's Cuba," *Newsweek,* April 17, 2000, p. 30ff.

Levin, Jordan. "Revolutionary Moves" *Los Angeles Times,* January 11, 1998, at www.cubanet.org

Murray, Mary. "Cuba Opens Offshore Oil to Foreigners," MSNBC News, November 29, 1999, at www.msnbc.com

Navarro, Mireya. "As Older Cuban Exiles Die, Young Pragmatists Emerge," *The New York Times,* December 6, 1997, p. A1.

Ojita, Mirta. "Divided Loyalties Tugging at Cuba's Children," *The New York Times,* February 18, 1998, A1.

———. "'You Are Going to El Norte,'" *The New York Times Magazine,* April 23, 2000, p. 68ff.

Parsa, T.Z. "Club Red," *New York Magazine,* November 17, 1997, pp. 36–43.

Putman, John J. "Evolution in the Revolution," *National Geographic,* June 1999, pp. 2–35.

Roca, Octavio. "Alicia Alonso—Mesmerizing at 76/ Cuban Dancer on Stage in 'United'," *San Francisco Chronicle,* May 13, 1995, at sfgate.com

Rohter, Larry. "Cuba Announces It Will Free 200 in Bow to Pope," *The New York Times,* February 13, 1998, A9.

———. "New Cuban Refugees Flee to Havana," *The New York Times,* October 20, 1997, p. 13.

Savold, David. "100 Minutes to Freedom," *Air & Space/Smithsonian Magazine,* December 1993/January 1994, at www.airspacemag.com

Sharp, Deborah. "Cubans See Elian's Case as a Kidnapping," *USA Today,* March 2, 2000, 5A.

———. "Dismay Follows Judge's Ruling in Miami," *USA Today,* March 2, 2000, p. 3A.

———. "Growing Up in Cuba," *USA Today,* March 22, 2000, 1A.

Shouler, Kenneth. "El Duque's Excellent Adventures," *Cigar Aficionado,* April 1999, pp. 79–98.

Suckling, James. "Unforgettable Cuba," *Cigar Aficionado,* June 1999, pp. 62–72.

Vecsey, George. "Cuba Gain Could Open Some Doors," *The New York Times,* May 4, 1999, D1.

Whitney, Craig R. "Castro Given Big Welcome by Mitterrand," *The New York Times,* March 14, 1995, p. 5.

FURTHER READING

Ada, Alma Flor. *Under the Royal Palms: A Childhood in Cuba.* New York: Atheneum, 1998.

Cannon, Terence. *Revolutionary Cuba.* New York: Thomas Y. Crowell, 1959.

Crouch, Clifford W. *Cuba.* Broomall, Pa: Chelsea House, 1997.

Fox, Mary Virginia. *Cuba.* San Diego: Lucent Books, 1999.

Galvan, Raul. *Cuban Americans.* Tarrytown, NY: Marshall Cavendish, 1995.

Hugh, Thomas. *The Cuban Revolution.* New York: Harper & Row, 1977.

Kennedy, Robert F. *Thirteen Days: A Memoir of the Cuban Missile Crisis.* New York: W.W. Norton, 1969.

Phillips, Ruby Hart. *Cuba: Island of Paradox.* New York: McDowell, 1960.

Rice, Earle, Jr. *The Cuban Revolution.* San Diego: Lucent Books, 1995.

Selsdon, Esther. *The Life and Times of Fidel Castro.* Broomall, Pa: Chelsea House, 1997.

INDEX